T0326536

Economic Aspects and Implications of Obesity

Volkswirtschaftliche Analysen

Herausgegeben von Elisabeth Allgoewer, Georg Hasenkamp, Wolfgang Maennig,
Christian Scheer und Peter Stahlecker

Band 14

PETER LANG
Frankfurt am Main · Berlin · Bern · Bruxelles · New York · Oxford · Wien

Elise Hefti

Economic Aspects and Implications of Obesity

PETER LANG
Internationaler Verlag der Wissenschaften

Bibliografische Information der Deutschen Nationalbibliothek
Die Deutsche Nationalbibliothek verzeichnet diese Publikation in der Deutschen Nationalbibliografie; detaillierte bibliografische Daten sind im Internet über <http://www.d-nb.de> abrufbar.

Zugl.: Hamburg, Univ., Diss., 2009

Gedruckt auf alterungsbeständigem,
säurefreiem Papier.

D 18
ISSN 1431-8739
ISBN 978-3-631-59338-7

www.peterlang.de

Table of Contents

Table of Figures

Abbreviations

BMI:	body mass index
BMR:	basal metabolic rate
BRFSS:	Behavioral Risk Factor Surveillance System
CDC:	Centers for Disease Control and Prevention
GEK:	Gmünder Ersatzkasse
IASO:	International Association for the Study of Obesity
kcal:	kilocalories
MEC:	marginal external costs
MPC:	marginal private costs
MRS:	marginal rate of substitution
MRT:	marginal rate of transformation
MSB:	marginal social benefit
MSC:	marginal social costs
NHANES:	National Health and Nutrition Examination Survey
OECD:	Organisation for Economic Co-operation and Development
TEE:	thermic effect of exercise
TEF:	thermic effect of food
WHO:	World Health Organisation

‘The vigorous, the healthy, and the happy survive and multiply.’

(Charles Darwin, The Origin of Species, 1859)

‘Zucker zaubert. Nimm deshalb mehr!’

(German TV commercial for sugar, 1950s)

Chapter 1. Introduction

1.1 Purpose of the Dissertation

While many public health issues have been solved and improved with the rise of affluent societies, their ascent has simultaneously led to new, wealth-related diseases. To begin with, there are caries and tooth decay, induced by increased consumption of sugar. Another wealth-related health problem is smoking, leading to various types of cancer, as well as cardiovascular and respiratory diseases. Excess drinking can also be added to this – probably incomplete – list. Caries as a disease can easily be avoided with dental care. Although the detrimental consequences of smoking have been known for more than four decades, the case of smoking is somewhat harder to solve. Since addiction is an important aspect of smoking, a balanced policy mix is required. Ever since the link between smoking and the numerous ensuing diseases has been publicly recognised,[1] a vast amount of research has been conducted and published in order to curb the smoking epidemic and, as a result, decrease the induced social cost. Despite the extensive implementation of political measures against smoking, tobacco use is nevertheless expected to cause a higher death toll than any other sickness, disease, or careless behaviour by 2030.[2] Nevertheless, in most industrialised countries, public opinion has turned against smoking.

---

1 Although the 1964 Surgeon General's Report is often quoted as the first publication to call attention to the health risks of smoking, the British Royal College of Physicians' 1962 report on smoking and health was the first to conclude that cigarette smoking causes lung cancer (see Royal College of Physicians 2002). In addition, it recommends a remarkably modern policy mix that includes education and information, restrictions on sales and advertising, tax measures, smoking restrictions, and help for those willing to quit. In contrast, the Surgeon General's Report relates smoking to a larger number of diseases, including numerous types of cancer, respiratory and cardiovascular diseases.

2 See World Bank 2003, p. 1.

Within the past two decades, an entirely new health problem has become increasingly important: The world has seen an unprecedented rise in overweight and obesity rates in a vast number of countries. Today, obesity ranks second to dental caries among nutritional abnormalities.[3]

In the United States, for example, almost one third of the adult population was obese in 2003-2004. The prevalence of overweight among children and adolescents exhibits a significantly increasing trend from the period 1999-2000 to the period 2003-2004: It has risen from 13.9 to 17.1 per cent. The prevalence of extreme obesity – defined by a Body Mass Index (BMI) equal to or larger than 40 – in 2003-2004 was 2.8 per cent in men and 6.9 per cent in women (for example, a BMI value of 40 is reached when an individual of 180 cm height weighs approximately 130 kilograms).[4] A recent study predicts that if current US trends continue, just about all American adults will be overweight or obese by the year 2048.[5] In Germany, the prevalence of overweight and obesity in 2005 amounted to 57.9 per cent among male adults and 41.5 per cent among females.[6] This trend is comparable in most affluent societies, that is in the industrialised world.

In industrialised states, adverse health behaviour has numerous economic implications. Obesity decreases productivity or may even render a person unable to work. It lowers life expectancy and results in comorbidities that, in turn, increase health care costs. Moreover, costs arise because the environment has to be adapted to persons with extremely high bodyweight: For example, ambulances, hospital beds, and operating tables have to be modified for obese persons. Furthermore, obesity has unfavourable demographic consequences as fertility is lowered. These additional costs are borne by society, either because those who have caused the costs cannot pay them or – in Germany – due to the principle of solidarity (In the German health insurance system, all insured must pay for the incurred costs, even if they do not contribute to them). Thus, obesity causes externalities that result in lower welfare. These externalities are caused

3 See Forbes 1987, p. 210.

4 See Ogden et al. 2006, pp. 1550/1551.

5 See Wang et al. 2008, p. 7.

6 See Bundesamt für Statistik 2007.

by private choices in favour of unhealthy behaviour but must be borne by society as a whole within the framework of the existing German insurance and social security system. Thus, everyone has to recompense for behaviour carried out only by specific members of society. Those performing adverse health behaviour are not held responsible for their actions. Their private consumption patterns put their health at risk. Still, they do not pay their way for the costs they have caused. Instead, they are subsidised by persons who actually care for and invest in their own health. Thus, every society is confronted with the question whether this kind of income redistribution is acceptable.

The above observations lead to the topic of this dissertation: Causes of obesity must be identified in order to determine a policy mix that can change the trends towards even higher obesity prevalence persisting in industrialised countries.

1.2 Organisation of the Dissertation

Chapter two starts with causes for the occurrence of obesity, first from the biological point of view, and then from a socioeconomic point of view. Within the framework of the medical elaborations, obesity as a concept is defined. From a medical point of view, bodyweight is determined interactively by the consumption of energy from food and the amount of energy spent on vital functions and physical activity. From a socioeconomic point of view, excess weight is influenced by the interaction of numerous aspects: These include economic, social, and informational aspects, as well as environmental factors and certain health-related behavioural patterns.

The third chapter is concerned with the economic consequences of obesity. Health and financial consequences are explained first. As a result of the health hazards of excess weight, obesity causes external costs. These stem from increased morbidity and mortality on the one hand and increased health care costs for prevention, diagnosis, and treatment on the other hand. The fact that these costs are not borne by obese individuals but by society as a whole – due to redistribution of income and higher health care contributions – is explained in the final section of this chapter.

Chapter four starts with a static model of consumer behaviour focussing on food consumption and its health consequences. In this chapter, the differentiation between health-conscious individuals and those lacking health-consciousness is introduced – this is the fundamental principle of this dissertation. In the subsequent paragraph, this model is extended to a dynamic framework which yields conditions for utility-maximising consumption decisions for overweight, normal-weight, and underweight individuals. The model is complemented by extensions relevant to food overconsumption, namely diet composition, the rate of time preference, addictive aspects, and dynamic inconsistency. Chapter four stresses the conditions under which instability can occur in a utility-maximising setting and the resulting policy implications.

Chapter five presents empirical work on systematic differences between obese and non-obese individuals and on the relation of other aspects of unfavourable health behaviour, such as smoking or a sedentary lifestyle, with socioeconomic status. As the same data source is used for all analyses, this chapter begins with a description of how the data is processed before the empirical analyses are conducted. Section 5.2 investigates whether education, employment, and income as measures of socioeconomic status significantly differ by weight level. Thereafter, section 5.3 describes whether socioeconomic status – as measured in 5.2 – differs by adverse health behaviour, namely excess weight, smoking, unbalanced nutrition, physical inactivity, and infrequent vaccination. All analyses are conducted separately by gender and ethnic background.

The consequences of chapters two to five for insurance design are described in chapter six. Here, the theoretical concepts of public goods and externalities, as well as moral hazard, and adverse selection are explained in the context of excess weight. Specific reference is made to preventive expenditures and risk differentiation. Chapters three, four, and six each conclude with a glossary explaining the use of symbols in the respective chapter.

In chapter seven, this dissertation concludes with a summary of the results obtained in chapters two to six, finding answers to the problems raised in the introduction. Finally, details on empirical studies and methodology are provided in the Appendix.

Chapter 2. Concept and Causes of Obesity

The following sections explain how overweight and obesity are defined, and why excess weight can occur. Furthermore, various factors leading to excess bodyweight are documented based on selected empirical studies. The determinants are classified into economic and social factors, informational aspects, environmental factors, health behaviours, and genetic influences.

2.1 The Biological Context

From a biological perspective, the relationship between the calories that are consumed by food intake and expended – for example, on vital functions or physical activity – is relevant for bodyweight. Obesity as a concept is defined in the subsequent section. Section 2.1.2 provides a clarification of the calorie balance.

2.1.1 Definition of Obesity

The definition of obesity is reliant on the Body Mass Index – for short, BMI – to distinguish between insufficient, normal, or excess bodyweight. Let the weight of a person be measured in kilograms, and the height in meters, then the formula

$$BMI = weight / height^2$$

indicates this person's Body Mass Index.[7]

---

7 See Insel et al. 2007, p. 345.

Following WHO (World Health Organisation) definitions, a person is underweight, normal weight, overweight, or obese according to the following BMI ranges:

- Underweight if BMI < 18.50
- Normal weight if 18.50 ≤ BMI < 25
- Overweight if 25 ≤ BMI < 30
- Obese if BMI ≥ 30.

Obesity is further subdivided into three classes: Class I, which is associated with moderate risk of comorbidities,[8] ranges from 30 to just under 35. A person suffering from class II obesity has a severe risk of experiencing comorbidities due to her BMI between 35 and just under 40. An individual with a BMI equal to or larger than 40 suffers from class III obesity and very severe risk of comorbidities.[9] The specific health risks of an increased BMI are described in section 3.1.

Since height remains constant for an adult person, variations in the BMI result from variations in the person's weight. However, the source of variations in weight is mainly reflected in the share of body fat. Practically all cases of overweight and obesity can be traced back to excess fat storage in the human body.

When food was in short supply – as it was centuries ago – the capacity to store fat was essential for survival. Today, in affluent societies, food is readily available at low cost. Thus, the once successful biological strategies for survival have become hazardous to many people's health.

Unfortunately, the BMI does not provide clear information on body composition. For example, a stocky person might be classified as overweight even though her body fat is within normal ranges, or a gracile person may be classified as underweight based on her BMI even though common sense indicates normality. As a result, health care professionals also use other methods to

---

8 'Comorbidity' is defined as the coexistence of medical problems with the initially diagnosed illness.

9 See WHO 2000, pp. 6-9.

assess body fat, for example waist circumference, fatfold measures, or hydrodensitometry.[10]

However, for the majority of persons, BMI appears to be a meaningful measure to distinguish between normal and abnormal weight.

A person will gain weight if calorie intake is higher than energy expenditure.[11] The calorie balance – resulting in stable bodyweight – is addressed in the following paragraph.

2.1.2 The Calorie Balance

The basis of a normal – that is, healthy – bodyweight lies in the balance between calorie intake and calorie expenditure. The risks associated with increased BMI are continuous and graded and begin at a level above 25.[12] Thus, a BMI level below or equal to 25 can be considered healthy (health hazards of underweight are not considered in this dissertation).

However, the balance between calories consumed and expended is a rather complicated process. For most, if not all humans, a stable equilibrium is not obtained by intuitive and unconscious decisions. While the amount of calorie intake by food consumption is a conscious act that can be observed, measured, and intentionally controlled, the amount of calories expended is not as easily checked and measured due to the different sources for which energy is needed.

When food is burned, energy is expended in the form of heat. The body's generation of heat is called 'thermogenesis'.[13] This heat is measured in calories.

---

10 See Whitney, Rolfes 2005, pp. 262-266.

11 The term 'energy expenditure' refers to the amount of energy, measured in kilocalories that the human body needs to maintain life functions or to perform a particular activity.

12 See WHO 2000, pp. 6-9.

13 See Whitney, Rolfes 2005, p. 256.

One kilocalorie consists of 1,000 calories. It equals the energy necessary to increase the temperature of one kg of water by one degree Celsius.[14]

The body expends energy for three main categories of thermogenesis:

- basal metabolism (maintains the basic processes of life, for example breathing, heart beating, kidney functions; the term 'metabolism' describes chemical reactions in living cells by which nutrients are broken down to yield energy, or rearranged into body structures)
- physical activity
- food consumption.

Of the daily energy requirements, basal metabolism accounts for roughly two thirds. The basal metabolic rate (BMR) can vary dramatically from person to person and, for the same individual, under different circumstances. An extensive list of the determinants of BMR is included in Appendix 8.2. The BMR equals the energy expended by an individual bodily and mentally at rest in a thermoneutral environment twelve to eighteen hours after a meal.[15]

The second category of calorie expenditure, physical activity, refers to voluntary movement of the muscles and support systems. Physical activity is the most variable component of energy expenditure, depending on muscle mass, bodyweight, and the activity performed. The energy spent on physical activity is called the thermic effect of exercise (TEE). Furthermore, the more frequent, more intense, and the longer the activity, the more energy is required.

The energy required to digest food and absorb nutrients from food intake is known as the thermic effect of food (TEF). It is proportional to the food energy absorbed and is usually estimated at six to ten per cent of energy intake, depending on the macronutrient that is digested (see paragraph on diet composition). However, the amounts vary for different portion sizes, frequency

14 See Insel et al. 2007, p. 16.

15 See Shils et al. 1998, p. 96.

of meals, and for different kinds of food (for example, it is generally higher for high-protein foods than for high-fat foods).[16]

Excess energy is stored as fat. Between meals, energy is derived from these storages. Unfortunately, in case of quick changes in bodyweight, energy is not only derived from fat storages, but the amounts of fluid and lean tissues are also affected. In the long term, the composition of weight lost or gained is approximately 75 per cent fat and 25 per cent lean tissues.[17]

2.2 Factors Inducing Overweight and Obesity

Overweight and obesity are determined by the imbalance between the amounts of calories consumed and expended. Generally, for a given level of physical activities, too many calories are consumed. The very simple lesson from this is "Eat less to improve your health, and save money at the same time". Therefore, an economic incentive exists, but the alarming trends towards overweight and obesity in affluent societies within the last few decades point out that this simple lesson does not suffice to solve the problems involved. However, the proportion of people following this lesson, thus consciously avoiding overweight and obesity, is unknown to us.

A vast amount of literature pertaining to excess weight has appeared within the last two decades (ten of the studies mentioned in the following paragraph have been published before the year 2000 with the earliest publication in 1992, 46 in or after 2000). The majority has been published in medical journals (i.e. American Journal of Preventive Medicine, Lancet, Obesity, Journal of Nutrition, Preventive Medicine), and the remaining ones have been taken in almost equal shares from economic journals (i.e. American Economic Review, Applied

16 See Whitney, Rolfes 2005, pp. 256-259.

17 See Whitney, Rolfes 2005, pp. 251/252.

Economics, Journal of Economic Perspectives, Quarterly Review of Economics and Finance), and from journals covering both fields (i.e. American Journal of Public Health, Journal of Human Resources, Journal of Health Economics). The publications in medical and economic journals approach the occurance of overweight and obesity from different angles: Publications in medical journals concentrate on the resulting effects on health and their treatment, often focussing on one specific factor at a time. In contrast, publications in economic journals try to find answers to behavioural questions related to the problem and the economic consequences. Thus, these publications attempt to include as many relevant factors as possible.

The following list includes studies using BMI as the dependent variable. Nevertheless, in addition to BMI, various measures and proxies of bodyweight, bodyfat, and nutrition are also frequently considered: weight gain, weight in pounds, skinfold thickness, waist-to-hip ratio, the percentage of the adult population that is obese, food supply trends, fat and saturated fat consumption, or the quantity of demand in specific food groups. Furthermore, one of the studies mentioned below concentrates on the allocation of time.

The risk of a chronic disease is determined by the interaction of genetic, environmental, social, and behavioural factors. Although the influence of genes on individuals' bodyweight is substantial, they alone fail to explain the trend in overweight and obesity prevalence the world has seen in recent decades. The impact induced by the factors listed below is often ambiguous and differs by the development stages of countries and societies, and even by age group. Therefore, the following list of factors is not necessarily exhaustive. Still, it covers the most important factors influencing overweight and obesity that have been identified so far. Notably, the following factors do not directly influence bodyweight (with the exception of soft drink consumption and physical activity) but generate behavioural patterns which, in turn, lead to overweight and obesity. The relevant factors identified in this dissertation are as follows:

- **Economic factors** influence the level of weight. Caloric intake obviously decreases with rising **income**. Still, the relationship is not necessarily linear: Several studies have found a negative quadratic or an inverse U-shaped effect of income on BMI. However, these results show variations over national and socioeconomic stages of development. While in developed countries, prevalence of obesity and overweight is highest among low-income groups, in China, for example, high-income groups have the highest obesity levels. Results also appear to differ in rural and urban areas. Studies have found **price increases** and / or imposing **taxes** to have a statistically negative influence on the consumption of snack foods and soft drinks. **Socioeconomic status**, which is usually constructed as an index consisting of education, occupation, and income, is generally negatively related to bodyweight. In developing countries, this relationship appears to be inverse U-shaped: Studies have found that in less developed countries, higher socioeconomic status tends to be associated with higher BMI. In contrast, in developed countries, lower socioeconomic status is often tied to overweight and obesity. Still, the relationship varies by race and ethnicity. Within the framework of this dissertation, occupational status is a decisive factor. However, most empirical studies do not specifically refer to occupation as such but include an index also containing other factors, mostly education and income (denoted socioeconomic status, social class, or socioeconomic position). Therefore, conclusions on the pure influence of employment can hardly be drawn. The few exceptions show that unemployed individuals are averagely heavier and gain weight at a faster rate. One study demonstrates that unemployed females are more likely to be overweight. Notably, the ratio of obese females is highest among the long-term unemployed (this is also evident in the empirical analyses included in this dissertation, see Appendix). In men, long-term unemployment is rather associated with underweight. Furthermore, a higher **cigarette price** is related to increased bodyweight.

- **Social factors** affect individuals' BMI. A person with a high level of **education** is less likely to suffer from excess bodyweight. The results on the influence of **age** are mixed: The relation is either found to be positive, inverse U-shaped, or quadratic. Most studies find that age increases obesity but beyond a certain point starts decreasing it. The influence of **other demographic variables** is equally ambiguous: Non-White, married individuals seem to be heavier, on average. In most studies, males have a higher bodyweight while females are often found to gain weight at a faster rate. **Food stamp participation** has been found to be related to a higher BMI, as have **family food insecurity** and **insufficiency**. In the US, **uninsured** or **publicly insured individuals** are more likely to be obese. The results on the influence of **immigration status** are mixed: Immigrants obviously display lower average bodyweight on arrival, but seem to blend in with additional years in the immigration country. The magnitude of weight gain may differ depending on the development stage of the emigration country. The norms and networks that enable collective action, the willingness of people to intervene for the good of a community, and the linkage of mutual trust within a community are constituents of **neighbourhood collective efficacy**, which has been found to be negatively related to adolescents' BMI.

- Sources of **information** seem to influence bodyweight. Food **advertising** has been found to be positively related to bodyweight. **Health information and health knowledge** can significantly lower overweight and obesity rates. Their effects apparently differ by gender. Even the most educated seem to benefit. The provision of various sources of nutrition-related information appears most effective.
- A range of **environmental factors** has an impact on BMI. The progress in **food processing technology** has dramatically reduced the time costs of food preparation and thus reduced food prices. This development has contributed to the rise in overweight and obesity prevalence. The **availability of energy-dense foods** is also positively related to bodyweight. In the United States, studies observe the consumption of ever more calories, more refined carbohydrates, more added sugars, and more total fats. These trends are different for males and females: Since the mid-1980's, many women have entirely quit consuming certain food categories with a high fat content. In contrast, men have rather reduced the amount of food consumed in these categories. In addition, BMI is positively associated with **urban**

sprawl (presumably as a consequence of increased automobile use and decreased physical activity), exposure to an **urban environment** (which may also be associated with lower levels of physical activity and changed dietary habits) and the **number of restaurants**. In contrast, studies find a **walkable environment** to decrease driving and increase physical activity, thus leading to reduced bodyweight. Nevertheless, the effect appears to be limited to individuals preferring walkability. Kelly Brownell, Director of the Rudd Center for Food Policy and Obesity at Yale, and Professor of Psychology and Professor of Epidemiology and Public Health at Yale, even went so far to coin the term "toxic environment". Although describing it as the "most radical" act against the obesity epidemic, he was the first person to propose a tax on calorie-dense food. Brownell explicitly accuses the US government of promoting unhealthy eating and physical inactivity as it subsidises the agricultural industry, lets the food industry influence national nutrition policy, does not sufficiently promote consumer information, and fails to counteract food advertising, unhealthy eating in schools, and high prices for healthy foods.[18]

- Bodyweight also varies with certain types of **health behaviour**. Among the range of sedentary behavioural patterns, **watching television** seems to play a special role as consuming snack food while watching TV is common practice. As a result, studies have found watching TV to increase BMI. Present **smoking** limits caloric intake, thus reducing bodyweight. The effect of past smoking is much smaller: After quitting, individuals often gain weight but after a while, their bodyweight converges to their usual, steady state weight. The impact of alcohol consumption is mixed: While most studies find **alcohol consumption** is related to lower BMI, some studies report a resulting increase in bodyweight. Being the prototypical junk food, the consumption of **soft drinks**, which contain sweeteners but few or no nutrients, is positively related to bodyweight. **Physical activity** lowers BMI, but studies find differently pronounced results by age group and gender. A recent study finds that Americans spend most of their time expending little

18 See Brownell 2005, pp. 52-54.

energy: US children and adults spend more than half of their waking time in sedentary behaviour.[19]

- In addition, bodyweight is genetically determined. The results of studies estimating the **genetic influence** on obesity usually range from 20 to 60 per cent. There is also evidence suggesting that genetic influences on children's bodyweight may be independent of those that influence BMI in adults, which would greatly complicate the search for genes affecting obesity as different genes seem to exert their influence at different periods in human development. In relatively few cases, genetics can be considered the sole reason for a person becoming obese, for example those suffering from the Prader-Willi syndrome.[20] However, most cases are not triggered by genetic mutations, but are caused interactively by genes and the environment: While a person's susceptibility to obesity appears to be genetically determined, slowly changing genetic patterns cannot explain the recent dramatic trends in weight gain.[21]

From an evolutionary point of view, natural selection has determined our eating habits and food preferences over many generations. While man's cravings for fat and sugar made perfect sense when energy was in short supply, today, the effortless availability of calories results in calorie overconsumption. For adaptations to evolve by natural selection, a vast amount of time is required. Accordingly, adaptations are mismatched with the current environment that has recently undergone rapid changes. One could say that human evolution fails to keep pace with today's speed of environmental changes.[22]

Details on the empirical studies leading to the above conclusions, as well as tables summarising these results, are provided in the Appendix.

---

19 See Matthews et al. 2008, p. 877.

20 A birth defect characterised by uncontrollable hunger, massive obesity, small stature, and cognitive impairment.

21 See Whitney, Rolfes 2005, pp. 282-285.

22 See Wilson 2007, pp. 51-57.

Chapter 3. The Consequences of Obesity

Having clarified the origins of redundant bodyweight in the precedent chapter, it is reasonable to take a look at the consequences of overweight and obesity. On the one hand, these consequences are reductions in health of the persons involved. On the other hand, obesity induces social cost that must be borne by society as a whole.

Figure 3-1: The Prevalence of Overweight and Obesity in Germany by Age Group [Per Cent]
(a) Women (b) Men
(Reference: Own construction [data obtained from Benecke, Vogel 2003, p. 17])

(a) Women

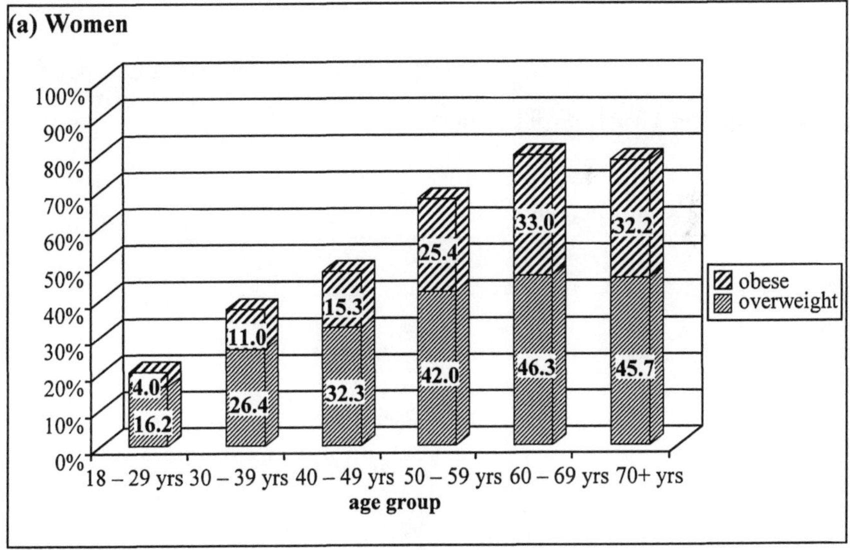

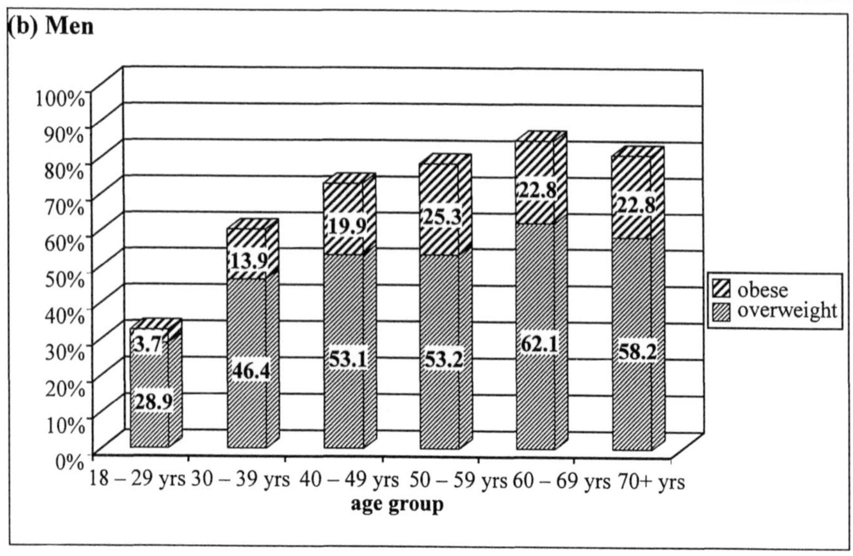

Figure 3-2: The Prevalence of Obesity Classes I, II, and III in Germany by Age Group [Per Cent]: Both Genders

(Reference: Own construction [data obtained from Haenle et al. 2006]; obesity classes are defined in paragraph 2.1.2, p. 6)

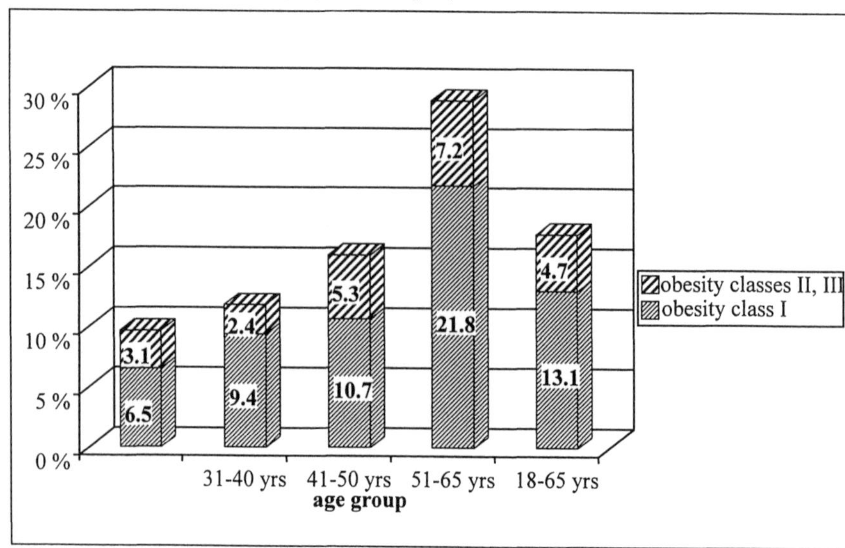

A recent study among 20,000 individuals aged fourteen to 80 years finds that 66.0 per cent of German males and 50.6 per cent of German females display a BMI larger than 25 and can, therefore, be classified as overweight. Roughly one fifth of the German population is obese: 20.5 per cent of men and 21.2 per cent of women. The fraction of those with excess bodyweight is positively correlated with age and negatively correlated with education and income.[23] In the same year, the International Association for the Study of Obesity (IASO) published slightly different figures showing that the fraction of the overweight and obese is higher in Germany than in any other member state of the European Union: Accordingly, 75.4 per cent of German males and 58.9 per cent of German females are overweight or obese. Germany is closely followed by the Czech Republic and Cyprus (73.2 and 72.6 per cent of overweight and obese males, 57.6 and 58.0 per cent of overweight and obese females, respectively). Obesity prevalence is highest in the Czech Republic followed by Cyprus and England (all values range between 26.6 and 23.7 per cent).[24]

As Figures 3-1 to 3-3 demonstrate, overweight and obesity seem to exhibit an inverse J-shaped relation with age for both genders and are negatively correlated with education.

---

23 See Max Rubner-Institut 2008, pp. XI-XV.

24 See International Association for the Study of Obesity 2008. Note that some of the figures are based on self-reported data and may, therefore, be underestimated. In addition, age range and year of survey may differ.

Figure 3-3: The Prevalence of Overweight and Obesity in Germany by Level of Education [Per Cent]: Both Genders

(Reference: Own construction ['Hauptschule' corresponds to a secondary general school, 'Realschule' to an intermediate secondary school, and 'Abitur' is the general qualification for university entrance; data obtained from Robert Koch-Institut (ed.) 2006, p. 114])

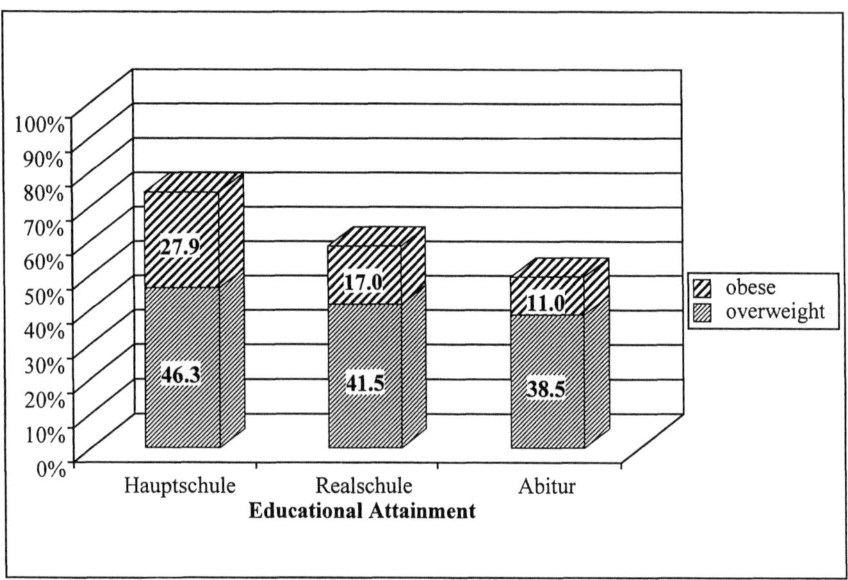

US obesity trends are clarified in Figure 3-4: In 1990, among states participating in the Behavioral Risk Factor Surveillance System (BRFSS), obesity prevalence in ten US states was less than ten per cent. In the remaining states, prevalence was lower than fifteen per cent. In 2006, only four states exhibited a prevalence of obesity of less than twenty per cent. Twenty-two states had a prevalence equal to or greater than 25 per cent. Two of these states (Mississippi and West Virginia) had a prevalence of obesity equal to or greater than 30 per cent.

The data are obtained from the Centers for Disease Control and Prevention (CDC), which define obesity in accordance with WHO criteria. Thus, individuals with a BMI equal to or larger than 30 are classified as obese.

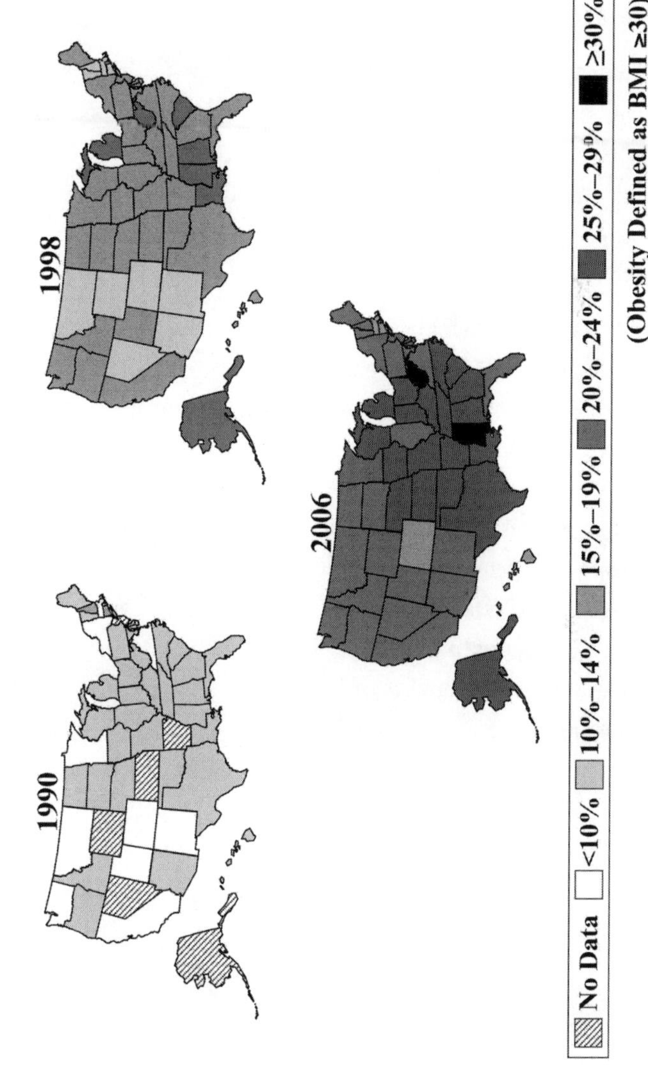
Obesity Trends Among U.S. Adults
BRFSS, 1990, 1998, 2006
1990
1998
2006
No Data
<10%
10%–14%
15%–19%
20%–24%
25%–29%
≥30%
(Obesity Defined as BMI ≥30)

3.1 The Health Hazards of Obesity

Various diseases are promoted by excess bodyweight. The chronic diseases attributable to obesity can be divided into four main categories:

- cardiovascular problems (i.e. hypertension, stroke, coronary heart disease)
- conditions associated with insulin resistance (i.e. non-insulin dependent diabetes mellitus)
- certain types of cancer, especially the hormonally related and large-bowel cancers (i.e. endometrial, ovarian, breast, cervical, and prostate cancer)
- gallbladder disease.

The relative risk[25] for an obese person to suffer from one of the above diseases varies with current BMI level, past BMI levels, and age. Furthermore, chances that an overweight or obese person becomes ill compared to the chance that the same illness occurs in a person within the normal weight range differs for different conditions. For example, the prevalence of high blood pressure in adults with a BMI of 30 is 38.4 per cent for men and 32.2 per cent for women, respectively, compared to 18.2 per cent for men and 16.5 per cent for women with a BMI below 25. Thus, the relative risk for men and women amounts to 2.1 and 2.0, respectively (in terms of Figure 3-5, the relative risk is then moderately increased). Although the impact of higher BMI levels varies in terms of magnitudes with age, gender, and ethnicity, the influence of an increased BMI on the conditions given in the following figure is unambiguous and evident.[26]

25 The ratio of the risk of disease in an obese person to the risk in the normal-weight population.

26 See Brown et al. 2000, pp. 608, 614.

Figure 3-5: The Relative Risk of Health Problems Associated with Obesity

(Reference: Own construction following WHO 2000, p. 43, all relative risk values are approximate, for a definition of relative risk cf. footnote no. 26)

Relative risk one to two **(Slightly increased risk)**	Relative risk two to three **(Moderately increased risk)**	Relative risk > three **(Greatly increased risk)**
Cancer	Coronary heart disease	Gallbladder disease
Reproductive hormone abnormalities	Hypertension	Non-insulin dependent diabetes mellitus
Polycystic ovary syndrome	Osteoarthritis (knees)	Dyslipidaemia
Impaired fertility	Hyperuricaemia	Insulin resistance
Low back pain	Gout	Breathlessness
Anaesthesia complications		Sleep apnoea
Fetal defects associated with maternal obesity		

The mortality ratio increases at BMI levels above 25 and more steeply above 27. At this level, health professionals have reason for concern.[27]

For both genders, the mortality ratio is lowest in the BMI range from twenty to 25. The risk of mortality is moderate for underweight individuals and increases almost linearly from a BMI of 25. For overweight and obese individuals, it is higher for men than for women.[28]

All in all, severe obesity leads to a twelvefold increase in mortality among those aged 25 to 35 years compared to their lean counterparts. The longer a person has suffered from redundant bodyweight, the higher the risk for the above diseases.

27 See Shils et al. 1998, p. 1396.

28 See Shils et al. 1998, p. 1400.

Controlling for possible biases, such as tobacco consumption and unintentional weight loss, the relationship between BMI and mortality becomes almost linear. Prior to the occurrence of chronic diseases, overweight and obese patients often suffer from conditions of mechanic origin caused by the carrying of excess weight, such as osteoarthritis, as well as from gout, pulmonary diseases, and psychological problems.[29]

3.2 The Financial Consequences of Obesity

For the reasons listed in the precedent paragraph, obesity causes varying amounts of direct health care expenditures. Hypertension is the most costly co-morbidity, followed by coronary heart disease and diabetes mellitus. Osteoarthritis, the different types of cancer, and stroke combined only amount to less than one fifth of total costs.[30]

Von Lengerke et al. (2006) assess the direct medical cost of obesity in different BMI groups and varying degrees of obesity among German adults. The authors compare respondents with normal bodyweight with those who are pre-obese, obese (class I), and severely obese (classes II and III) in accordance with WHO classifications. They find that those suffering from severe obesity cause substantially higher costs compared to the other groups under consideration: For example, average annual costs resulting from general practitioner visits increase linearly from € 43.47 for persons within the normal weight range to € 75.59 for the severely obese. The costs for pharmaceuticals that are only available on prescription are also significantly higher for the severely obese. The same applies to the average costs for inpatient services, which may be as much as five times higher for the severely obese than for all other groups. The following figure il-

29 See WHO 2000, pp. 39-57.

30 See Comptroller and Auditor General 2001, p. 17.

lustrates the total direct medical costs for the severely obese compared to costs induced by the other groups mentioned:

Figure 3-6: Annual Direct Medical Cost per Capita by BMI Class [€]
(Reference: Own construction [including inpatient services, outpatient services, and pharmaceuticals; data obtained from von Lengerke et al. 2006, p. 114])

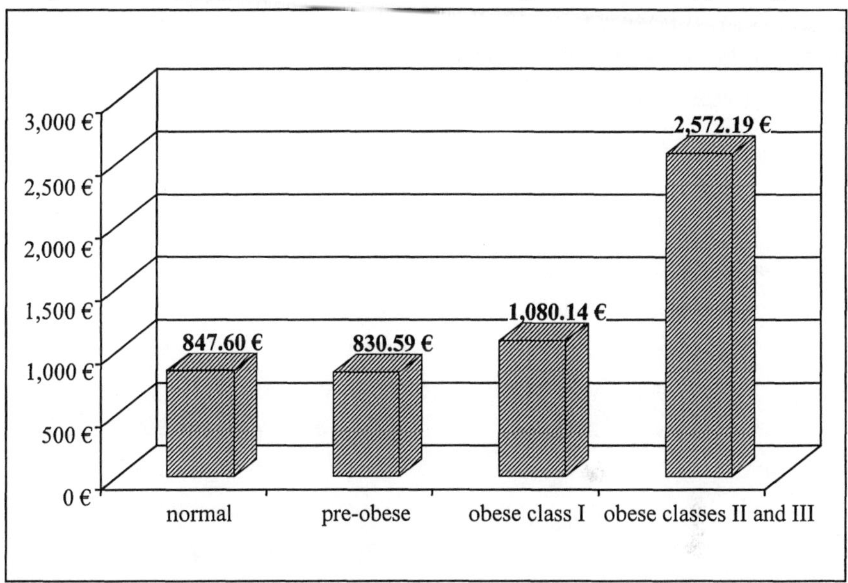

Costs for those suffering from obesity class I are 25 per cent higher than for individuals with normal weight. In contrast, severely obese persons cause costs that are three times higher on average than those within the normal weight range.[31] Due to the fact that the highest cost increases can be found in the obese class, as opposed to mere overweight, health care costs are likely to continue rising as rates of increase are higher in the obese group than in the overweight group.

Health care costs of overweight and obesity not only vary with BMI category, but also with age and race. The rise in health expenditures associated with ex-

31 See von Lengerke et al. 2006, pp. 110-114.

cess bodyweight is similar for both genders but most dramatic for Whites, especially for inpatient stays, office visits, and medications. Healthcare expenditures rise with higher BMI for all adult age groups starting in the middle age (approximately from 35 years of age). The relative cost increase becomes more substantial with age.[32]

In Germany, diseases of the heart and circulatory system are the predominant single cause of premature death. In 1990, 43.8 per cent of all deaths could be attributed to such conditions, in large part potentially induced by unhealthy nutrition.[33]

Three basic categories of costs resulting from obesity must be distinguished: To start with, there are the medical costs of preventing, diagnosing, and treating obesity itself and its associated comorbidities. These costs are referred to as **direct costs**. Moreover, there are morbidity costs which stem from earnings lost due to obesity-related diseases. Furthermore, mortality costs occur when an individual dies prematurely and his future earnings are lost. Morbidity and mortality costs combined are referred to as **indirect costs**. The pain family and friends experience when a person suffering from excess weight becomes sick or dies represents another category of costs. As these costs are **intangible**,[34] they can hardly be quantified. Thus, they are not included in studies concerning obesity-attributable costs. These cost categories combined add up to the social cost. Social costs constitute the private costs of an action plus the external costs (costs induced by an action that are not imposed on the agent deciding on this action, but on other members of society).[35] Social costs and their occurrence are explained in detail in section 3.3.

In addition to the direct individual cost of health treatment, indirect individual obesity-related costs occur: Excess bodyweight also has a negative influence on

32 See Wee et al. 2005, pp. 161-163.
33 See Kohlmeier et al. 1993, p. 14.
34 See Hajen et al. 2006, p. 225.
35 See Varian 1992, p. 433.

the marriage and labour market (occupational attainment[36] and wages[37]). Still, these costs are internal to the individual, and do not contribute to the social costs which may justify government intervention. Furthermore, they can hardly be quantified and are thus neglected in this dissertation.

To my knowledge, only two studies are concerned with the social costs attributable to obesity in Germany. Sander and Bergemann (2003) estimate the economic burden of obesity in Germany in accordance with WHO classifications. The diseases considered in their analysis include non-insulin dependent diabetes mellitus, myocardial infection, hypertension, and stroke. In their approach, the annual treatment costs for each condition are multiplied by the proportion of the disorder in the population that is attributable to obesity. Minimum and maximum values are defined to account for variations in odds ratios and relative risks which are used to calculate the above proportions. Direct costs considered include outpatient treatment, medication including over-the-counter drugs, hospitalisation, and rehabilitation. The indirect costs that are taken into account are due to mortality, work loss, and disability. In Germany, about 12.24 million adults were obese at the time of the study. Of these, an average of 2.9 million, which is equal to approximately 24 per cent, suffer from the selected comorbidities. Annual costs attributable to the four comorbidities combined and obesity incur social costs amounting to € 4,240 m (€ 2,034 m in direct and € 2,206 m in indirect costs) in the base case. The minimum and maximum values are € 2,709 m and € 5,682 m, respectively.[38]

36 See Morris 2006 for a cross-sectional analysis of the effect of BMI on occupational attainment which displays unambiguous statistically significant evidence of a negative impact of obesity measures on labour market outcomes. The results are consistent with other studies suggesting obesity-related discrimination at the workplace.

37 See Baum, Ford 2004, whose results suggest that obesity affects wages independently of actual health limitations. Instead, the authors suggest that obese individuals may invest less in training, that they are discriminated against concerning training opportunities, and / or that obese workers display certain behavioural patterns. For a more thorough discussion of the subject, see Appendix 10.2.

38 See Sander, Bergemann 2003, pp. 248-252.

In the second study, German health expenditures are associated with various diseases caused by nutrition (coronary heart disease, non-insulin dependent diabetes mellitus, hypertension, gout, lipometabolic disorders, gallbladder disease, different types of cancer). Obesity-attributable costs are then calculated using relative risks. Again, minimum and maximum values are defined to account for variations in relative risks and prevalence, and obesity is defined as a BMI of at least 30. As a result, the social costs of obesity in Germany amount to a minimum of DM 11.1 billion and a maximum of DM 19.3 billion (approximately € 5.7 billion and € 9.9 billion, respectively). The result is equal to between 3.5 per cent and 6.1 per cent of total health expenditures. Similar studies conducted in other countries yield similar results with respect to the percentage of health expenditures attributable to obesity (1 per cent to 5.5 per cent), thus reassuring the above calculation.[39]

Due to the restricted availability of data, calculating the direct and indirect costs of obesity is not straightforward. An example of reasonable and detailed calculations despite the incompleteness of information is a study developed by the Comptroller and Auditor General for the United Kingdom.[40]

As a result, social costs due to obesity in England are estimated at £ 2,628.9 m or € 3,753.5 m (direct costs: £ 479.4 m or € 684.5 m, indirect costs: £ 2,149.5 m

39 See Schneider 1996, pp. 369-372.

40 The direct costs in this study comprise the cost of treating obesity itself and the cost of treating the consequences of obesity. For the costs of treating obesity, the unit cost data is multiplied by the incidence of these events. The cost of treating obesity-attributable diseases was estimated by calculating the relevant population attributable risk proportion, using the relative risk. These figures were multiplied by the unit costs of treatment. The indirect costs consist of earnings lost due to premature mortality and earnings lost due to sickness. To estimate earnings lost as a consequence of mortality, the number of deaths attributable to obesity in England was estimated by applying the proportion of obesity-attributable deaths to the number of age- and sex-specific deaths in England. To estimate the years of life lost, data on residual life expectancy by age and sex were applied. These figures were finally multiplied by mean annual earnings data. To estimate earnings lost due to morbidity, the authors multiplied the days lost due to associated diseases by the proportion of each disease attributable to obesity to estimate of the number of days off work attributable to obesity. This was then multiplied by mean daily earnings figures.

or € 3069.0 m). The direct cost is driven primarily by the costs of treating the consequences of obesity, which account for 98 per cent of the total. The most significant cost drivers by far are hypertension, coronary heart disease, and non-insulin dependent diabetes mellitus, followed by osteoarthritis and stroke. Of the indirect cost of obesity, 61 per cent can be attributed to sickness absence, and the remainder to premature mortality.[41] Many studies use the same approach to estimate obesity-attributable costs in a specific country. The main differences are that many studies neglect indirect costs and / or choose other conditions related to obesity.

An approach to estimating the burden of obesity in the European Union is based on the 2002 trend levels of obesity for each member state and the above report published by the UK National Audit Office. By assumption, a country with the same level of health expenditures as England but an average adult obesity level that is, for example, one fifth higher, is assumed to face obesity-attributable costs that are one fifth higher than health expenditures in England. A country with the same level of obesity but half the overall health expenditures is assumed to face half the amount of obesity-related costs. Thus, total direct and indirect cost of obesity for the fifteen EU member states in 2002 is estimated to be approximately € 32.8 billion per year.[42]

In a study conducted for the United States, taking hypertension, diabetes, cardiovascular disease, gallbladder disease, cholecystectomy, and colon and postmenopausal breast cancer into account, the social costs of obesity are estimated at US $ 39.3 billion, or 5.5 per cent of health expenditures in 1986. At least 40 per cent of the arising costs were attributable to severe obesity alone.[43] Total costs attributable to excess weight in the Unites States are projected to double every ten years by the year 2030, thus amounting to US $ 860 to 956 billion which corresponds to sixteen to eighteen per cent of total US health care costs.[44]

41 See Comptroller and Auditor General 2001, Appendix 6, pp. 57-61.

42 See Fry, Finley 2005, pp. 359/360.

43 See Colditz 1992, pp. 503S-507S.

44 See Wang et al. 2008, p. 7.

Comparing health care costs in the US by diagnosis, diseases of the circulatory system, which include, among others, hypertension, stroke, and heart disease, account for US $ 127.8 billion or seventeen per cent of total personal health care expenditures. As in Germany, such conditions, therefore, represent the most expensive disease category.[45]

Estimating the social cost arising from obesity is especially difficult for children. As children are not involved in the labour market, indirect costs of their conditions are ignored. In present studies, only health expenditures are taken into account: One approach focuses on hospital costs and three related diseases, as well as obesity-related diseases, for which obesity was listed as a secondary diagnosis.[46] A more sophisticated study takes a larger number of diseases into account as with the increasing attention that is paid to obesity, an increasing number of conditions has been related to redundant bodyweight.[47] Still, the results ignore the fact that a large percentage of obese children is likely to remain obese as adults and will, as a result, cause substantial economic costs in the future.

When calculating the costs of obesity, mortality must not only be considered in order to calculate forgone earnings, but also to account for lower health expenditures due to differential mortality. As a result, direct health care costs may be as much as 25 per cent lower than many studies suggest.[48]

3.3 Theoretical Aspects: Public Goods, Externalities, and Social Costs

Having demonstrated and quantified the observable consequences of overweight and obesity above, the theoretical economic analysis follows. In addition to the mere occurrence of social costs arising from obesity – which is clarified in the

45 See Hodgson, Cohen 1999, p. 123.

46 See Wang, Dietz 2002, p. E81-1.

47 See Johnson et al. 2006, pp. 171/172.

48 See Allison et al. 1999, pp. 1196-1198.

following section – their consequences on the insurance market are elucidated within the framework of moral hazard and adverse selection. In the first place, in order to understand why overweight and obesity induce costs, pure and impure public goods must be defined, as well as the closely related concept of externalities. Furthermore, a model of impure public goods is elaborated which is appropriate for the case of nutrition.

Two concepts are necessary to define the pure public good: nonrivalry and nonexcludability. These concepts clarify how pure public goods systematically differ from pure private goods.[49]

Due to its **nonrivalry**, every individual is able to consume the same quantity of the pure public good. The enjoyment of other consumers is not decreased by an additional consumer. Therefore, once a certain amount of the public good has been provided, the additional cost of provision to another consumer is zero.

Nonexcludability means that no-one can be excluded from consuming the good. The preclusion is either technically impossible or prohibitively costly.[50]

In contrast, a pure private good is **rival** and **excludable.**[51] It provides benefits only to the person who has paid a certain price for it. Therefore, it is excludable from those who haven't paid. In addition, once the benefits have been rendered, the good is not available to others. Accordingly, the private good is rival.

A common example for a pure private good is food: A price must be paid, and once it has been eaten, it does not provide benefits for others. However, this consideration ignores the consequences of food intake on health, in turn affecting health insurance rates and lifetime productivity.

As expressed in the following figure, the pure public good (point A) and the pure private good (point B) are extreme points on a scale.[52]

---

49 See Samuelson 1954, pp. 387-389.

50 See Mas-Colell et al.1995, p. 360.

51 See Rosen 2005, p. 56.

52 See Connolly, Munro 1999, p. 59.

Figure 3-7: Pure Public vs. Pure Private Good
(Reference: Own construction following Connolly and Munro 1999, p. 59)

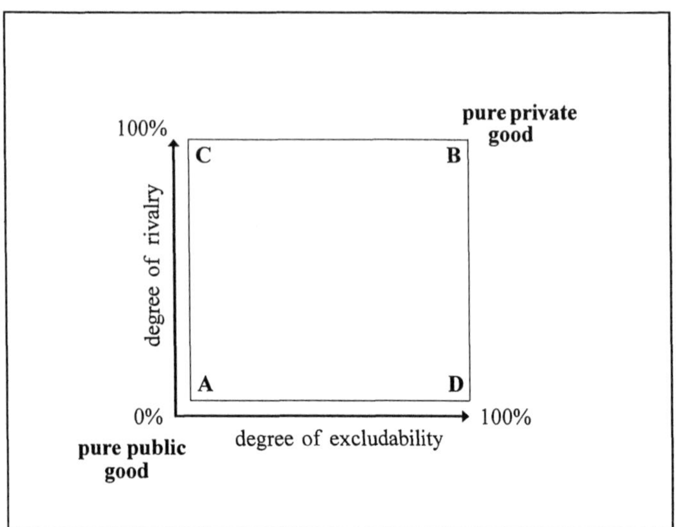

As shown in Figure 3-7, goods vary in their degree of publicness. A public good can be congestible. As a result, the benefits to existing consumers are nonrival up to a certain point; afterwards they are diminished by additional consumers. This is the point of congestion (point C in Figure 3-7). Still, benefits cannot be excluded.

Public goods can also be price-excludable: Their benefits can be sold to a limited number of people before they are consumed. Consequently, the degree of excludability is larger than in the pure public good case. When such goods remain nonrival, they are called club goods (point D in Figure 3-7).[53]

Having explained how public goods differ from the standard pure private good, it must now be clarified which properties are relevant to the occurrence of social costs to society: Externalities, which are defined in this section, often share

53 See Hyman 1996, p. 129.

characteristics of public goods.[54] Other agents in the economy cannot be excluded from their effects, making the externality nonexcludable. If every agent is affected by the externality to the same degree, the externality will also be nonrival. Furthermore, externalities can be generated as a result of public good provision.

Externalities can arise under a number of different circumstances. The case of incompleteness or absence of markets is relevant to obesity, as many consequences of excess bodyweight are not reflected in market transactions. The market may be incomplete for several reasons: To start with, the costs of operating the market can be too high. This applies to many categories of social costs attributable to obesity: The market for health care does not differentiate between obese individuals and those with normal weight in a manner that makes obese individuals pay their way for the costs they have caused. Neither does the structure of government payments associated with sickness and death. The market may also be incomplete due to lack of information.

In addition, the number of buyers and sellers may be too small. Finally, it might be impossible to enforce property rights.[55] The last two cases are hardly relevant to obesity and resulting externalities.

Theoretically, there are three distinct types of externalities: When it comes to **technological externalities**, the objective functions of several agents are correlated. The correlation is not captured by the market mechanism and, as a result, cannot be considered when prices are determined. The absence of market relations may result in discrepancy from an ideal market on which every agent pays for the costs he induces. **Pecuniary externalities** are a consequence of market relations, indicating the scarcity of goods or resources when market prices change. They do not cause market failure. In the case of **psychological externalities**, an individual's utility is affected by other persons' levels of utility or consumption without a physical or market relationship. Both pecuniary and psychological external effects are irrelevant to the following considerations.

54 See Connolly, Munro 1999, pp. 72/73.

55 See Cornes, Sandler 1996, p. 42.

Technological external effects can arise from both production and consumption, and they can have positive or negative consequences for third persons' utility. Due to the possible occurrence of market failure, technological externalities may justify government interventions.[56] Common examples of government interventions are taxes or subsidies.

The occurrence of external effects leads to a deviance from the perfectly competitive market. The perfectly competitive market ensures an efficient market outcome.

According to the First Fundamental Welfare Theorem, an equilibrium allocation achieved by a complete set of competitive markets will necessarily be Pareto-efficient. If there is a complete set of markets, every relevant good will be traded at publicly known prices. Therefore, when markets are incomplete and give rise to externalities, this theorem is violated. In addition, the complete markets assumption implicitly requires that the characteristics of traded goods are observable by all market participants.[57] Thus, the market outcome can be inefficient in the presence of externalities.

For pure public goods, the conditions that must be fulfilled to achieve a Pareto-optimal market outcome are slightly different from the pure private good case. As pure public goods simultaneously provide benefits to all consumers in the economy, each individual's valuation must be accounted for when deciding on the allocation of resources. If the utility of any individual is maximised and other agents' utility levels are held constant, and production efficiency still holds, the marginal rate of substitution, aggregated over all agents, will equal the marginal rate of transformation.

In the case of pure public goods, exchange efficiency must not be fulfilled as due to the simultaneous provision of benefits to all consumers, public goods are not exchanged.[58]

56 See Fritsch et al. 2003, pp. 90-92.

57 See Mas-Colell et al. 1995, pp. 308/309.

58 See Cornes, Sandler 1996, p. 23.

To provide an example for a distorted market outcome, assume there are two individuals, i and j, and two goods. While $good_1$ gives rise to an externality, $good_2$ can be considered a vector of standard goods that do not lead to such consequences. i's utility increases with every unit of the two goods consumed. j's utility also rises in $good_2$, but decreases with every unit of $good_1$ that is consumed by i. While i's utility depends solely on her own consumption of both goods, j's utility is also subject to the amount of $good_1$ consumed by individual i. j's marginal rate of substitution is determined by the amount of $good_1$ consumed by individual i and her own consumption of $good_2$ as both are arguments of j's utility function. With only two individuals in the economy, Pareto-efficiency requires the following equation to hold:

$$MRS_i + \frac{\partial U_j / \partial good_{2j}}{\partial U_j / \partial good_{1i}} = MRT \qquad (3.1)$$

$$\frac{\partial U_i}{\partial good_{1i}} > 0; \frac{\partial U_i}{\partial good_{2i}} > 0; \frac{\partial U_j}{\partial good_{1i}} < 0; \frac{\partial U_j}{\partial good_{2j}} > 0$$

Under perfect competition, i's MRS exactly equals the ratio of the market prices of the two goods produced. While MRS_i equals the marginal rate of transformation (MRT) – which, on a competitive market, is also equal to the ratio of goods prices – MRS_j violates condition (3.1).[59] Thus, the externality induces a suboptimal allocation which results in a loss of welfare.

In Figure 3-8, consider a producer or consumer who makes his decision on quantity q based on the costs he has to pay, the marginal private costs (MPC). In the case of a negative externality, the action causes additional costs that are not reflected in the marginal private costs. These are the marginal external costs (MEC). The sum of both represents the marginal social costs (MSC):

59 See Connolly, Monro 1999, p. 75.

$$MPC + MEC = MSC \quad (3.2)$$

As the marginal external costs are not taken into account when making the decision on quantity q, production or consumption of the good will be too high (q_0 will be produced or consumed instead of q_{opt} as the marginal external costs are not considered).[60] The allocation of resources is, therefore, inefficient.

The marginal social benefit (MSB) is denoted by the dotted line. Social cost incorporates the total of all costs associated with an economic activity. It includes both costs borne by the economic agents directly involved in the decision and the resulting economic activity and also all costs borne by society at large. In presence of a negative externality, social costs are higher than private costs.

When making a decision, for example whether to consume a good or not, the individual weighs the private benefits against the private costs. Thus, the external cost or benefit is ignored. Prices only reflect private costs and benefits.[61] As the external cost is not considered, the market is incomplete and the market outcome is inefficient.

Now that the occurrence of externalities and resulting costs has been explained, one should distinguish three basic categories of social costs resulting from obesity: **Direct costs** are directly associated with either medical treatment of the disease or consequences of the treatment.[62] Thus, they must be paid by the sick person herself. They comprise the costs of preventing, diagnosing, and treating obesity itself and its associated comorbidities. Furthermore, there are **morbidity costs** which stem from earnings lost due to obesity-related diseases. Finally, **mortality costs** occur when an individual dies prematurely and her future earnings are lost.[63]

60 See Hyman 1996, pp. 91/92.
61 See Connolly, Munro 1999, p. 73.
62 See Rychlik 1999, p. 36.
63 See Hajen et al. 2006, p. 225.

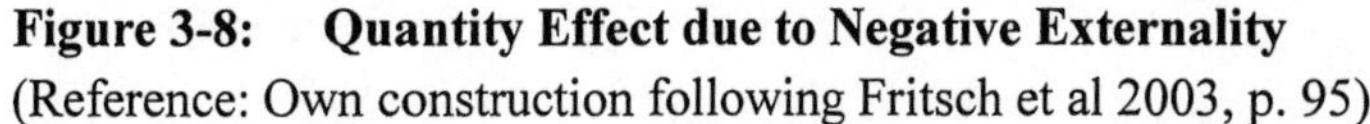

Figure 3-8: Quantity Effect due to Negative Externality
(Reference: Own construction following Fritsch et al 2003, p. 95)

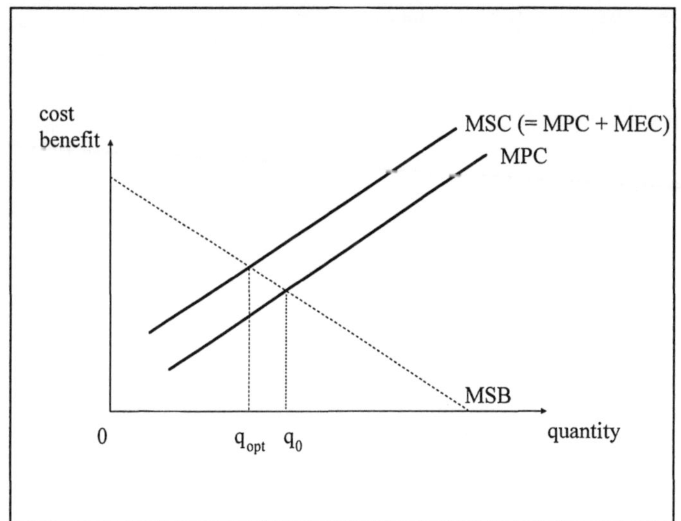

Indirect costs quantify the production loss as a consequence of illness or death and must be borne by society at large. They comprise both mortality and morbidity costs. In contrast to direct costs, indirect costs cannot be directly traced back to the illness.[64]

The pain family and friends experience when a person suffering from excess weight becomes sick or dies represents another category of costs. As these costs are intangible,[65] they can hardly be quantified. Thus, they have not been included in studies concerning obesity-attributable costs.

The categories of social costs attributable to overweight and obesity are illustrated in detail in Figure 3-9.

Notably, the direct costs of prevention, treatment, and diagnosis can lead to increased health care premiums not only for the sick person but for all those in-

64 See Rychlik 1999, pp. 38/39.
65 See Hajen et al. 2006, p. 225.

sured. In this case, the medical costs are indirect in nature because they are borne by society as a whole. In contrast, if health care premiums only rise for the patient causing these costs, they will be direct costs.

Figure 3-9: Obesity-Specific Social Cost Categories
(Reference: Own construction)

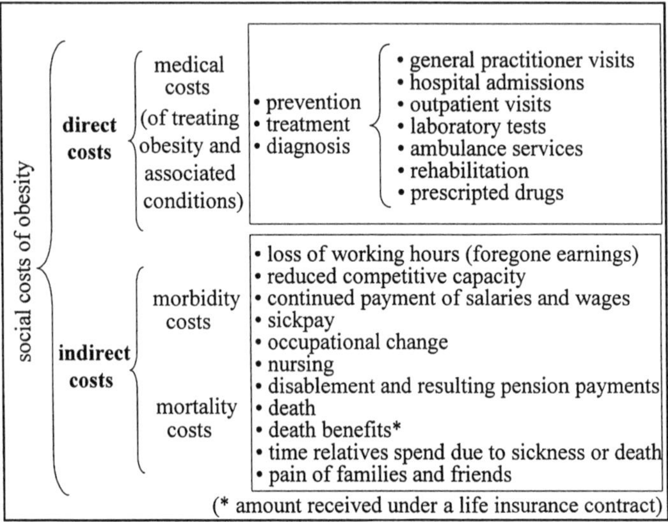

With such an extensive list of social cost categories at hand, one must be careful not to double-count costs or benefits: For example, if the foregone benefit of lost productivity is counted as social costs, then the continued payment of wages and salaries must not be considered. Both amounts are different aspects of the same cost.[66]

As stated before, the pure public and the pure private good are extreme points on a scale. Pure public goods can hardly be found in reality. The case of the **impure public good** is more common in real life. Public impurity can be attributed to at least three factors: To begin with, multiple outputs of a single good can

66 See Folland et al. 2001, p. 82.

exist. Furthermore, the benefits provided can either be only partially rival or partially excludable.[67] Notably, private consumption (or production) activities can generate externalities.[68]

Formally, the impure public good appears twice in an individual's objective function. Once, it appears as a private commodity. In addition, it appears in combination with the quantities consumed by other agents, representing its publicness.

To provide an example for impure public goods, assume individual i's utility depends on the consumption of food F and other (non-food) goods and services, L, as well as on the level of health H. As described in the preceding chapter, the level of health is influenced by food consumption. Furthermore, public health (denoted PH) depends on the individual states of health of all n agents in the economy. A high level of public health provides positive utility as it leads to lower health expenditures and allows for a high level of productivity in the economy. On a personal level, good health is desirable as sickness provides disutility:

$$U_i = U_i(F_i, H_i(F_i), L_i; PH(H_1(F_1),...,H_i(F_i),...,H_n(F_n)) \quad (3.3)$$

$$i = 1,...,n$$

$$\frac{\partial U_i}{\partial F_i} > 0; \frac{\partial U_i}{\partial H_i(F_i)} > 0; \frac{\partial U_i}{\partial L_i} > 0; \frac{\partial U_i}{\partial PH} > 0$$

Thus, food consumption as an impure public good simultaneously gives rise to health as a private characteristic and to the public characteristic PH. The level of the public characteristic depends on the levels of health of individuals 1 to n which, in turn, depend on their diet.

67 See Cornes, Sandler 1996, p. 542.

68 See Musgrave et al. 1994, p. 77.

As a result, i's utility not only depends on her own health, but also on the health habits of all other agents in the economy. The market outcome can only be optimal if the impure publicness of a good is accounted for. The optimal market outcome in the impure public good case is between the pure private and the pure public good case. As a result, the optimal solution can only be obtained in a free market with a correction of the relative prices.[69]

3.4 A Microeconomic Framework for Food Choices

Equation (3.3) shows that within the framework of this dissertation, food as a determinant of health is an impure public good. For this reason and due to the complex nature of food choices, standard approaches to consumer theory do not fit the present framework. An appropriate framework is provided by Kelvin J. Lancaster's approach to consumer theory. At the core of his theory lies the idea that goods give rise to various characteristics, and that utility is derived from these characteristics as opposed to goods.

The following elaborations draw on both Lancaster's works concerning consumer theory (Lancaster 1966, 1971) and impure public goods (Lancaster 1976). In the case of food, relevant characteristics are quantitative and objectively measurable. Examples for such characteristics are caloric content, the content of specific vitamins, or the fat content. Which characteristics a person considers important is a question of personal preferences. Figure 3-10 illustrates that different edibles can give rise to the same characteristics (albeit these characteristics are usually offered in varying amounts):

The columns of the matrix below describe the characteristics (caloric, protein, carbohydrate, and fat content) that can be derived from 100g of three edibles (cornflakes, low-fat milk, bacon). The rows depict the relative amount of the characteristics of 100g of each of these edibles: It can easily be seen that the

69 See Lancaster 1976, pp. 132-135.

caloric content of cornflakes is more than seven times higher than that of low-fat milk. However, its fat content is less than twice as high, each number referring to the same weight.

Figure 3-10: Consumption Technology Matrix
(Reference: Own construction following Lancaster 1971, pp. 17/18)

Goods / Characteristics	Cornflakes (100g)	2% Low-fat Milk (100g)	Bacon; Cooked Breakfast Strips (100g)
Calories [no. kcal]	361.0	50.0	461.0
Protein [g]	7.1	3.3	30.4
Carbohydrates [g]	85.7	4.5	4.3
Fat [g]	3.6	2.0	34.8

Consequently, consumers can choose between several different goods collections (in the present context, we name these collections 'food baskets') in order to achieve the same aim in terms of characteristics. Individual preference orderings then rank the collections of characteristics. Individuals have an ordinal (and subjective) utility function U on characteristics and rationally maximise the utility gained from a collection of characteristics, subject to the budget constraint. Lancaster uses 'consumption technology matrix' as a term for the matrix describing the relation between the food basket and the respective characteristics.

Figure 3-10 depicts a consumption technology matrix. The question remains as to whether which characteristics collection an individual prefers. In contrast, previous approaches to consumer theory ask which *goods* collection is preferred.

From the consumer's point of view, a budget is spent on goods so as to maximise utility. Goods prices determine which goods collections are affordable. The affordable goods collections are ranked in accordance with the characteristics they provide to the consumer. Goods are related to these characteristics via the consumption technology matrix. This matrix is objective and quantifiable. The resulting characteristics are the same for all consumers and can hence be called 'objective'. The choice of the characteristics collection is based on personal preferences and is thus an individual choice. This choice gives rise to a personal, subjective element, such as taste. As a result, Lancaster's theory explicitly separates universal properties of demand from personal, subjective properties of demand, which depend on individual preferences and taste.

Consequently, subject to the budget constraint, the consumers' choice consists of two separate decisions: The **efficiency choice** determines the characteristics frontier. The characteristics frontier contains the most efficient combinations of goods to achieve a characteristics collection, given the budget value. It is thus comparable to the production possibilities frontier in production theory. The associated efficient goods collection is the same for all consumers facing the same constraints and goods and can, therefore, be called objective.

Individuals' **private choice** constitutes which point on the frontier the consumer prefers. This choice is subjective. Here, individual tastes can be taken into consideration.[70]

In the case of two goods, the consumer faces the following standard budget constraint:

$$M = price_1 \cdot good_1 + price_2 \cdot good_2 \tag{3.4}$$

M denotes the budget. The above equation determines the affordable combinations of goods. Nevertheless, consumers are not interested in the goods as such, but in the characteristics they provide. Under the assumption that $good_1$ and $good_2$ provide a number of z characteristics (denoted ch), the above equation becomes:

70 See Lancaster 1966, pp. 139/140.

$$M = price_1 \cdot ch_1 + price_1 \cdot ch_2 + ... + price_1 \cdot ch_z$$
$$+ price_2 \cdot ch_1 + price_2 \cdot ch_2 + ... + price_2 \cdot ch_z \quad (3.5)$$

Equations (3.4) and (3.5) are related via the consumption technology matrix. Now, the budget also determines which collections of characteristics the consumer can afford. In terms of Lancaster, all affordable characteristics add up to the characteristics frontier. Then, individuals decide which characteristics collection to choose based on their preferences. In the case of food, these preferences will be different for different individuals (for example, vegetarians value other characteristics than meat eaters, and construction workers need more calories than office workers or fashion models). Therefore, individuals attach different weights to the respective characteristics. This is illustrated in the Characteristics-Preferences Matrix CP:

Figure 3-11: Characteristics-Preferences Matrix
(Reference: Own construction)

Characteristics / Preferences	ch_1	ch_2	...	ch_z
pr_1	γ_{11}	γ_{12}	...	γ_{1z}
pr_2	γ_{21}	γ_{22}	...	γ_{2z}
...	...	...	...	...
pr_k	γ_{k1}	γ_{k2}	...	γ_{kz}

$0 \leq \gamma_{ij} < 1$ for all $i = 1,...,k$

$$\sum_{j=1}^{z} \gamma_{ij} = 1$$

The weight individuals attach to characteristic ch based on their preference pr is denoted γ_{ij}. There are k individuals and z characteristics. Now, the vector of characteristics as quoted in equation (3.5) is written in matrix form and denoted CH. CH is then multiplied by matrix CP:

$$CP \cdot CH = \begin{pmatrix} \gamma_{11} & \gamma_{12} & \cdots & \gamma_{1z} \\ \gamma_{21} & \gamma_{22} & \cdots & \gamma_{2z} \\ \cdots & \cdots & \cdots & \cdots \\ \gamma_{k1} & \gamma_{k2} & \cdots & \gamma_{kz} \end{pmatrix} \begin{pmatrix} ch_1 & 0 & \cdots & 0 \\ 0 & ch_2 & \cdots & 0 \\ \cdots & \cdots & \cdots & \cdots \\ 0 & 0 & \cdots & ch_z \end{pmatrix} = \begin{pmatrix} CH_1 \\ CH_2 \\ \cdots \\ CH_r \end{pmatrix} \tag{3.6}$$

$$CH_i = \gamma_{i1} \cdot ch_1 + \gamma_{i2} \cdot ch_2 + \ldots + \gamma_{iz} \cdot ch_z$$

CH_i is a fixed combination of characteristics satisfying the individual's preferences. CH_i can be normalised, for example by setting ch_1 equal to 1. Then, the preferred characteristics collection is assigned a price. As a consequence, the consumer's decision is a standard price-quantity decision.

Now, assume there are three categories of goods: Food F, all goods and services except for food (denoted L), and medical care C. Each category provides a certain number of characteristics: There are a food characteristics, b characteristics of non-food goods, and c characteristics of medical care. Again, the number of individuals is k. The Characteristics-Preferences Matrix is depicted in Figure 3-12.

The fixed combination of characteristics is derived as in equation (3.6). Again, a price is assigned to the normalised characteristics collections. Based on this, individuals choose a combination of goods of each category providing the preferred characteristics collection.

In the subsequent chapter, food is considered a determinant of good health. Notably, there is a physical upper limit to good or optimal health. F and C influence health. Appropriate nutrition and medical care can both improve health when it is suboptimal. In this case, their marginal utility is positive. With continued consumption of a healthy diet and medical care, their marginal utility first becomes zero and can then also become negative. The focus of this dissertation is the influence of nutrition on health. Thus, medical care is neglected in the following.

Figure 3-12: Characteristics-Preferences Matrix: Food, Non-food, Medical Care
(Reference: Own construction)

			Characteristics								
			Food			**Non-food**			**Medical care**		
			ch_1	**...**	**ch_a**	**ch_{a+1}**	**...**	**ch_{a+b}**	**ch_{a+b+1}**	**...**	**ch_{a+b+c}**
Preferences	**Food**	**pr_1**	γ_{11}	...	γ_{1a}	0	0	0	0	0	0
		...	...	...	...	0	0	0	0	0	0
		pr_k	γ_{k1}	...	γ_{ka}	0	0	0	0	0	0
	Non-food	**pr_1**	0	0	0	γ_{1a+1}	...	γ_{1a+b}	0	0	0
		...	0	0	0	...	...	...	0	0	0
		pr_k	0	0	0	γ_{ka+1}	...	γ_{ka+b}	0	0	0
	Medical care	**pr_1**	0	0	0	0	0	0	γ_{1a+b+1}	...	γ_{1a+b+c}
		...	0	0	0	0	0	0	...	...	...
		pr_k	0	0	0	0	0	0	γ_{ka+b+1}	...	γ_{ka+b+c}

Characteristics can be subject to satiation effects, meaning the consumer does not have positive interest in further quantities of this specific characteristic. Two types of satiation effects can be observed: The consumer can either have zero interest in the characteristic (i.e. further amounts of vitamin A after the recommended daily intake has already been achieved) or negative interest (i.e. calories from fat). The former shall be referred to as **open satiation**, the latter as **closed**

satiation. Closed satiation does not make a characteristic and, in turn, a good irrelevant beyond a certain level of consumption. It rather causes a switch in preferences from positive to negative. Again, satiation in this model refers to a characteristic, not to a good. In addition, not all characteristics are necessarily satiable.[71] Satiation effects and their consequences within the framework of health are further elaborated in the subsequent chapter (see Figures 4-2 and 4-4).

71 See Lancaster 1971, pp. 147-156.

Glossary

a:	number of food characteristics
b:	number of non-food characteristics
c:	number of characteristics of medical care
C:	medical care
ch:	consumption characteristic
CH:	vector of characteristics
CP:	Characteristics-Preferences Matrix
F:	food
F_n:	food basket
h, i, j:	index for individuals
H:	state of health
k:	number of individuals
L:	non-food goods and services
M:	budget
PH:	public health
pr:	preference
q:	quantity
q_{opt}:	optimal quantity
U:	utility function
z:	number of characteristics
γ_{ij} :	weight valuing characteristics

Chapter 4. Obesity from a Microeconomic Perspective

In the present chapter, a consumer model referring to food consumption decisions is developed. Moreover, the static model is extended to a dynamic framework. Further extensions of the model include specific reference to diet composition, the rate of time preference, addictive aspects, and dynamic inconsistency. Figure 4-1 illustrates the main differences between the model and its extensions with respect to standard assumptions in microeconomic theory.

4.1 The Static Model

The present section approaches obesity as a phenomenon from an individual perspective. The core of the model is the microeconomic theory of consumer behaviour. In addition, some empirical facts are considered: On average, obese persons have a lower socioeconomic status. Thus, they are less educated and earn less. Obesity also appears associated with unemployment. In the following, the lack of human capital, of which health is an important aspect, is – by assumption – traced back to a feature which causes the above empirical observations. This feature is referred to as 'health consciousness' in this dissertation. Thus, the population is differentiated into two groups. These groups are denoted P_1 and P_2, respectively. Health-conscious group P_1 is more highly educated and thus able to find employment and receive a higher income.

The fact that this group has made an effort to receiving higher education can be attributed to consciousness in general which simultaneously leads to reasonable decisions concerning health.

Figure 4-1: The Static Model, the Dynamic Model, and Extensions: Main Differences
(Reference: Own Construction)

	Concave utility function	**Exponential discounting / Constant rate of time preference**	**Normal goods**	**Comments**
4.1 Static Model	+ / -	(-)	+	A Concave utility function and the deviation from concavity are both analysed.
4.2 Dynamic Model	+	+	+	All standard assumptions are fulfilled.
4.2.1 Diet Composition	+	+	+	In contrast to 4.2, the process of digestion is differentiated with respect to fat and carbohydrates.
4.2.2 Rate of Time Preference	+	-	+	The rate of time preference increases with higher deviation from optimal weight.
4.2.3 Addictive Aspects	+	+	-	An addictive good is introduced.
4.2.4 Dynamic Inconsistency	+	-	+ / -	Quasi-hyperbolic discounting is introduced; its combination with an addictive good is also analysed.

As a result, short-term taste and price advantages of cheap, energy-dense foods are neglected in favour of the long-term health effects that stem from healthy food.

Group P_2's decisions systematically differ from P_1's decisions as this group lacks health consciousness. P_2 individuals do not pursue higher education and care less for their health. As a result, they are more often unemployed and have less disposable income. They prefer junk food as it provides more calories per monetary unit.

P_2 individuals may understand the health information they receive but do not bear the consequences. This view is consistent with the fact that the types of food which should be primarily consumed or avoided are common knowledge. Although even the most educated persons could not quantify the exact number of calories they consume from fats, proteins, and carbohydrates with a given meal, many people manage to balance their energy intake with energy expenditure, thus keeping their weight stable. Therefore, it is unlikely that more detailed food labelling will be effective in reducing overweight and obesity rates unless health information is actually processed (which may happen as a consequence of constant reminiscence of food quality).

Furthermore, the following elaborations are based on the observation that health food is more costly than junk food. Thus, diet quality depends on income. On a per-calorie basis, increased consumption of fats and sugars leads to savings on food expenditures. Recent studies show that the major trends in US food supply point to a greater availability of low cost, energy-dense foods. Between 1985 and 2000, retail prices for fresh fruit and vegetables increased by 118 per cent, and prices for total fruit and vegetables increased by 89 per cent. By contrast, price increases were only 35 per cent for fats and oils, and 20 per cent for carbonated soft drinks.[72] Although the proportion of disposable income that is spent on food is continuously decreasing, Americans are becoming fatter and fatter. Thus, diets obviously become cheaper (relative to the number of calories)

72 See Putnam et al. 2002, p. 15.

and more energy-dense (more loaded with refined grains, added fats, and added sugars) at the same time.[73]

This approach explicitly considers limited resources and the higher costs of a healthy diet. The contribution of the growing price gap between healthy and unhealthy food to rising obesity rates is taken into account. Given that energy-dense foods are often more palatable and are usually perceived less satiating, there is obviously potential for food overconsumption. A healthy but inexpensive diet may require some sacrifices in taste.

In the following, individuals pursue a high level of health. A high level of health is desirable as illness provides disutility, and because good health is a prerequisite for productivity on the labour market. In order to achieve a favourable state of health, consumers spend their disposable income on the food basket F, on non-food goods L (all other goods and services, that is), and on medical care. Medical care helps recover a high level of health in case of illness. By contrast, diet choices are necessary to maintain the present level of health or can improve the state of health, usually independently of illness. To maximise utility, optimal consumption levels of food, non-food, and medical care must be found. These will sustain the optimal level of health which, in turn, enables the individual to maximise income. Noteworthy, the optimal state of health (which is achieved when the marginal benefits of improved health equal the marginal costs of investments in health) may differ from the maximally achievable level of health. As this dissertation is concerned with obesity as a phenomenon, the optimal value for medical care is exogenously determined, like all health-related goods and services except for food. Thus, by assumption, the level of health (denoted H) is solely influenced by diet choices. H is increased by food consumption for underweight individuals (BMI below 18.5). Adequate nutrition maintains the state of health in the normal weight range. At the upper limit of the normal weight range is the satiation point beyond which health is deteriorated by food overconsumption.

73 See Drewnowski 2004, p. 159.

Figure 4-2: Health and Satiation
(Reference: Own construction)

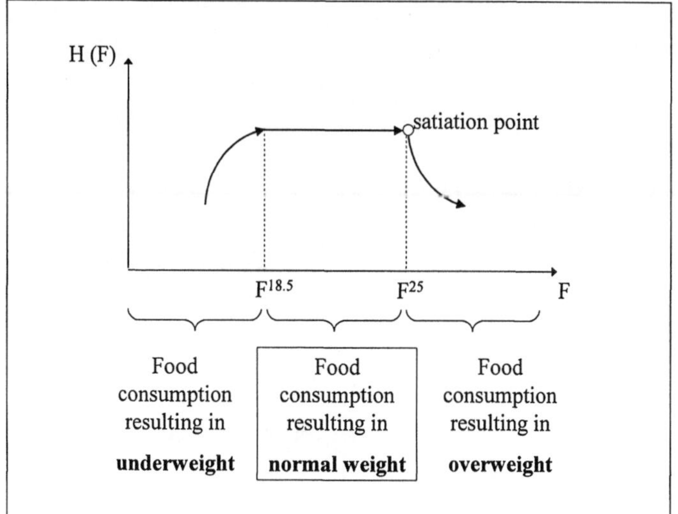

Physically, a BMI range between 18.50 and 25 is optimal (that is, a normal weight level in accordance with WHO criteria). In the above figure, $F^{18.5}$ refers to a food basket leading to a BMI at the lower limit of the normal weight range. F^{25} denotes food consumption resulting in a BMI at the upper limit of the same weight range. Above this weight range, individuals are overweight (or obese from a BMI value of 30). As a result, marginal health differs by weight level:

- $H'(F) > 0$ for BMI values below 18.5
- $H'(F) = 0$ for BMI values from 18.5 to just under 25
- $H'(F) < 0$ for BMI values equal to or higher than 25.

The present approach may not have been appropriate before excess weight became a global health problem: Previously, individuals simply had to maximise the amount of calories consumed. Today, calories are readily available in vast amounts at low prices. Therefore, the benefits of food consumption must be weighed against their costs.

The food basket that will be chosen is endogenous. The utility function depends on the food basket F, non-food goods L, and the food-dependent state of health H:

$$U = U(F, L, H(F)) \qquad (4.1)$$

$$\frac{\partial U}{\partial F} > 0; \frac{\partial U}{\partial L} > 0; \frac{\partial U}{\partial H(F)} > 0; \frac{\partial H}{\partial F} > 0, = 0, < 0$$

As described on the previous page, the value of marginal health depends on a person's current weight level (underweight, normal weight, or overweight). The marginal utilities from F, L, and H are all positive. Notably, only conscious individuals derive positive utility from health. By assumption, income depends on H(F). As a result, the budget constraint is:

$$F \cdot G + L \cdot I = M + \alpha \cdot H(F) \qquad (4.2)$$

$$\alpha > 0$$

G denotes the price for the chosen food basket F, I the price for the chosen collection of other goods and services L. M refers to the budget. The influence of health on income is directly proportional and determined by α. Within the normal weight range, the level of health (maintained by appropriate nutrition) remains constant. Thus, the maximally achievable budget (denoted M_{max}) also remains constant within this interval:

$$M_{max} = M + \alpha \cdot H(F) \qquad (4.3)$$

For BMI values below 18.5, disposable income increases until M_{max} is reached. For BMI values above 25, disposable income decreases. In order to determine an optimal consumption bundle, the budget constraint (4.2) and the slope of the indifference curve must be given. In accordance with (4.1), the slope of the indifference curve is:

$$\left.\frac{dL}{dF}\right|_{\bar{U}} = -\frac{U_F + U_H \cdot H'}{U_L} \tag{4.4}$$

Within the normal weight range, marginal health equals zero. Thus, within this interval, the above equation becomes:

$$\left.\frac{dL}{dF}\right|_{\bar{U}} = -\frac{U_F}{U_L} \tag{4.5}$$

This standard situation occurs even though marginal utility from health is positive. For BMI values above 25, marginal health from food consumption is negative. Thus, indifference curves level off, their slope first becomes less, and may even become positive. This is a consequence of the satiating characteristics of food: In terms of Lancaster (see precedent chapter), an individual is neutral towards the caloric content of food within her normal weight range as a result of open satiation. At the upper limit of normal weight, further calorie consumption provides disutility. In this range, food is subject to closed satiation. By contrast, other goods and services always provide positive utility.

In the overweight range, the budget equation remains unchanged. Notably, H(F) is decreasing in this range. The slope of the budget constraint is:

$$\frac{dL}{dF} = \frac{\alpha \cdot H'(F)}{I} - \frac{G}{I} = \frac{-(G - \alpha \cdot H'(F))}{I} \tag{4.6}$$

In this range, marginal health is negative. As a result, the numerator of the above fraction is larger than the food price, G:

$$(G-\alpha\cdot H'(F))>G \tag{4.7}$$

Thus, the budget constraint is steeper in the overweight than in the normal weight range. Simultaneously, the slope of indifference curves has decreased. Thus, optimal food consumption must lead to a BMI value equal to or smaller than 25 as the corner solution is binding (point A in Figure 4-3). For the underweight range, the argumentation is analogue: Within this range, marginal health is positive. Therefore, the following holds:

$$(G-\alpha\cdot H'(F))<G \tag{4.8}$$

Thus, the slope of the budget constraint is smaller than in the normal weight range. Simultaneously, indifference curves are steeper:

$$\left.\frac{dL}{dF}\right|_{\bar{U}}=\frac{-(U_F+U_H\cdot H')}{U_L} \tag{4.9}$$

Therefore, due to the binding corner solution, optimal food consumption must lead to a BMI value of at least 18.5 (point B in Figure 4-3). Under the assumption that health influences income, indifference curves thus have a kink in their upper range. As stated before, their slope becomes less or even positive due to the satiation point. The budget constraint is also kinked, its slope becomes larger in this range. As a consequence, indifference curves touch the budget constraint between $F^{18.5}$ and F^{25} (point C in Figure 4-3).

Figure 4-3: Solution of the Static Model: Health-Dependent Income
(Reference: Own construction)

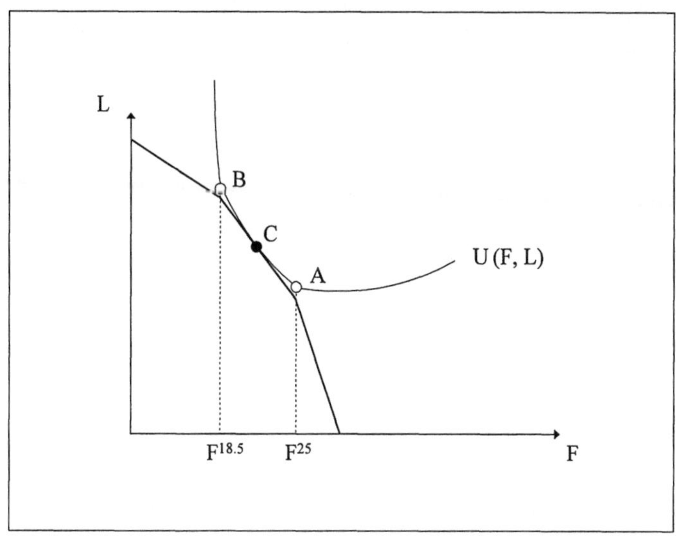

Notably, in this range, the price ratio equals the MRS. Otherwise, a corner solution occurs and point A in the above figure is realised. Below normal BMI values, indifference curves are steeper, and the budget equation is less sloped. Therefore, the tangent point is in the normal weight range or a corner solution in point B occurs. The chosen value of F is consequently either equal to $F^{18.5}$ or to F^{25} or lies between these two values. As a result, utility maximisation leads to a healthy bodyweight.

Health-conscious individuals have a direct and an indirect incentive to sustain a favourable state of health:

- $U_H(F) > 0$ provides a **direct** incentive for good health
- $M_{max} = M + \alpha \cdot H(F)$ provides an **indirect** incentive.

The direct incentive is a sufficient condition provided all other health aspects are optimal. If they are not optimal, the indirect incentive constitutes a necessary condition.

Now, assume disposable income is independent of health. The achievable budget is simply denoted M. Then, the budget equation is:

$$F \cdot G + I \cdot L = M \tag{4.10}$$

As a result, the slope of the budget constraint is:

$$\frac{dL}{dF} = -\frac{G}{I} \tag{4.11}$$

Therefore, the budget constraint is not kinked. As the utility function and the different values for marginal health (depending on the weight range) remain unchanged compared to the situation with health-dependent income, the slope of the indifference curve and its kinks remain unchanged, as well. As a result, the conclusions are equivalent with and without the indirect incentive for good health. Thus, health-dependent income is not a prerequisite for a solution that is binding in the normal weight range. A rational person deriving positive utility from health optimally chooses a BMI value between 18.5 and 25.

Under the assumption that good health enhances productivity, thus increasing income, the following holds:

- In the underweight range, the indifference curve (steeper than in the normal weight range) and the budget constraint (less sloped than in the normal weight range) are both kinked – thus, a corner solution occurs in point B
- In the normal weight range, the budget constraint is tangent to the indifference curve
- In the overweight range, the indifference curve (less sloped than in the normal weight range or even positively sloped) and the budget constraint (steeper than in the normal weight range) are both kinked – thus, a corner solution occurs in point A.

Under the assumption that income is independent of the state of health, the kinks in the budget constraint do not appear. Still, the same conclusions on tangency and corner solutions hold. Again, the value of F is either equal to $F^{18.5}$ or to F^{25} or lies between these two values as values outside of this range are never chosen due to the shape of the indifference curve (see Figure 4-4).

Figure 4-4: Solution of the Static Model: Health-Independent Income
(Reference: Own Construction)

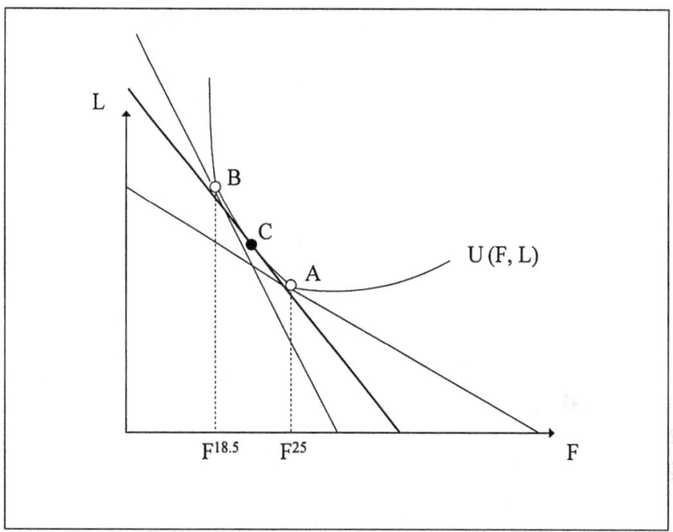

Obviously, within this framework, obesity does not occur. Still, obesity is a widespread phenomenon in the industrialised world. This is where the distinction between conscious and unconscious individuals comes into play: A health-unconscious individual does not gain utility from health:

$$U_H(F) = 0 \tag{4.12}$$

Health as an input into the utility function may be neglected due to lack of education, or simply due to a generally apathic attitude towards life. However, as argued before, this aspect leads to lower disposable income. In turn, lower income may result in the consumption of more energy-dense food (i.e. junk food) as it provides more calories per monetary unit. The price of healthy food (healthy in the sense of low fat content and comparatively few calories) is larger than the price of junk food. Now, assume healthy food is relevant to P_1 individuals as P_1 individuals care for their health. Moreover, they are employed and have a higher income. As a result, their budget constraint is steeper than P_2's budget constraint.

In this case, P_2 individuals rationally choose a state of overweightness as depicted in Figure 4-5 (F* denotes utility-maximising food consumption), unless food prices are increased sufficiently so tangency of budget constraint and indifference curve is obtained within the normal weight range – for example by taxing junk food.

Figure 4-5: Rational Overeating
(Reference: Own construction)

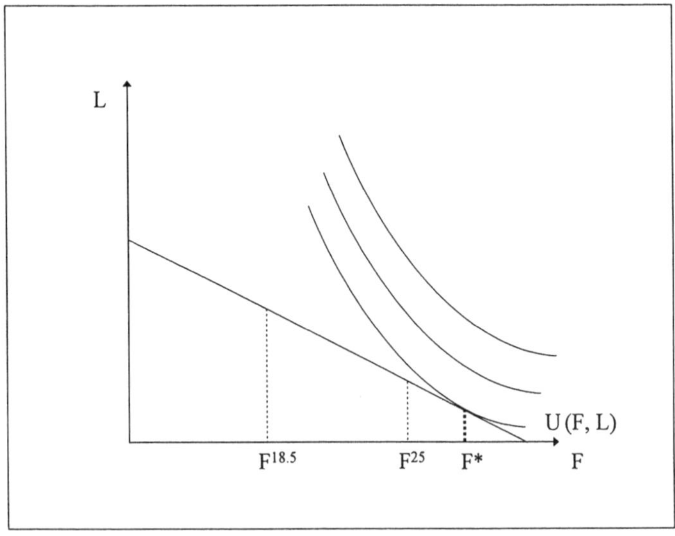

So far, the model is static. However, a static approach to the present problem is inappropriate. For example, the amount of calories necessary to attain normal weight changes with age due to a reduction in BMR. In addition, lifestyle varies over time: Individuals may change their profession or start (or quit) a physical activity. As a consequence, $F^{18.5}$ and F^{25} change because a different food basket is chosen. If a person does not react to such changes, she will leave the normal weight range. Thus, habit persistence may lead to overweight or obesity. In addition, good health usually leads to longevity. Such aspects cannot be considered in a static model.

4.2 The Dynamic Model

Within the framework of this model – which draws on Grossman's (1972) work on the demand for health – the level of an individual's health depends on her allocation of resources. Individuals choose their level of health comparable to choosing a certain level of consumption. A particular level of health is desired because sickness reduces productivity: With a worse state of health, more time is lost due to weight-related sickness. In addition, a low state of health itself causes disutility as a consequence of reduced well-being. Food is purchased for the sake of maintaining a healthy level of weight, and for its taste. Thus, food is considered an intermediate product in the production of health, and in addition to the demand for food due to its palatability, the demand for food is a derived demand. All non-food goods and services are inputs into the production function and give rise to an aggregate commodity. Again, the introduction of the aggregate commodity is based on Lancaster's approach to consumer theory as explained in the precedent chapter.

The dynamic approach allows for a distinction between stock and flow variables. In the following elaborations, food enters the utility function twice: As a stock variable (bodyweight, or more precisely the deviation from the physically optimal weight level) and as a flow variable (taste and palatability provide immediate satisfaction – food consumption in period t is denoted F_t in the utility function). The central proposition of the model is that health is a durable stock. Due to the intertemporal nature of the present approach, health does not depend on food consumption as such, but on the deviation from a physically optimal level of bodyweight, BW*. Again, the optimal weight level is exogenously determined in accordance with WHO criteria. Due to this slight alteration, the state of health is now weight-dependent (as opposed to food-dependent in the precedent paragraph): The further the deviation from BW*, the lower the state of health. On the one hand, weight is augmented due to food consumption. On the other hand, bodyweight depreciates over time at rate δ_t, which equals the metabolic rate. This rate depends on several factors, such as the individual's age or body composition. The amount of energy expenditure in each period is proportional to current bodyweight. Therefore, δ_t is multiplied by BW_t in the equation of motion. Individuals have intertemporal utility functions U_t. Utility is defined from the period of birth, period 0, to the final period T in which the individual dies. Utility is increased by health (which, in turn, is decreased by the deviation from the optimal level of weight, D_t), and by food consumption, F_t, and the consumption of other goods and services L_t:

$$U_t = U_t(H_t(D_t), F_t, L_t) \tag{4.13}$$

$$\frac{\partial U_t}{\partial H_t(D_t)} > 0; \frac{\partial H_t}{\partial D_t} < 0; \frac{\partial U_t}{\partial F_t} > 0; \frac{\partial U_t}{\partial L_t} > 0$$

$$U_t' > 0; U_t'' < 0$$

By assumption, the utility function is continuous, twice differentiable, and concave.[74]

74 Provided that the utility function is of the von Neumann-Morgenstern type, a strictly concave utility function implies risk aversion since the individual prefers a payoff that occurs with certainty to a lottery that yields the same expected payoff. The fact that people are risk-averse is well-established, see, for instance, the seminal work by Arrow

Deviation D_t from optimal weight BW* is derived in the following way:

$$D_t = (BW^* - BW_t)^2 \tag{4.14}$$

The consumption of food and of other goods and services provides enjoyment. Reductions in the level of health provide disutility and increase sick time TL_t:

$$\frac{\partial TL_t}{\partial H_t(D_t)} < 0 \tag{4.15}$$

The change in bodyweight from one period to the next, $B\dot{W}_t$, equals the amount of energy intake J_t (depending on net calories and on the time for food preparation and consumption, TF_t), deducted by the calories expended on metabolism:

$$J_t - \delta_t BW_t = BW_{t+1} - BW_t = B\dot{W}_t \tag{4.16}$$

While F_t denotes the specific foods consumed and refers to its taste and palatability, J_t denotes the actual amount of energy derived from food consumption. This differentiation is appropriate as different types of food provide varying amounts of calories.

Put differently, bodyweight is a result of the following equation:

(1963, pp. 959/960) or Pratt (1964, p. 127). This train of thought implies that risk-averse individuals are more slender, and that weight depends on the level of risk aversion. These hypotheses appear plausible as excess bodyweight increases the likeliness of disease, and proneness to disease can be decreased by avoiding an unhealthy BMI. Similarly, risk-averse individuals will refrain from smoking and immoderate alcohol consumption.

$$BW_{t+1} = BW_t \cdot (1-\delta_t) + J_t \tag{4.17}$$

Under the restrictive assumption that the metabolic rate remains stable throughout life, current bodyweight can also be expressed as:

$$BW_t = BW_0 \cdot (1-\delta)^t + J_1 \cdot (1-\delta)^{t-1} + J_2 \cdot (1-\delta)^{t-2} + \ldots + J_t \tag{4.18}$$

This representation illustrates that the path of an individual's bodyweight starts at birth weight BW_0 – which is approximately equal for everyone – and afterwards solely depends on calorie intake and energy expenditure.

There are two separate household production functions. One describes food consumption and the time spent on preparing and enjoying food:

$$J_t = J_t(F_t, TF_t) \tag{4.19}$$

TF_t is a time input. The second production function refers to the aggregate consumption commodity K_t:

$$K_t = K_t(L_t, TA_t) \tag{4.20}$$

TA_t denotes the time input, L_t represents the goods and services input into the production of commodity K_t.

There are two constraints. The first constraint is a time constraint:

$$TL_t + TF_t + TA_t + TW_t = TZ \tag{4.21}$$

Accordingly, the total amount of time, TZ, must be exhausted by its possible uses in every period t. As the total amount of time remains stable for every period in a person's lifetime, TZ does not require a time index. TL_t represents sick time, TF_t and TA_t are time inputs into the two production functions, and TW_t denotes hours worked.

The second constraint refers to the budget:

$$\sum \frac{F_t G_t + L_t I_t}{(1+r)^t} = \sum \frac{W_t \cdot TW_t}{(1+r)^t} + A_0 \tag{4.22}$$

On the left hand side of the above equation, expenses for food (its price is denoted by G_t) and for other goods and services (I_t denotes their prices) are summed up and discounted. The rate of interest is given by r. On the right hand side, wage rate W_t is multiplied by the hours worked, TW_t, summed up over all periods and discounted. Discounted initial assets A_0 are added. Thus, the right hand side of the equation represents the present value of lifetime earnings.

Substituting for TW_t from the time constraint and inserting it into the budget constraint yields the 'full wealth constraint':

$$\sum \frac{F_t G_t + L_t I_t + W_t (TL_t + TF_t + TA_t)}{(1+r)^t} = \frac{W_t \cdot TZ}{(1+r)^t} + A_0 = R \tag{4.23}$$

R denotes full wealth. On the left hand side of the above constraint, expenses for food and other goods are added to the wage rate multiplied by the remaining possible uses of time, which is equal to the opportunity cost of work: Time inputs into the production of the aggregate commodity and bodyweight and time lost due to sickness, each multiplied by the wage rate. This notation clearly illustrates that sickness is costly as it decreases the time available for work, thus reducing lifetime wealth. The rational consumer maximises intertemporal utility as described by equation (4.13) subject to constraints (4.19), (4.20) and (4.23).

Therefore, in order to maximise utility, the individual chooses how to allocate time (between work and leisure time, and leisure time can be spent investing in weight and in other activities) and which commodities to purchase (food or other goods and services). The level of health is determined as a result of the above decisions.

The two household production functions (4.19) and (4.20) are assumed homogenous of degree one in all inputs. In the following, time and money input into food consumption equal the amount of calories consumed times their marginal costs, m_t:

$$m_t J_t = F_t G_t + W_t TF_t \tag{4.24}$$

Furthermore, time and money input into consumption of the aggregate commodity also equal expenditures on other goods and services. Their marginal costs are denoted by n_t:

$$n_t K_t = L_t I_t + W_t TA_t \tag{4.25}$$

Thus, both the monetary and time costs of food and other goods are taken into account. In continuous time, the full wealth equation becomes:

$$R = \int e^{-rt}(m_t J_t + n_t K_t + W_t TL_t)dt \tag{4.26}$$

Substituting the equation of motion (4.16) into the above expression yields:

$$R = \int e^{-rt}(m_t\delta_t BW_t + m_t\dot{B}W_t + n_t K_t + W_t TL_t)dt \tag{4.27}$$

The Lagrangian of the above problem is:

$$\int U_t(H_t(D_t), F_t, L_t) - \lambda e^{-rt}(m_t\delta_t BW_t + m_t\dot{B}W_t + n_t K_t + W_t TL_t)dt \tag{4.28}$$

The Lagrange multiplier is denoted by λ. As the maximisation problem is dynamic, the Euler equation must be developed. The above objective functional is simplified in the following way:

$$U_t(H_t(D_t), F_t, L_t) - \lambda e^{-rt}(m_t\delta_t BW_t + m_t\dot{B}W_t + n_t K_t + W_t TL_t) = Q \tag{4.29}$$

Therefore, the Euler equation to determine the optimal path of bodyweight becomes:

$$\frac{\partial Q}{\partial BW_t} - \frac{d}{dt}\cdot\frac{\partial Q}{\partial \dot{B}W_t} = 0 \tag{4.30}$$

The individual terms of the Euler equation are:

$$\frac{\partial Q}{\partial BW_t} = \frac{\partial U_t}{\partial H_t}\cdot\frac{\partial H_t}{\partial D_t}\cdot\frac{\partial D_t}{\partial BW_t} - \lambda e^{-rt} m_t\delta_t - \lambda e^{-rt} W_t \frac{\partial TL_t}{\partial H_t}\cdot\frac{\partial H_t}{\partial D_t}\cdot\frac{\partial D_t}{\partial BW_t} \tag{4.31}$$

$$\frac{\partial Q}{\partial \dot{B}W_t} = -\lambda e^{-rt}\cdot m_t \tag{4.32}$$

$$\frac{d}{dt}\cdot\frac{\partial Q}{\partial \dot{B}W_t}=-\lambda e^{-rt}\dot{m}_t+\lambda e^{-rt}rm_t \qquad (4.33)$$

As the utility function is assumed to be continuous, twice differentiable, and concave, the extremum is a maximum.

The following condition ensures utility maximisation:

$$\left(\frac{\partial U_t}{\partial H_t}\cdot\frac{\partial H_t}{\partial D_t}\cdot\frac{\partial D_t}{\partial BW_t}\right)\cdot\frac{1}{\lambda}e^{rt}-W_t\cdot\frac{\partial TL_t}{\partial H_t}\cdot\frac{\partial H_t}{\partial D_t}\cdot\frac{\partial D_t}{\partial BW_t}=m_t(r+\delta_t)-\dot{m}_t \qquad (4.34)$$

On the right hand side, the marginal cost of the time and money input into calorie intake is multiplied by the rate of interest and the metabolic rate. The rate of change of the marginal cost of the time and money input into food consumption is deducted from this expression. Thus, the right hand side of equation (4.34) may be interpreted as the consumer cost of healthy bodyweight. On the left hand side, there is a wage penalty from excess weight, $W_t\cdot\frac{\partial TL_t}{\partial H_t}\cdot\frac{\partial H_t}{\partial D_t}\cdot\frac{\partial D_t}{\partial BW_t}$. Therefore, the higher wage rate W_t, the higher the opportunity cost of weight-related illness. In addition, the left hand side contains marginal utility components.[75] Thus, it represents the value of the marginal product of healthy weight. Optimally, the marginal product equals the consumer cost of healthy weight.

Except for three terms, the individual components of equation (4.34) are positive:

75 There is evidence for a wage penalty in excess to the penalty in the model which depends solely on sick time. Three hypotheses are quoted in existing literature: In the first place, obesity may lower wages as a result of decreased productivity or workplace discrimination. Moreover, low wages may cause obesity as cheaper food is more energy-dense. Furthermore, unobserved variables may cause both lower wages and obesity. For a more thorough discussion of the subject, see Appendix 8.3.

- Deviation from optimal weight provides disutility: $\frac{\partial H_t}{\partial D_t} < 0$
- The lower the level of health, the more time is lost due to sickness: $\frac{\partial TL_t}{\partial H_t} < 0$
- The algebraic sign of $\frac{\partial D_t}{\partial BW_t} = \frac{\partial (BW^* - BW_t)^2}{\partial BW_t}$ depends on the level of weight:

A. $\frac{\partial D_t}{\partial BW_t} < 0$ if $BW_t < BW^*$ (the individual is underweight)

B. $\frac{\partial D_t}{\partial BW_t} = 0$ if $BW_t = BW^*$ (individual weight is physically optimal)

C. $\frac{\partial D_t}{\partial BW_t} > 0$ if $BW_t > BW^*$ (the individual is overweight).

In case B, the left hand side of the utility-maximising condition becomes zero. This result is *independent* of health-consciousness ($\frac{\partial U_t}{\partial H_t} > 0$) or unconsciousness. Thus, if a normal-weight individual optimises her utility, the following must hold:

$$m_t(r + \delta_t) = \dot{m}_t \tag{4.35}$$

The rate of change in the marginal costs of food consumption must equal the marginal costs of food consumption multiplied by the interest rate and the metabolic rate. Notably, the metabolic rate decreases with age.

In case C, the first part of the left hand side of equation (4.34) up to the minus sign is negative. The second part – which is deducted from the first – is positive. Thus, the left hand side of this equation is negative. Therefore, the following must hold for health-conscious individuals:

$$m_t(r+\delta_t) < \dot{m}_t \tag{4.36}$$

For overweight individuals who are health-unconscious, the same conclusion holds as only the first part of the utility-maximising condition includes a utility component. Therefore, the rate of change in the marginal costs of food consumption is also larger than the marginal costs of food consumption multiplied by the interest rate and the metabolic rate, but the difference between these two is smaller than for health-conscious individuals.

In case A, the following holds for health-unconscious individuals:

$$m_t(r+\delta_t) > \dot{m}_t \tag{4.37}$$

For health-conscious individuals, the same relation between the rate of change in the marginal costs of food consumption and the marginal costs of food consumption (multiplied by the interest rate and the metabolic rate) holds, and the difference is larger than for health-unconscious individuals.

Figure 4-6 summarises the above results ($\dot{m}_t$ is substituted by $m_{t+1}-m_t$). For normal-weight individuals, the marginal costs of food consumption (multiplied by interest rate r and by the basal metabolic rate, δ_t) remain stable over time. In the long run, interest rate r reflects the rate of inflation (as the nominal interest rate constitutes the real interest rate plus the rate of inflation). The basal metabolic rate, δ_t, decreases with age.[76] Thus, in equilibrium, individuals adapt their marginal costs of food consumption to the level of prices and to the age-dependent decrease of the BMR.

Therefore, if individuals neglect the fact that fewer calories are necessary for their vital functions as they become older, their weight will rise. The table below shows that case B represents a stable equilibrium. Case A is also stable as it ap-

76 The basal metabolic rate changes as a reaction to numerous factors – age is one of them, see Figure 8-1.

proaches the state of equilibrium due to the decreasing marginal costs of food consumption over time. Due to their higher decrease in marginal costs, health-conscious persons approach the equilibrium at a faster rate than health-unconscious individuals. Theoretically, case C is stable as it approaches the state of equilibrium, as well. In case of overweightness, the marginal costs of food consumption rise over time until the state of equilibrium is reached. Again, the equilibrium is approached at a faster rate by health-conscious than by health-unconscious individuals.

Figure 4-6: Consumer Cost of Healthy Weight by Weight Status Category

(Reference: Own construction)

Population subgroup / Weight status category	I. health-conscious $\frac{\partial U_t}{\partial H_t} > 0$	II. health-unconscious $\frac{\partial U_t}{\partial H_t} = 0$
A. Underweight	$m_t(r+\delta_t) > m_{t+1} - m_t$	$m_t(r+\delta_t) > m_{t+1} - m_t$, smaller difference than for A.I
B. Normal Weight	$m_t(r+\delta_t) = m_{t+1} - m_t$	
C. Overweight	$m_t(r+\delta_t) < m_{t+1} - m_t$	$m_t(r+\delta_t) < m_{t+1} - m_t$, smaller difference than for C.I

$1 \geq r \geq 0$

$1 \geq \delta_t \geq 0$

Notably, as all cases depicted in Figure 4-6 maintain or approach a stable equilibrium, *obesity does not occur within the present framework.* This result holds independently of the level of health-consciousness. This framework is suitable for persons who gain weight and then successfully diet, or for those who unintentionally lose weight and then decide to gain weight until their normal weight is reached. The question remains as to whether which aspect of this framework must be adapted for obesity to occur. The budget (and time) constraint is observable and objective and, therefore, remains unchanged. Consequently, the assumed preference order is questionable, and concavity of the utility function may have to be abandoned for a framework appropriate to obesity. However, deviations from concavity can hardly be modelled in a dynamic framework and are only considered in the static model.

Furthermore, the basal metabolic rate also depends on body composition (see Figure 8-1). As an increase in fat tissue lowers the BMR, the metabolic rate is lower in overweight individuals than in their normal-weight counterparts. If the BMR approaches zero, marginal costs will only be adapted to inflation. Thus, convergence to normal weight is delayed. This line of reasoning offers an alternative interpretation: Current trends in overweight and obesity suggest that the period of convergence may be longer than a person's lifetime. Thus, convergence rather occurs in theory than in real life.

However, the political implications are the same for both interpretations. Informational measures to overcome current obesity trends are unlikely to be successful. Individuals rather react to financial incentives. Such incentives could be provided by a tax on fatty food ('fat tax'), or by an insurance scheme charging individuals with the costs resulting from self-inflicted illness as described in chapter six.

4.2.1 Diet Composition

In the previous paragraph, food digestion as a process is greatly simplified. It is assumed that the metabolic rate remains stable, and it is proportional only to current bodyweight but independent of a range of other decisive factors, such as age. Furthermore, there is only one energy store in the basic model, represented by bodyweight. Moreover, the composition of a person's diet has been neglected so far. For a more realistic model, the process of building up and breaking down energy stores should be differentiated with respect to the energy-yielding nutrients. The following paragraphs describe in detail how the human body stores energy, and how these stores are depleted. They may yield further insight whether nutrient-specific taxation is a promising political approach to curbing the obesity epidemic.

There are three energy-yielding nutrients: Carbohydrate, protein, and fat. As food is burned in the body, heat is released. This heat, called the heat of combustion, is measured in calories. The heat of combustion values for the three energy-yielding nutrients are: one gram of carbohydrates yields 4.2 kcal, one gram of protein 5.65 kcal, and one gram of lipid 9.45 kcal.[77]

Despite providing energy when it is metabolised, alcohol is not a nutrient. It is not essential and does not have a necessary function in the body. As overconsumption of alcohol can have dramatic consequences, it is broken down rather than stored. Therefore, alcohol does not meet the definition of a nutrient.[78] Still, it yields energy: seven kcal per gram of pure alcohol. It can also be converted into fat tissue.[79]

Fuel for energy can be supplied directly by the diet or by endogenous storage depots in the body. The relative contributions to the fuel mixture seem to follow a hierarchy consistent with:

- the storage capacity of the body for each macronutrient in relation to its intake
- the energy cost of converting the ingested nutrient into a form with greater storage capacity
- the fuel needs of the specific body tissues.

Thus, the priorities are: Alcohol is broken down before protein, which is metabolised before carbohydrate, which is used before fat. **Alcohol** has highest priority for oxidisation because it can be toxic if it accumulates in the body tissues.

77 See Spallholz et al. 1999, p. 202.

78 See Insel et al. 2007, p. 304.

79 See Whitney, Rolfes 2005, p. 9.

As body **proteins** are functional in nature, a storage pool for excess amino acids does not exist, either.[80] Proteins are essential for all living systems: Genetic information is retained as proteins, they are used to build biological membranes, act as enzymes, hormones, and receptors of information.[81]

Carbohydrate can be stored as glycogen, but storage is limited. If carbohydrates are not provided with food intake, their stores are used up within 24 hours. Glycogen is primarily stored in the liver and muscles, of which the approximately 150 g stored in the liver are metabolised especially easily.[82] Overall, a typical adult stores between 200 and 500 g of glycogen.[83] Conversion of carbohydrate into fat is energetically expensive and requires about twenty per cent of the energy contained in the carbohydrate.[84]

Fat is stored in the fat tissue primarily as triglycerides. From an evolutionary point of view, fat stores can be considered a reserve for times of food shortage. Therefore, unlike the storage of carbohydrate, the storage of fat is virtually unlimited.[85]

Independent of its source, excess energy is stored as fat. For approximately 3,500 kcal eaten in excess, one pound of fat is stored.[86]

For example, an adult male with a bodyweight of 70 kg stores fifteen kg of triglyceride in his adipose tissue (which correspond to 115,000 kcal), six kg of protein in his muscle mass (25,000 kcal), 350 g of glycogen in his liver and muscle (1,400 kcal), and 25 g of glucose or lipid in his body fluids (100 kcal).[87]

Overweight and obese individuals have accordingly higher energy reserves. An individual with adequate food intake metabolising 1,800 kcal per day oxidises 160 g of triglyceride from his adipose tissue. If these reserves are completely

80 See Stipanuk 2000, pp. 435/436.
81 See Rehner, Daniel 2002, pp. 218-220.
82 See Rehner, Daniel 2002, p. 175.
83 See Stipanuk 2000, p. 435.
84 See Insel et al. 2007, p. 285.
85 See Rehner, Daniel 2002, p. 175.
86 See Whitney, Rolfes 2005, p. 234.
87 See Stipanuk 2000, p. 426.

used up at a constant rate, triglyceride stores could provide energy for 75 days. Storage of lipids does not require water for dissolvement. Therefore, lipid stores need relatively little space. Compared to the triglycerides, dimension and energy of glycogen stored in the liver and muscle are of minor importance.[88]

A person's fat depot can expand in two ways: By increasing the size or the number of fat cells. The number of fat cells in the human body is almost unlimited. The adipose reservoir can reach huge dimensions if caloric intake remains high over a prolonged period of time. Once fat cells are formed, it seems difficult to dedifferentiate them. Even if weight is lost, their number appears to remain fixed although some decrease in number with weight loss has been reported.[89]

In addition, storage of dietary fat in adipose tissue is very efficient with 97 to 98 per cent. The amount of fat oxidised is not proportional to its intake. Fat oxidisation equals total energy intake less the amounts of alcohol, protein, and carbohydrate that are oxidised (the amounts that are taken in but not oxidised are converted into fat).[90]

Excess consumption of carbohydrates shifts the body's fuel preferences towards burning more carbohydrate and fewer fatty acids. The remaining fat intake goes directly to storage rather than being oxidised. Thus, overconsumption of carbohydrate can lead to an increase in body fat although the carbohydrates themselves are not converted into fat. In addition, the inefficient conversion of carbohydrates into fat is avoided.[91]

Consequently, overconsumption of carbohydrates leads to weight gain and can be crucial to remaining or becoming overweight or obese.[92]

After carbohydrate stores have been used up, fat and protein are the primary fuels. Fat stores are used up at a faster rate than protein stores. As fat stores are

88 See Rehner, Daniel 2002, p. 487.
89 See Shils et al. 1998, p. 1407.
90 See Stipanuk 2000, pp. 435/436.
91 See Insel et al. 2007, pp. 283-285.
92 See Whitney, Rolfes 2005, pp. 234/235.

exhausted, protein breakdown accelerates. Excess protein, beyond what is necessary to replenish the overall body pool of amino acids, also heads to fat storage.[93] Still, this process is only relevant when adipose tissue has already been converted into energy.

Considering that humans evolved largely in a subsistence environment, the bias towards efficient energy storage and defending body energy is hardly surprising.[94]

Experts recommend a combination of the three energy-yielding nutrients for healthy subjects in the following ratios:

- 45 to 65 per cent energy from carbohydrates
- twenty to 35 per cent energy from fat
- ten to 35 per cent energy from protein.[95]

In addition to its function as an energy store, fat is an endocrine organ: A hormone called leptin, which was discovered in 1994, influences hunger and satiation via the hypothalamus. Thus, it is involved in regulating bodyweight. The amount of leptin circulating in a person's blood is proportional to her adipose tissue. In healthy individuals, increased bodyweight leads to an increase in the level of leptin in the blood, in turn reducing food intake and increasing energy expenditure. High levels of leptin in obese individuals can indicate a dysfunction in the regulation described.[96]

A complex regulatory system involving integration of neural and hormonal inputs and outputs from the hypothalamic brain centres regulates energy intake and output to achieve and defend a steady state. As a result of an increase in energy intake, bodyweight rises. This rise is accompanied by increases in energy expenditure. Finally, bodyweight stabilises when energy intake equals energy consumption. When energy intake decreases, bodyweight decreases, as well. The decrease is accompanied by a reduction in energy expenditure. Bodyweight

93 See Insel et al. 2007, p. 289-292.
94 See Stipanuk 2000, p. 429.
95 See Whitney, Rolfes 2005, p. 18.
96 See Rehner, Daniel 2002, pp. 513-515.

stabilises when energy intake equals energy consumption. As positive or negative energy balance is largely a condition of positive or negative fat balance, a stable bodyweight may only be reached at the point where body fat mass has increased sufficiently so fat intake equals fat oxidisation. Therefore, a stable bodyweight is reached when fat balance is achieved. Balances of the other nutrients are preferentially achieved at the expense of fat oxidisation.[97]

As explained before, energy expenditure can be decomposed into three main compounds: The basal metabolic rate and the thermic effects of food and exercise.

Different macronutrients produce different thermic effects proportional to the food energy taken in: Protein is generally found to produce a TEF of fifteen to thirty per cent (that is, this amount of the bond energy in the protein is spent in the process of utilising the constituent amino acids, either oxidising them or incorporating them into body proteins). The metabolic cost of either oxidising carbohydrate or storing it as glycogen is six to eight per cent. The cost of converting excess carbohydrate to fat is twenty per cent. Studies have shown that net conversion of carbohydrate to fat only occurs in situations of massive and sustained carbohydrate overfeeding. The net metabolic cost of either oxidising or storing ingested fat is only two to three per cent of the energy consumed. [98] For alcohol, it accounts for twenty per cent of energy intake. [99]

For the thermic effect of exercise, the specific type of physical activity performed is crucial to energy expenditure. Carbohydrates present in muscle, liver, and body fluids are the major fuel for physical performance. Duration and intensity of exercise determine the mix of the fuel used. In resting or light activity, about 60 per cent is derived from free fatty acids and triglycerides in muscles. At moderate levels of activity, fat and carbohydrate contribute about equal

97 See Stipanuk 2000, pp. 436/437.

98 See Stipanuk 2000, p. 420.

99 See Whitney, Rolfes 2005, pp. 256-259.

amounts as energy sources. Carbohydrate becomes more and more important as the intensity of exercise increases.[100]

Figure 4-7 illustrates the most important facts described in this paragraph so far (energy expenditure on basal metabolism by gender is given in accordance with the Harris-Benedict equation):

Figure 4-7: Energy Consumption, Storage, and Expenditure
(Reference: Own construction)

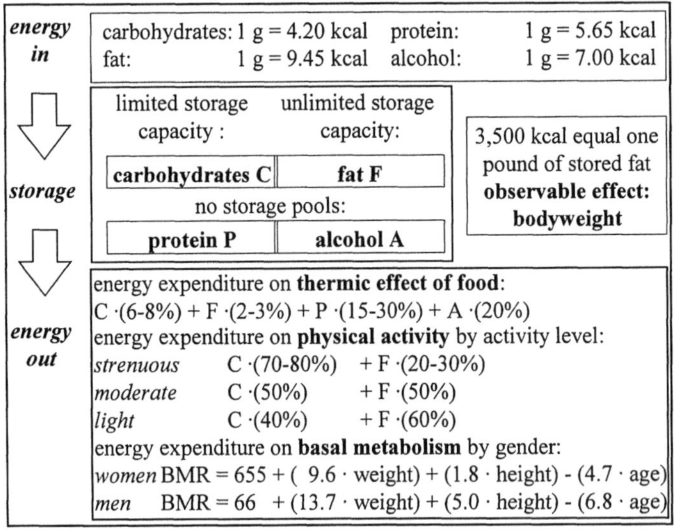

In the following, net calories will be considered. As the energy lost due to the thermic effect of food is directly proportional to the amount of macronutrient or alcohol consumed, gross calories can easily be converted into net calories. Considering that the TEF differs by nutrient, net calories must be determined in accordance with the following equations:

100 See Shils et al. 1998, p. 62.

$$f_t^C = 0.94 \cdot F_t^C \tag{4.38}$$

$$f_t^F = 0.98 \cdot F_t^F \tag{4.39}$$

$$f_t^P = 0.85 \cdot F_t^P \tag{4.40}$$

$$f_t^A = 0.80 \cdot F_t^A \tag{4.41}$$

The TEF is assumed to be at the lower bound of the ranges given in Figure 4-7. Gross calorie consumption is denoted by F_t. The upper index refers to C for carbohydrates, F for fat, P for protein, and A for alcohol. Net calories by nutrient are consequently expressed as f_t^C, f_t^F, f_t^P, or f_t^A, respectively.

Consumption of protein is essential on a daily basis. Still, for excess protein consumed, a storage pool does not exist. Theoretically, excess proteins can be converted into body fat so their energy is stored. For simplicity, I will assume in the following that protein consumption is adequate, so neither too little protein is consumed nor excess amounts. Therefore, neither a stock of protein nor the consumption of protein itself will appear in the model. Its treatment in the model could be very similar to that of carbohydrates due to the upper storage limit for both nutrients, so the inclusion of protein will hardly deliver additional insight. Furthermore, alcohol consumption is neglected for simplicity.

Nutrient-specific treatment is reasonable as carbohydrates are suspected of triggering addiction.[101] Furthermore, the tendency to replace energy from fat with carbohydrates in order to avoid the inefficient conversion of carbohydrates into fat decisively contributes to excess weight.

In contrast to carbohydrate, fat has unlimited storage capacity. In addition, all other nutrients that are consumed in excess amounts can be converted into fat,

101 See Richards et al. 2007.

albeit at the expense of some of their energy which is used up in the conversion process. Again, the deviation from optimal weight is decisive for the level of health which, in turn, provides positive utility.

As a result, the utility function takes the following form:

$$U_t = U_t(f_t^C, f_t^F, H_t(D_t); L_t) \tag{4.42}$$

$$\frac{\partial U_t}{\partial f_t^C} > 0; \frac{\partial U_t}{\partial f_t^F} > 0; \frac{\partial U_t}{\partial H_t(D_t)} > 0; \frac{\partial H_t}{\partial D_t} < 0; \frac{\partial U_t}{\partial L_t} > 0$$

$$U_t^{'} > 0; U_t^{''} < 0$$

By assumption, the utility function is continuous, twice differentiable, and concave.

The consumption of carbohydrates, f_t^C, and fat, f_t^F, provides utility as it is essential for the body and due to taste and palatability. Consumption of other goods L_t and good health – diminished by rising deviation from optimal bodyweight – also provide positive utility. In this context, the fat stock is decisive for bodyweight. Variability in lean body mass is much smaller than variability in body fat, and the decisive portion of weight variation is due to body fat content.[102] This approach intuitively makes sense as this dissertation is concerned with overconsumption of food, not with undernourishment.

Virtually all of the energy represented by stored fat can contribute to net fuel energy for the body.[103] Even if carbohydrates are not converted into fat, a diet rich in carbohydrates may significantly contribute to an increase in bodyweight: Carbohydrates are burned first for immediate energy supply to avoid their costly conversion into adipose tissue. Under such circumstances, the main part of fat consumed goes directly to storage.[104] Therefore, the stock of body fat can be

102 See Forbes 1987, p. 173.

103 See Stipanuk 2000, p. 427.

104 See Insel et al. 2007, pp. 283-285.

used as a proxy for bodyweight. As the index in the following equation points out, bodyweight solely depends on fat in this context:

$$D_t = (BW^F * - BW_t^F)^2 \tag{4.43}$$

Again, the time a person can devote to work becomes less the lower the stock of health:

$$\frac{\partial TL_t}{\partial H_t(D_t)} < 0 \tag{4.44}$$

The human body stores the energy taken in as efficiently as possible. Therefore, carbohydrates are firstly converted into glycogen. In this conversion process, six to eight per cent of the energy is used up. This corresponds to the TEF and has already been taken into account. In contrast, once the carbohydrate stock is full, additional carbohydrates are stored as fat. In this process, approximately twenty per cent of the energy is lost. Storage of fat in the adipose tissue is especially energy-efficient: Only two to three per cent of its energy is used up. As a result, fat storage is not directly proportional to fat intake but also depends on the amount of carbohydrates taken in.

The above elaborations make clear that the balance of carbohydrate in the human body is achieved at the expense of fat oxidisation.

For simplicity, the rate of depreciation, δ_t^F, includes two channels of energy expenditure, namely the energy expended for physical activity and the energy necessary to maintain the basic processes of life, the basal metabolic rate. Taking adaptive processes of the human body when energy supplies change into consideration makes matters more complicated. Therefore, these effects are summed up in a single parameter for the time being. Obviously, not all physiological processes referring to food intake and energy consumption can reasonably be considered at the same time. Still, the present model is flexible enough to incorporate one aspect of interest at a time.

The stock of carbohydrates is commodity-specific as it is only determined by carbohydrate consumption and expenditure. Adipose tissue, in contrast, is not commodity-specific as it is determined by fat and carbohydrate consumption. Once the stock of carbohydrates is full, further calories from carbohydrate replace calories from fat. Thus, once the total daily energy requirement is reached, both calories from carbohydrate and from fat decrease utility. They are, therefore, subject to closed satiation (for details on satiation, see paragraph 3.3). Still, calories from carbohydrates are subject to closed satiation to a different degree due to their more costly conversion into fat tissue. Thus, they provide less disutility. Notably, these negative effects are taken into account in parameter H_t (D_t) and the resulting increase in sick time.

Under the assumption that carbohydrate supply is at least adequate, and taking into account that the amount of body fat is decisive for weight, the change in bodyweight can be expressed as follows:

$$BW_{t+1}^F - BW_t^F = B\dot{W}_t^F = 0.8 \cdot J_t^C + J_t^F - \delta_t^F BW_t^F \tag{4.45}$$

In the following, the energy intake depends on net calories and on the time for food preparation and consumption, TF_t. It is denoted by J_t. The upper index denotes the source of energy (C for carbohydrates, F for fat). There are two interdependent equations of motion:

$$J_t^C = \frac{B\dot{W}_t^F + \delta_t^F BW_t^F - J_t^F}{0.8} \tag{4.46}$$

$$J_t^F = B\dot{W}_t^F + \delta_t^F BW_t^F - 0.8 \cdot J_t^C \tag{4.47}$$

In contrast to the basic model, there are now three separate household production functions, one describing carbohydrate intake, one describing fat intake, and the other referring to the consumption of other goods and services:

$$J_t^C = J_t^C(f_t^C, TF_t^C) \tag{4.48}$$

$$J_t^F = J_t^F(f_t^C, f_t^F, TF_t^F) \tag{4.49}$$

$$K_t = K_t(L_t, TA_t) \tag{4.50}$$

Again, TA_t denotes a time input, and L_t represents the goods and services input into the production of commodity K_t. The term f_t^C will only contribute to the stock of fat if the upper limit of carbohydrate storage is reached. This situation is likely to occur when food is available in sufficient amounts on a daily basis.

The budget constraint now differentiates between prices for carbohydrates, G_t^C, and fat, G_t^F:

$$\sum \frac{f_t^C \cdot G_t^C + f_t^F \cdot G_t^F + L_t I_t}{(1+r)^t} = \sum \frac{W_t \cdot TW_t}{(1+r)^t} + A_0 \tag{4.51}$$

The time constraint contains the aggregate preparation and consumption time of both nutrients, TF_t^C and TF_t^F:

$$TL_t + TF_t^C + TF_t^F + TA_t + TW_t = TZ \tag{4.52}$$

Substituting for TW_t from the time constraint and inserting it into the budget constraint yields the new 'full wealth constraint':

$$\sum \frac{f_t^C \cdot G_t^C + f_t^F \cdot G_t^F + L_t I_t + W_t (TL_t + TF_t^C + TF_t^F + TA_t)}{(1+r)^t} = \frac{W_t \cdot TZ}{(1+r)^t} + A_0 = R \quad (4.53)$$

As in the preceding section, the rational consumer maximises intertemporal utility subject to the above constraints.

The marginal costs of time and money input into carbohydrate consumption are denoted by l_t, the marginal costs of time and money input into fat consumption are denoted by o_t, and time and money input into consumption of the aggregate commodity is represented by n_t:

$$l_t J_t^C = f_t^C G_t^C + W_t TF_t^C \quad (4.54)$$

$$o_t J_t^F = f_t^F G_t^F + W_t TF_t^F \quad (4.55)$$

$$n_t K_t = L_t I_t + W_t TA_t \quad (4.56)$$

In contrast to the basic model, only the latter two household production functions can reasonably be assumed to be homogenous of degree one in their inputs. This result stems from carbohydrate consumption. Doubling the amount of carbohydrate intake which is – at least partly – converted into fat tissue does not double the amount of energy stored, but twenty per cent of the energy is lost in the conversion process.

In continuous time, the modified full wealth equation becomes:

$$R = \int e^{-rt}(l_t J_t^C + o_t J_t^F + n_t K_t + W_t TL_t)dt \tag{4.57}$$

Substituting the equations of motion into the above expression yields:

$$R = \int e^{-rt}(l_t([B\dot{W}_t^F + \delta_t^F BW_t^F - J_t^F] \cdot \frac{1}{0.8}$$
$$+ o_t[B\dot{W}_t^F + \delta_t^F BW_t^F - 0.8J_t^C] + n_t K_t + W_t TL_t)dt \tag{4.58}$$

The Lagrangian of the above problem is:

$$\int U_t(f_t^C, f_t^F, H_t(D_t); L_t) - \lambda e^{-rt}(BW_t^F(o_t\delta_t^F + \frac{l_t\delta_t^F}{0.8})$$
$$+ \dot{B}W_t^F(o_t + \frac{l_t}{0.8}) - \frac{l_t J_t^F}{0.8} - 0.8 \cdot o_t J_t^C + n_t K_t + W_t TL_t)dt \tag{4.59}$$

The Lagrange multiplier is denoted by λ. As in the precedent paragraph, the Euler equation is determined and solved in order to determine the utility-maximising condition (for details see Appendix).

The following condition ensures utility maximisation:

$$(\frac{\partial U_t}{\partial H_t} \cdot \frac{\partial H_t}{\partial D_t} \cdot \frac{\partial D_t}{\partial BW_t^F}) \cdot \frac{1}{\lambda} e^{rt} - W_t \cdot \frac{\partial TL_t}{\partial H_t} \cdot \frac{\partial H_t}{\partial D_t} \cdot \frac{\partial D_t}{\partial BW_t^F}$$
$$= (o_t + \frac{l_t}{0.8})(r + \delta_t^F) - \dot{o}_t - \frac{\dot{l}_t}{0.8} \tag{4.60}$$

The left hand term of the above equation is identical to the left hand side of the first order condition in the precedent paragraph. On the right hand side, the model now differentiates between marginal costs of carbohydrate and fat consumption, as well as its change from one period to the next. Thus, it becomes obvious that the composition of a person's diet with respect to nutrient contents (i.e. low fat content) is decisive for bodyweight.

The individual components of equation (4.60) are positive, except for three terms:

- Deviation from optimal weight provides disutility: $\frac{\partial H_t}{\partial D_t} < 0$
- The lower the level of health, the more time is lost due to sickness: $\frac{\partial TL_t}{\partial H_t(D_t)} < 0$
- Again, the algebraic sign of $\frac{\partial D_t}{\partial BW_t^F} = (-2) \cdot (BW^* - BW_t^F)$ depends on the level of weight:

  A. $\frac{\partial D_t}{\partial BW_t^F} < 0$ if the individual is underweight

  B. $\frac{\partial D_t}{\partial BW_t^F} = 0$ if individual weight is physically optimal

  C. $\frac{\partial D_t}{\partial BW_t^F} > 0$ if the individual is overweight.

In an analogous manner to the precedent paragraph, Figure 4-8 summarises the results ($\dot{l}_t$ is substituted by $l_{t+1} - l_t$ and $\dot{o}_t$ by $o_{t+1} - o_t$, respectively).

For normal-weight individuals, the marginal costs of carbohydrate and fat consumption (multiplied by interest rate r and by the basal metabolic rate, δ_t^F) remain stable over time. The denominator of the marginal costs of carbohydrate consumption stems from the energy loss of approximately twenty per cent in the conversion process to fat. In equilibrium, individuals adapt their marginal costs of food consumption to the level of prices and to variations in the BMR. As in the precedent paragraph, case B represents a stable equilibrium, and cases A and C are theoretically stable as the marginal costs converge to the equilibrium (the marginal costs decrease in case A and increase in case C). Again, health-conscious persons approach the equilibrium at a faster rate than health-unconscious individuals in both cases.

Figure 4-8: Consumer Cost of Healthy Weight by Weight Status Category: Diet Composition
(Reference: Own construction)

Population subgroup / Weight status category	I. health-conscious $\frac{\partial U_t}{\partial H_t} > 0$	II. health-unconscious $\frac{\partial U_t}{\partial H_t} = 0$
A. Underweight	$(o_t + \frac{l_t}{0.8})(r + \delta_t^F) > o_{t+1} - o_t + \frac{l_{t+1} - l_t}{0.8}$	$(o_t + \frac{l_t}{0.8})(r + \delta_t^F) > o_{t+1} - o_t + \frac{l_{t+1} - l_t}{0.8}$, smaller difference than for A.I
B. Normal Weight	$(o_t + \frac{l_t}{0.8})(r + \delta_t^F) = o_{t+1} - o_t + \frac{l_{t+1} - l_t}{0.8}$	
C. Overweight	$(o_t + \frac{l_t}{0.8})(r + \delta_t^F) < o_{t+1} - o_t + \frac{l_{t+1} - l_t}{0.8}$	$(o_t + \frac{l_t}{0.8})(r + \delta_t^F) < o_{t+1} - o_t + \frac{l_{t+1} - l_t}{0.8}$, smaller difference than for C.I

$1 \geq r \geq 0$

$1 \geq \delta_t^F \geq 0$

Notably, virtually the same conclusions hold as in paragraph 4.2. The assumption of a concave utility function may have to be abandoned, or a person's lifetime may be shorter than the period of convergence in overweight individuals. Therefore, the same political conclusions hold. The essential result of this paragraph is the relevance of the fat-carbohydrate ratio in a diet, indicating the usefulness of a tax rate depending on the fat content in food.

4.2.2 The Rate of Time Preference

In the dynamic setting so far, the accumulation of weight has been described as a rational decision with standard assumptions concerning preferences, goods, and the rate of discounting. Although the utility-maximising conditions suggest convergence to a state of equilibrium despite a present deviation from physically optimal bodyweight, many individuals do not seem to be able to decide on a certain level of weight and maintain it. Therefore, the assumption of a stable rate of time preference is abandoned in the following in order to analyse whether the stability results attained so far change as a consequence.

The rate of time preference can be interpreted as the marginal rate of substitution at which individuals are willing to exchange current consumption for consumption in the future. The present value of a future benefit is smaller the higher the rate of time preference and the larger the time span between the presence and the gain.

The rate of time preference has occasionally been analysed in health-related contexts to explain behavioural patterns that can be observed in reality.[105] One of the key benefits of a variable rate of time preference is the fact that patterns which might otherwise point at irrational behaviour can be explained in a rational manner. The present paragraph particularly builds on Becker and Mulligan (1997) as their elaborations nicely correspond to the approach of this

105 See, for example, Fuchs, Zeckhauser 1987, pp. 264/65 for a discussion of the application of time preference to health, Johannesson, Johansson 1997 for an estimation of the rate of time preference in the context of additional years of life, and for a short survey of similar studies on p. 53, Grossman 1972 and Johansson 1996 for a model of time preference depending on age, or Yaniv 2002 for an application to food overconsumption. Fuchs 1982 and Becker and Mulligan 1997 examine the correlation between time preference and health.

dissertation described in the beginning of this chapter according to which "consciousness" – or lack thereof – leads to systematic differences between two population subgroups.

To some extent, Becker and Mulligan (1997) build on an idea originally developed by Eugen von Böhm-Bawerk (1891), namely that individuals should "be able to form a mental picture of what will be the state of our wants, needs, feelings, at any particular point in time." While this visualisation of future states requires effort, he argues that "the present always gets its rights. It forces itself upon us through our senses."[106] For the case of food consumption, the fact that the influence of the presence can hardly be circumvented is obvious.

In their model of time preference, Becker and Mulligan allow individuals to make expenditures in order to become less impatient. As a result, more weight is attached to future consumption in the current period. The discount function β can be influenced with expenditures on patience, EP. EP represents the time and effort spent on envisioning future pleasures. This time and effort cannot be spent in market or home production. Schooling also determines the level of EP. β is not fixed but evolves in accordance with propinquity of future utilities:

$$\beta(EP) > 0; \beta'(EP) \geq 0; \beta''(EP) \leq 0 \qquad (4.61)$$

for all EP ≥ 0. The discount function is an increasing function as more resources spent on imagining future pleasures increase the weight that is attached to them in the present. Depending on the level of EP, future consumption can even become more important than present consumption. Utility is maximised over lifetime subject to a budget constraint. The budget constraint includes expenditures on patience. Optimality requires marginal utility of consumption in any period t, adjusted by the rates of interest and discount, to equal marginal utility of wealth. As time and effort spent on EP cannot be used on home or market production,

106 Böhm-Bawerk 1891, book 5, chapter I, paragraph 10.

the marginal benefit of investment in the rate of time preference must also equal the marginal utility of wealth in order to attain the optimal level of EP.[107]

An age-dependent rate of time preference has occasionally been assumed, as well as empirically observed. A weight-dependent rate of time preference has similar consequences. This approach is reasonable as the health consequences of obesity are comparable to those of twenty years' aging (from age thirty to age fifty) with respect to chronic medical conditions. In addition, obesity decreases health-related quality of life to an even greater extent than twenty years' aging (by more than two points compared to just under 1.5 points on a scale from zero to 100).[108]

In the preceding paragraphs, it is implicitly assumed that the rate of time preference equals the interest rate, r. This assumption is abandoned in the following. Still, for the sake of simplicity, it is assumed that interest rate r remains constant. Lifetime utility must be maximised in accordance with the following equation:

$$V = \sum_{t=0}^{T} \beta_t(D_t) \cdot U_t(F_t, L_t, H_t(D_t)) \tag{4.62}$$

$$\frac{\partial U_t}{\partial F_t} > 0; \frac{\partial U_t}{\partial L_t} > 0; \frac{\partial U_t}{\partial H_t(D_t)} > 0; \frac{\partial H_t}{\partial D_t} < 0$$

Here, utility per period is discounted by β before it is summed up over lifetime. The discount factor depends on the deviation from optimal bodyweight and may vary over time. β obeys the following rules:

$$\beta_t(D_t) > 0; \beta_t^{'}(D_t) \geq 0; \beta_t^{''}(D_t) \geq 0 \tag{4.63}$$

107 See Becker, Mulligan 1997, pp. 733-739.
108 See Sturm 2002, pp. 247/48.

Thus, the larger the deviation from physically optimal weight, the higher the rate of discount. With a high rate of discount, less weight is attached to future consequences. It could be argued that a person's attitude towards healthy bodyweight becomes more and more fatalistic the further out of reach optimal weight is. As a result, the discount function is an increasing function. It is convex as further deviation from optimal weight increases the rate of discount at an even higher rate.

Maximisation is subject to the same wealth constraint as the basic problem described in section 4.2:

$$R = \int e^{-rt}(m_t J_t + n_t K_t + W_t TL_t)dt \tag{4.64}$$

Again, an Euler equation must be determined to maximise utility over lifetime. Only one of the individual components changes compared to the basic model. The new term is:

$$\frac{\partial Q}{\partial BW_t} = (\frac{\partial U_t}{\partial H_t} \cdot \frac{\partial H_t}{\partial D_t} \cdot \frac{\partial D_t}{\partial BW_t}) \cdot \beta_t + (\frac{\partial \beta_t}{\partial D_t} \cdot \frac{\partial D_t}{\partial BW_t}) \cdot U_t$$

$$- \lambda e^{-rt} m_t \delta_t - \lambda e^{-rt} W_t \frac{\partial TL_t}{\partial H_t} \cdot \frac{\partial H_t}{\partial D_t} \frac{\partial D_t}{\partial BW_t} \tag{4.65}$$

As a result, the following condition ensures utility maximisation:

$$((\frac{\partial U_t}{\partial H_t} \cdot \frac{\partial H_t}{\partial D_t} \cdot \frac{\partial D_t}{\partial BW_t}) \cdot \beta_t + (\frac{\partial \beta_t}{\partial D_t} \cdot \frac{\partial D_t}{\partial BW_t}) \cdot U_t) \cdot \frac{1}{\lambda} e^{rt} - W_t \cdot \frac{\partial TL_t}{\partial H_t} \cdot \frac{\partial H_t}{\partial D_t} \cdot \frac{\partial D_t}{\partial BW_t}$$

$$= m_t(r + \delta_t) - \dot{m}_t \tag{4.66}$$

The right hand side of the equation, representing the marginal cost of nutrition, is the same as in the basic model (see paragraph 4.2). On the left hand side, describing the benefits of nutrition, β_t as a function is added. In contrast to paragraph 4.2, the question whether convergence leads to a stable equilibrium depends on the absolute size of the terms on the left hand side of the above equation. In the following,

- $(\frac{\partial \beta_t}{\partial D_t} \cdot \frac{\partial D_t}{\partial BW_t}) \cdot U_t \cdot \frac{1}{\lambda} e^{rt}$ is referred to as **Term I**
- $W_t \cdot \frac{\partial TL_t}{\partial H_t} \cdot \frac{\partial H_t}{\partial D_t} \cdot \frac{\partial D_t}{\partial BW_t}$ is denoted **Term II.**

The results of the present section will be identical to those presented in section 4.2 if Term I is sufficiently small and / or Term II is sufficiently large. By contrast, instability will occur if Term I is sufficiently large and / or Term II is sufficiently small. For example, this may be the case if the increase in the rate of discount with rising deviation from optimal weight – $\frac{\partial \beta_t}{\partial D_t}$ – is large (which is probable as it is assumed that a person's attitude towards healthy bodyweight becomes more fatalistic the further out of reach optimal weight is, see equation (4.63)) or if the wage rate W_t is small, which is likely to occur as a result of the wage penalty for overweight individuals, especially for women (see paragraph 8.3). Figure 4-9 summarises the results by weight status category.

The table depicts the conditions under which cases A and C are instable. Obviously, if the opposite holds, cases A and B will be stable and equivalent to the results presented in section 4.2.

An extension to two different discount rates at which individuals discount consumption goods, on the one hand, and health, on the other hand, intuitively makes sense. Nevertheless, the analysis will be complicated further.

Figure 4-9: Consumer Cost of Healthy Weight by Weight Status Category: Variable Rate of Time Preference
(Reference: Own construction)

Population subgroup / Weight status category	I. health-conscious $\frac{\partial U_t}{\partial H_t} > 0$	II. health-unconscious $\frac{\partial U_t}{\partial H_t} = 0$
A. Underweight	$m_t(r+\delta_t) < m_{t+1} - m_t$ if Term I is sufficiently large and / or Term II is sufficiently small	$m_t(r+\delta_t) < m_{t+1} - m_t$ if Term I is sufficiently large and / or Term II is sufficiently small, smaller difference than for A.I
B. Normal Weight	$m_t(r+\delta_t) = m_{t+1} - m_t$	
C. Overweight	$m_t(r+\delta_t) > m_{t+1} - m_t$ if Term I is sufficiently large and / or Term II is sufficiently small	$m_t(r+\delta_t) > m_{t+1} - m_t$ if Term I is sufficiently large and / or Term II is sufficiently small, smaller difference than for C.I

$1 \geq r \geq 0$
$1 \geq \delta_t \geq 0$
$1 \geq \beta_t \geq 0$

4.2.3 Addictive Aspects of Food Consumption

So far, this dissertation shows that in order to explain recent obesity trends, standard microeconomic assumptions may have to be abandoned. In the subsequent paragraph, a variable rate of time preference has been introduced. In this paragraph, utility is discounted in a conventional way, but the possibility that food has addictive capacity is analysed. In addition, as it is assumed that carbohydrates trigger addiction, this paragraph may also yield further insight whether nutrient-specific taxation represents a promising political approach. The present paragraph is based on the seminal Model of Rational Addiction developed by Gary S. Becker and Kevin M. Murphy (1988).[109]

As this section deals with the addictive aspects of food consumption, the definition of addictive behaviour must be clarified. Generally, to meet the definition of a harmful addiction, a consumption process must exhibit reinforcement, tolerance, and withdrawal. **Reinforcement** describes an increase in the strength of response: The more an individual has consumed in the past, the more she wishes to consume today. **Tolerance** implies that current consumption of a given amount of the addictive substance provides less utility today the higher consumption in the past. This effect occurs as the subject becomes accustomed to consuming the addictive good. Therefore, tolerance leads to increased current consumption.[110] **Withdrawal** points to the physical and psychological symptoms of decreased or discontinued use of the addictive substance.[111]

Often, the concept of adjacent complementarity is mentioned within the framework of addictions. Accordingly, current consumption of an addictive good depends on the level of its consumption in the very previous period, not on consumption at a distant point in time.[112]

One of the decisive features of the framework of Rational Addiction is its ability to explain addictive consumption under consistent maximisation of stable preferences over time.

---

109 To my knowledge, the Becker-Murphy model has been applied to food consumption twice: John H. Cawley (1999) estimates a modified Rational Addiction regression model, and Timothy J. Richards, Paul M. Patterson, and Abebayehu Tegene (2007) test for addiction to individual nutrients as opposed to food in general. However, both analyses neglect the fact that theoretically, addiction is triggered by a psychological stock variable that cannot be observed, the 'ability to enjoy eating' (Cawley uses BMI to proxy this stock). The incorporation of both stocks with different depreciation rates and different degrees of complementarity and substitutability is crucial to the occurrence of binges which are frequently observed in food consumption.

110 See Becker et al 1991, p. 237.

111 See Chaloupka 1991, p. 723.

112 See Ryder, Heal 1973, pp. 1-5.

In this approach, the consumer is fully aware of the habit-forming effects of her behaviour.[113] As a result, she will have correct perceptions of the future costs of her actions – as opposed to the myopic consumer who only realises that actions or consumption of a specific good in the past influence *current* actions through an accumulated stock of habits.[114] (The main difference between a mere habit and an addiction lies in the intensity: A habit can turn into an addiction when the effects of past on present consumption are strong enough to be destabilising.)[115]

The optimal solution will determine maximum obtainable utility from the initial value of assets, the initial stock of consumption capital, the person's earnings function, and the price structure. In theory, current consumption depends on current and anticipated prices, future consumption, and the addictive stock. The empirical estimation equation is developed by differencing the first-order conditions for optimal consumption. It contains past, current and anticipated prices, as well as past and future consumption, thus reflecting the interdependence of past, present, and future.

Numerous studies have found empirical support for this model, mostly for the case of tobacco consumption, but also for alcohol, caffeine, cocaine, and heroin.[116]

Apparently, food consumption differs from the consumption of other goods. Many people intend to lose weight but don't adhere to their diet. Thus, they display cyclical consumption patterns. In order to explain the incident of cyclical consumption, two stocks of consumption capital must be differentiated:[117] Weight is the detectable stock, while the stock of 'eating capital' (the ability to

113 See Iannaccone 1986, p. 95.

114 See Grossman 1995, pp. 158/159.

115 See Becker 1992, p. 329.

116 See, for instance, Becker, Murphy 1988, p. 687, Cameron 1997, p. 401, Bardsley, Olekalns 1999, p. 233, Gruber, Köszegi 2001, p. 1293 for tobacco consumption, Bentzen et al. 1999, p. 271 for alcohol, Bask, Melkersson 2004, p. 379 for tobacco and alcohol combined, Olekalns, Bardsley 1996, p. 1103 for caffeine, Grossman, Chaloupka 1998, p. 449 for cocaine, and Bretteville-Jensen 1999, pp. 401-403 for heroin.

117 The occurence of two stocks is also more realistic as the assumption that consumption of an addictive good will only generate one durable consequence seems implausible.

enjoy eating, or the accumulated psychological consequences of eating experience that trigger addiction) remains unobservable. This approach draws on a model developed by Engelbert J. Dockner and Gustav Feichtinger (1993). By contrast, the Becker-Murphy Model contains one addictive stock. In order to generate cycles of overeating and dieting, one stock must be adjacently complementary with eating and have the higher depreciation rate. The stock with the lower depreciation rate must display adjacent substitution with eating. Within this framework, binges do not stem from irrational or inconsistent behaviour as could be intuitively assumed. They are caused by a consistent dynamic maximisation process.[118]

It is assumed that the individual derives utility from consuming carbohydrates, F_t^C, and from consuming proteins, F_t^P. In this context, carbohydrate consumption is assumed to be addictive (this presumption is empirically supported[119]). By contrast, F_t^P is a standard good. The addictive capacity of carbohydrates is captured in the stock of consumption capital, S_t which, in turn, affects utility. As an alternative to the understanding of S_t as the stock of consumption capital, S_t can also be interpreted as the degree of addiction.

In the following, food consumption generates two stocks, S_t and BW_t. In the utility function, BW_t is captured via the deviation from optimal weight, D_t, which is derived as in the precedent paragraphs. Both stocks influence food intake in the adjacent period, one of them positively and the other negatively (in the case of overweight individuals, which is assumed here). Thus, eating capital displays an addictive effect, while weight counterbalances addiction due to its satiating effect. The utility function is:

$$U_t = U_t(F_t^C, F_t^P, S_t, H_t(D_t)) \tag{4.67}$$

$$\frac{\partial U_t}{\partial F_t^C} > 0; \frac{\partial U_t}{\partial F_t^P} > 0; \frac{\partial U_t}{\partial S_t} > 0; \frac{\partial U_t}{\partial H_t(D_t)} > 0; \frac{\partial H_t}{\partial D_t} < 0$$

118 See Becker, Murphy 1988, pp. 693/694.

119 See Richards et al. 2007.

All of the above depend on time t. By assumption, U_t is concave in carbohydrate and protein intake, in the addictive stock, and in health. As carbohydrates are the addictive good, F_t^C generates both stocks S_t and BW_t while F_t^P represents a standard good.

$$\dot{S}_t = F_t^C - \varphi_t \cdot S_t \tag{4.68}$$

$$B\dot{W}_t = F_t^C - \delta_t^C \cdot BW_t \tag{4.69}$$

By assumption, $\varphi_t > \delta_t^C$. The depreciation rate φ_t measures the exogenous rate of disappearance of the physical and mental consequences that have been caused by the addictive good. The maximisation procedure is analogue to the optimising problem described for the standard Model of Rational Addiction and features a combined time and budget constraint and time-consistent utility maximisation. The decisive features for the occurrence of cyclical consumption patterns are the counterbalancing effect of the desire to eat and the dislike for weight, and the adjacent complementarity with respect to both stocks.[120]

Cyclical consumption is described in Figure 4-10. Eating capital S_t has the higher depreciation rate than bodyweight BW_t. S_t reacts quicker to changes in food consumption than bodyweight BW_t. To start with, food consumption increases due to its positive correlation with eating capital. As bodyweight continues to increase, eating levels off. Lower food consumption quickly depreciates eating capital, which keeps food consumption at a low level even after weight starts to fall. When weight is at a sufficiently low level, eating starts to rise and the cycle starts all over again.

These cycles are a side-effect of consistent dynamic utility maximisation. Notably, they will only occur if food is perceived as satiating. Therefore, the existence of two stocks is a prerequisite to this realistic feature.

120 See Dockner, Feichtinger 1993, pp. 257-260.

Figure 4-10: Cycles of Overeating and Dieting
(Reference: Own construction following Dockner, Feichtinger 1993, p. 261)

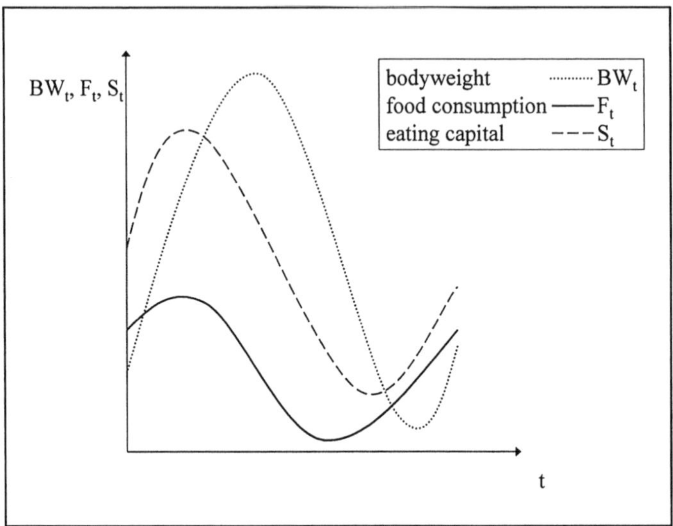

In addition to the stable limit cycles depicted above, the accumulation of two stocks of consumption capital can also lead to explosive (or damped) oscillations, depending on whether the eigenvalues appearing in the dynamics of the optimal solution are complex with positive (negative) real parts. For stable limit cycles to arise, the real parts must equal zero.[121]

Consequently, the incorporation of addictive aspects of food consumption allows for instability despite time-consistent maximisation of a concave utility function. As the addictive aspects stem from carbohydrates – which is empirically supported – this paragraph also stresses the importance of nutrient-specific taxation, although in this case on carbohydrates.

121 For a detailed solution see Dockner, Feichtinger 1993, pp. 257-260.

4.2.4 Dynamic Inconsistency

So far, this dissertation has presented three types of deviations from standard microeconomic assumptions leading to instability. In this section, as in the section on the weight-dependent rate of time preference, the assumption of time-consistent discounting is abandoned. In contrast to paragraph 4.2.2, the discount function is now not an exponential function, but a hyperbola. This allows for different short-term and long-term decisions, which intuitively seems plausible in the context of food consumption. In addition, recent examinations of neural processes seem to support hyperbolic discounting as an appropriate framework for food consumption decisions. The question remains as to whether this type of discounting can account for instability, as well, and which political implications can be derived.

There are many different definitions of economic rationality.[122] As a standard microeconomic assumption, it is understood that rational behaviour implies consistent maximisation of an individual's utility function.[123] In a dynamic setting, consistent maximisation means that at any point in time, the same decisions are made. This assumption is fulfilled when lifetime utility is discounted exponentially. In this case, the rate of time preference is constant.[124]

Therefore, for every unit of time, the exponential curve loses the same constant proportion of its remaining height. As a result, values that are discounted exponentially always have the same relationship when compared to one another, independent of the point in time when the comparison is made.[125] Thus, decisions based on exponential discounting are consistent over time.

In contrast to exponential discounting, which is widely used in conventional utility theory, hyperbolic discounting can account for preference reversals. Preference reversals can frequently be observed in reality and could also be found in

122 See Meyer 1999, pp. 7-10 for a short survey.

123 This widely used definition is in accordance with, for example, Becker 1962, p. 1.

124 See Samuelson 1937, p. 156.

125 See Ainslie 1975, p. 471.

experimental set-ups with animals and humans. For example, a person currently dieting may attempt to lose a certain amount of weight in the long run, but still choose to have a piece of cake right now. Thus, the short-run decision represents a deviation from the long-run plan the individual had decided on before making the short-run decision. Graphically, this reversal of preferences can be observed when the curves of the discount function that are applied to two rewards cross. Accordingly, distant rewards are discounted at a lower rate than immediate rewards.

In order to cross, the discount function must be more concave than the exponential curve. Hyperbolas fulfil this requirement.[126]

In an economic framework, the possibility of time-inconsistent behaviour was first outlined by Robert H. Strotz (1956). He developed a utility function which changes as time passes. The value of the discount function depends on both the time span between a future date and the present date, as well as on the calendar date.[127] Thereafter, behavioural psychologists found evidence for hyperbolic discounting, which in their field has become known as Herrnstein's matching law.[128]

Figure 4-11 clarifies the occurence of preference reversals in the case of hyperbolic discounting. The figure displays the present value of delayed rewards of different magnitudes, B_1 and B_2 ($B_1 < B_2$), as a function of time. In panel A, conventional exponential discounting is depicted. The smaller, sooner reward B_1 is preferred over the larger, more distant reward B_2 irrespective of the point in time when the decision is made. The individual always prefers B_1 as the exponential curves don't intersect. In the lower panel B, the decision depends on the point in time: At time t_1, B_2 is preferred over B_1. In contrast, the opposite is true at time t_2. Preferences are reversed at the point of intersection of the hyperbolas.

126 See Loewenstein, Prelec 1992, p. 580.

127 See Strotz 1956, p. 167.

128 See, for example, Chung, Herrnstein 1967, Ainslie 1974, Kirby 1997 for experimental evidence, Herrnstein 1970 for the first formulation of the matching law.

Figure 4-11: Exponential vs. Hyperbolic Discounting
(Reference: Own construction following Kirby 1997, p. 55)

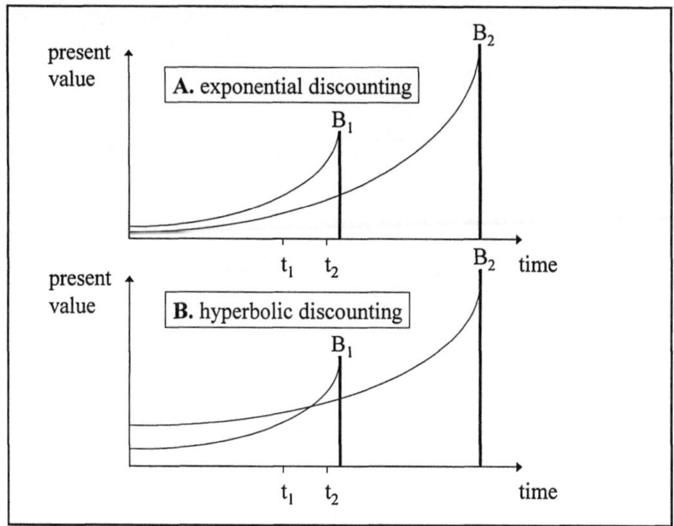

In addition to the violation of the stationarity property (also referred to as the **common difference effect** which states that preferences between two delayed outcomes can switch), there are three patterns frequently observed in reality which cannot be accounted for by conventional exponential discounting: To start with, according to the **absolute magnitude effect**, discount rates vary inversely with the size of the reward. Furthermore, there is a **gain-loss asymmetry**, which implies that losses are discounted at a lower rate than gains. Finally, individuals demand a higher compensation for delaying a reward than they are willing to give up to speed consumption up by the same time span. Thus, a **delay-speedup asymmetry** exists.[129] Hyperbolic discounting can account for these anomalies.

A third kind of discount functions, called quasi-hyperbolic discount functions, maintains most of the analytical tractability of exponential functions while retaining the decisive feature of dynamic inconsistency:

129 See Loewenstein, Prelec 1992, pp. 574-578, or see Thaler 1981 for a crisp description of the first three anomalies and a related experimental set-up.

$$V = U_0 + \rho \sum_{t=1}^{T} \sigma^t U_t dt \tag{4.70}$$

$$0 < \rho < 1;\ 0 < \sigma < 1$$

V denotes lifetime utility, ρ and σ are discount parameters. The above equation implies a discrete discount function with values $\{1, \rho\sigma, \rho\sigma^2, \rho\sigma^3, \ldots\}$.[130] If ρ=1, the above expression simplifies to the standard exponential function.

Quasi-hyperbolic discounting was first proposed by Edmund S. Phelps and Robert A. Pollak in 1968. In their article, discounting is applied to intergenerational saving.[131] In addition to its analytical tractability, hyperbolic discounting is applicable to many fields, such as saving and consumption decisions[132] or health, especially addiction.[133] Recently, brain scans have shown that hyperbolic discounting as a mathematical formulation well describes processes in the human brain involved in decision-making concerning food and addictive substances.

According to brain scans with functional magnetic resonance imaging, two separate neural systems are involved when deciding between reward options that are varied by delay. Parts of the limbic system, which are heavily innervated by the midbrain dopamine system, are preferentially activated when dealing with immediately available rewards. These refer to ρ as a decision parameter (see equation 4.70). In contrast, regions of the lateral prefrontal cortex and posterior pa-

---

130 See Laux, Peck 2007, p. 8.

131 See Phelps, Pollak 1968, p. 186.

132 See, for example, Laibson 1997 for an analysis of the influence of commitment technology when time inconsistency is common knowledge, Diamond, Köszegi 2003 for an extension of Laibson's savings model with endogenous retirement, Huang et al. 2006 for a theoretical and empirical analysis of consumption in the context of temptation and self-control.

133 See, for example, Laux, Peck 2007 for a simplified model of rational addiction with hyperbolic discounting, Raineri, Rachlin 1993 for a theory of addiction based on learning to increase the consumption rate, Gruber, Köszegi 2004 for an analysis of time-inconsistent smoking decisions, Robberstad, Cairns 2007 for an empirical examination whether health-related decisions are non-stationary.

rietal cortex are engaged with intertemporal choices, irrespective of delay. Thus, these decisions refer to σ. For choices between immediate and delayed outcomes, decisions are obviously determined by the relative activation of both systems. When ρ is engaged, the earlier option will be chosen, while a greater influence of the σ-system leads to a decision in favour of the later option. Limbic and paralimbic cortical structures have consistently been implicated in impulsive behaviour, and drug addiction is commonly thought to involve disturbances of dopaminergic neurotransmission in these systems. As a result, many factors other than temporal proximity, such as smell or touch of the desired object, are associated with impulsive behaviour. Therefore, the interaction of the two constants expresses competition between lower level, automatic processes that may reflect evolutionary adaptations to a particular environment – represented by ρ – and the more recently evolved uniquely human capacity for abstract reasoning and future planning, which is described by σ.[134]

In addition, there is evidence that two classes of signals regulate food intake: While short-term signals determine portion sizes, long-term signals attempt to adjust bodyweight and may refer to an individual's fat storage in general. As a result of the interaction of the two kinds of signals, bodyweight is supposed to remain fairly constant despite varying levels of activity and food intake. Interestingly, similar mechanisms regulating bodyweight can be observed for various mammals. As a consequence, the ratio of energy consumption to bodyweight is almost the same for humans and many mammals (approximately 0.7).[135] Notably, this approach does not contradict the occurrence of cyclical consumption described in the previous paragraph: Cyclical food consumption and the resulting variations in bodyweight can frequently be observed in individuals. The two kinds of signals discussed in the present section have evolved to maintain bodyweight constant, but obviously, the regulatory mechanism fails in some individuals – resulting in food overconsumption – and serves its purpose in others.

134 See McClure 2004, pp. 503-506.

135 See Kandel et al. 1996, pp. 630-635.

A study of brain activity during food presentation finds significant increases of the whole brain metabolism, and a different reaction to mere food ingestion (influenced by feelings of hunger or satiety) than to the reward associated with food that is influenced by its palatability. One of the regions where the most significant changes were observed, the orbitofrontal cortex, has previously been shown to be linked with drug craving in drug-addicted subjects.[136]

In comparison to lean control subjects, morbidly obese subjects exhibit enhanced sensitivity in the brain regions where sematosensory maps of the mouth, lips, and tongue are located. The same area is involved with the perception of taste. As many especially palatable kinds of food are relatively energy-dense, such differences in brain activity may contribute to food overconsumption and obesity.[137]

Despite characteristic mechanisms of action, virtually all drugs have a common feature: They directly or indirectly influence the mesocorticolimbic pathway. Just like the consumption of drugs, such as heroine or cocaine, the consumption of food or water and sexual activity lead to a release of dopamine in the brain.[138]

As a result of the above considerations, quasi-hyperbolic discounting is an appropriate discount function for analysing food preferences. Jonathan Gruber and Botond Köszegi (2001) introduce quasi-hyperbolic discounting to the framework of the Becker-Murphy Model of Rational Addiction. However, the authors are unable to empirically distinguish between exponential and hyperbolic discounting in their application to smoking.[139]

Within their framework, the addictive stock evolves according to

$$\dot{S}_t = \varphi_t \cdot (F_t^C + S_t) - S_{t+1} \tag{4.71}$$

136 See Wang et al. 2004, pp. 1791-1795.

137 See Wang et al. 2004, pp. 1151-1154.

138 See Thompson 2001, p. 173.

139 See Gruber, Köszegi 2001, p. 1263.

As before, the addictive good is denoted F_t^C, while the normal good is represented by F_t^P. The rate of depreciation of the addictive stock is denoted by φ_t. By assumption, utility is additively separable in F_t^C and F_t^P:

$$V = U_t(F_t^C, F_t^P, S_t) = U_t(F_t^C, S_t) + U_t(F_t^P) \tag{4.72}$$

There are two kinds of hyperbolic discounters: naïve agents are not aware of their self-control problem. Therefore, they ignore the resulting preference reversal. Sophisticated agents know their self-control problem and plan correspondingly.

In order to time-consistently maximise utility, a standard Euler equation can be used. Maximisation is more difficult under the time-inconsistent framework: Sophisticated agents' plans are modelled by a subgame-perfect equilibrium. The sophisticated agent in the periods comprised by the plan (the 'intertemporal selves') represents the players participating in the game, the vectors of consumption are the strategies that can be followed. Naïve agents are neglected in the analysis. It turns out that both exponential and hyperbolic discounters will decrease consumption as a result of anticipated price increases if the degree of addiction to F_t^C is sufficiently high. Thus, both approaches lead to virtually identical conclusions. Still, the justification for government intervention is different.[140]

The authors don't justify government intervention with rational addictiveness, but with self-control problems resulting from the inconsistency of long-run and short-run preferences and with a misperception problem: Agents fail to correctly predict their own future behaviour. As a result, they do not act in their best interest. Consequently, agents' long-run preferences – which would induce optimal consumption if they were adhered to – are used as a starting point to maximise social welfare. The resulting positive optimal tax can correct the self-con-

140 See Gruber, Köszegi 2001, pp. 1280-1285 and Gruber, Köszegi 2004, pp. 1965-1967.

trol problem at the margin. While the Model of Rational Addiction under time-consistent dynamic maximisation justifies government intervention based on externalities, the present approach addresses internalities as the greatest harm is done to the addict himself. Therefore, the justification of tax intervention is radically different under the assumption of hyperbolic discounting.[141]

The distinction between addictive and non-addictive substances is vital in this context: Assume an agent suffers from self-control problems. Then, taxing the harmful, addictive good imposes less of a burden on the agent than taxing an equally harmful, non-addictive good. The reason is that an addictive good not only directly induces harm, but that it also increases the short-run desire to consume. The above is true for both naïve and sophisticated agents.[142]

Thus, this paragraph also stresses the importance of nutrient-specific taxation. In this context, instability arises from the introduction of an addictive good. Therefore, the tax should be based on the carbohydrate content of food. The political implications are the same as in the precedent paragraph, although they are differently justified: Rather than preventing externalities, individuals are kept from harming themselves due to internal effects.

141 See Gruber, Köszegi 2001, pp. 1285-1289.
142 See Gruber, Köszegi 2004, pp. 1269/70.

Glossary

A_0:	initial assets
B:	reward
BW*:	physiologically optimal level of weight
BW_0:	birthweight
BW_t (BW_t^F):	bodyweight (fat-dependent bodyweight)
$\dot{BW}_t$ ($\dot{BW}_t^F$):	rate of change in (fat-dependent) bodyweight
D_t:	deviation from the physiologically optimal level of weight
EP:	expenditures on patience
F*:	optimal (utility-maximising) level of food consumption
$F^{18.5}$ (F^{25}):	food consumption resulting in a BMI of 18.5 (25)
F_t ($F_t^A, F_t^C, F_t^F, F_t^P$):	food consumption (of alcohol, carbohydrates, fat, protein)
f_t ($f_t^A, f_t^C, f_t^F, f_t^P$):	net calorie consumption (of alcohol, carbohydrates, fat, protein)
G_t (G_t^C, G_t^F):	food price (of carbohydrates, of fat)
H_t:	state of health
I_t:	price of non-food goods and services
J_t (J_t^C, J_t^F):	energy consumed (from carbohydrates, from fat)
K_t:	aggregate consumption commodity
l_t:	marginal costs of carbohydrate consumption
$\dot{l}_t$:	rate of change in marginal costs of carbohydrate consumption
L_t:	non-food goods and services
M:	budget
M_{max}:	maximally achievable budget
m_t:	marginal costs of food consumption
$\dot{m}_t$:	rate of change in marginal costs of food consumption
n_t:	marginal costs of consumption of non-food

	goods and services
o_t:	marginal costs of fat consumption
$\dot{o}_t$:	rate of change in marginal costs of fat consumption
P_1:	fraction of the population with consciousness
P_2:	fraction of the population without consciousness
Q:	objective functional
R:	full wealth
r:	rate of interest
S_t:	addictive stock
$\dot{S}$:	rate of change of the addictive stock
T:	length of life
t:	time index
TA_t:	time input into consumption of the aggregate commodity
TF_t (TF_t^C, TF_t^F):	time input into food preparation and consumption (of carbohydrates, of fat)
TL_t:	sick time
TW_t:	working hours
TZ:	total amount of time
U_t:	utility function
V:	lifetime utility
v:	scalar parameter
W_t:	wage rate
α:	influence of health on income
β:	discount function
δ_t (δ_t^C, δ_t^F):	rate of depreciation of bodyweight (of calories from carbohydrates, from fat)
θ_i:	slope parameter
λ:	Lagrange multiplier
ρ, σ:	discount parameters
φ_t:	rate of depreciation of the addictive stock
ψ:	degree of deviation from constant discounting

Chapter 5. Empirical Analysis

Based on the differentiation between health-conscious and health-unconscious individuals, the precedent chapter demonstrates that obesity only occurs in health-unconscious persons. By assumption, consciousness also refers to other aspects of life. As a result, conscious individuals are assumed to be more highly educated, able to find employment, and to receive a higher income. Therefore, in the present chapter, systematic differences in education, employment status, and income between normal-weight subjects and those suffering from redundant bodyweight are examined in order to find out why some persons care for their health and others do not. For this purpose, US data from a total number of 430,912 persons is analysed to investigate possible relations between their BMI and the above aspects of their socioeconomic status. Then, correlations between several aspects of behaviour that are harmful to health are evaluated. The chapter closes with an analysis of the relation between these health-related behavioural patterns and socioeconomic status.

5.1 Data

In the present section, data from the 2007 Behavioral Risk Factor Surveillance System (BRFSS) are analysed. The 2007 data file is available at *http:// www.cdc.gov/brfss/technical_infodata/surveydata/2007.htm#data* in ASCII or SAS Transport format.

The BRFSS is a data source intended to monitor risky health behaviour that is associated with chronic diseases, preventable infectious diseases, injuries, and death. It was established in 1984 by the Centers for Disease Control and Prevention. The cross-sectional survey is the largest continuously conducted telephone health survey in the world. All 50 US states, the District of Columbia, and Puerto Rico participate in the system (The Virgin Islands and Guam merely conduct point-in-time surveys). Subjects are aged eighteen years and older and live in households. The survey consists of three components: The core, optional modules, and state-added questions. The core includes demographic questions, as well as questions on health-related perceptions, conditions, and behaviour. The core questions are asked by all states. The modules pertain to specific topics, such as asthma, arthritis, or cardiovascular health. The states choose whether they want to include a specific module in their survey. The modules are designed by the CDC. In contrast, states develop the state-added questions. Due to its standardised questions, BRFSS data are comparable over time and across states.[143]

Data of comparable quality (regarding period and frequency of survey, number of subjects, and comprehensiveness of questions concerning health and demography) is not available for Germany in the field of health. However, the assumption that findings based on BRFSS can be transferred to other industrialised countries is plausible, especially since in such countries, recent trends in weight gain are similar.

In the following, all analyses are conducted separately by gender, as well as individually for three ethnic groups: White, Black, and other ethnic origin. As a result, there are six separate estimations for each analysis. The analyses are conducted with SPSS 15.

The basic data file as downloaded from the BRFSS website contains 270,161 female and 160,751 male subjects. As BMI is the main variable of interest and the standard BMI scale cannot be applied in case of pregnancy, pregnant women are removed from the sample. Thus, 3,309 subjects are deleted. This leaves 266,852 women in the sample. Of these, those responding 'White' to the question "Which one of these groups would you say best represents your race?" are included in the White sample (5,146 cases), those responding 'Black' in the Black one (623 cases). All others (2,528 cases) are included in the subsample

143 See CDC 2007.

denoted 'Others'. 258,555 subjects have not answered the above question. They are sorted into ethnic groups by their response to "Which one or more of the following would you say is your race?". If 'White' is the only race chosen, subjects are denoted 'White' (n = 215,536). The same procedure applies to Black subjects (n = 23,488). All other answers, including those who refused to answer this question, are included in 'Others' (n = 19,525). As a result, there are 220,682 White females, 24,111 Black females, and 22,059 females with other ethnic background. Male subjects are divided into three groups in an analogous manner. The three groups consist of 135,428 White males, 10,918 Black males, and 14,405 men with other ethnic background. Thereafter, subjects who didn't know or refused to provide information on either height, weight, or both at any point of the survey are removed from the sample (this includes subjects who didn't answer either question in the first place but provided information on further enquiry). As a result, the subsamples consist of 207,489 White females, 22,496 Black females, and 19,694 females with other ethnic background. In the male samples, 133,574 White, 10,594 Black, and 13,537 Other subjects remain. The descriptive statistics of these samples by gender and ethnic group are presented in the Appendix (BMI categories are established in accordance with WHO criteria as described in chapter two). For the descriptive statistics, the variables of interest are: reported weight (in pounds and in kilograms), reported height (in inches and in metres), computed BMI based on this information, and BMI category. BMI is not directly included in the BRFSS questionnaire but calculated from the self-reported information on weight and height. Such information is presumably subject to reporting error. Therefore, the data on weight and height must be corrected before reliable BMI values can be determined.

The correction follows John H. Cawley (1999). He uses data from the Third National Health and Nutrition Examination Survey (NHANES III) conducted from 1988 to 1994. The data set consists of 31,311 subjects who were not only surveyed but also underwent a physical examination. Thus, it contains reported height and weight, as well as weight and height measured in a medical examination. The given age range differs from the age range relevant to this dissertation (seventeen to 40 years of age as opposed to a minimum age of eighteen). As higher age is correlated with higher bodyweight and higher weight is correlated with more severe underestimation, the corrections made in this dissertation are likely to be more moderate than they would be if all adults were included (Due to the age range considered, Cawley's calculations are based on 3,547 male and 3,854 female respondents).

He calculates the average reporting error separately by gender, race / ethnicity, age, classification of actual weight, classification of reported weight, and by the time lag between survey response and examination. Per cent reporting error is defined as:

$$([\text{reported value} - \text{measured value}] / \text{measured value}) \cdot 100$$

As a result, overestimates become positive and underestimates are negative.[144]

The BRFSS data file is corrected for reporting error using Cawley's results on height and weight. Thus, it is assumed that the relationship between reported and actual height and weight is the same in both data sets. Details on his results can be found in Appendix 8.6.

Based on the corrected values, BMI and BMI category are established. As a consequence of the corrections, the percentage of women in the underweight and normal categories decreases for all ethnic groups. In contrast, the percentage of women in the pre-obese and obese categories rises. The percentage of White men also decreases in the underweight and normal categories. The reverse is true for Black and Other men. The descriptive statistics of the corrected sub-samples are included in the Appendix, as well.

After correcting for reporting error, the data set must be inspected for potential outliers and extreme values. Subjects with a corrected BMI value below 15 are removed from the sample as they are suspected to be extremely underweight for psychological conditions which are not of interest here. As body fat reserves can

144 See Cawley 1999, pp. 79-84.

grow almost boundlessly, the upper bound is determined in a different manner using mean and standard deviation of the respective subsample:

$$\text{upper bound} = \text{mean} + 7.5 \cdot \text{standard deviation}$$

Values above this upper bound are deleted, as well. Thus, values exceeding 74.12, 86.625, and 78.58 for White, Black, and Other women are removed, respectively. The corresponding upper limits for men are 66.36, 70.97, and 68.855. As a result, the sample is reduced to 407,022 subjects (249,446 women, 157,576 men).

The descriptive statistics of the new subsamples are presented in Appendix 8.7. Again, BMI categories are established in accordance with WHO criteria as described in chapter two.

As a consequence of the removal of outliers and extreme values, the mean values hardly change while the standard deviation is reduced in most cases (or it remains equal). Skewness is slightly reduced in all subsamples. Kurtosis is reduced in all cases, as well. It is considerably decreased by the removal of outliers and extreme values for White men and Black women. The percentage values of BMI categories for men are virtually unchanged: Ratios are slightly higher for underweight Black and Other men, and for pre-obese males of other ethnic origin. For females, only the normal BMI category remains unchanged. The ratio of underweight women is now lower (except for Black females), while the ratios of pre-obese and obese women have increased as a result of the removal of outliers (except for Black obese women and for women of other ethnic origin in the pre-obese and obese category).

The descriptive statistics show that less than one third of the male population is in the normal weight range, and less than 40 per cent of the females. Obesity prevalence is highest among Blacks of both genders. The spread of BMI values is particularly large in the Black population, as well, and it is generally smaller for the male than for the female subsamples. Average BMI is highest for Black females, and lowest for White Women. The standard deviation of height is almost identical for all subsamples. Average height is similar for all ethnic groups of the same gender. The histograms show that the distribution of BMI values is right-skewed: Skewness is positive for all subsamples. In all cases but one, kurtosis is above three and, therefore, all subsamples are heavy-tailed (except for Black women). Still, the deviation from the value of three is moderate.

5.2 Differences in Socioeconomic Status between Obese, Pre-Obese, and Normal-Weight Persons

As described in section 4.1, a fundamental assumption of this dissertation is the significant difference between population subgroups P_1 and P_2. These population subgroups differ concerning their consciousness. Group P_1 is conscious. As a consequence, it is more highly educated, able to find employment, and receives a higher income. Group P_2 lacks consciousness. Therefore, P_2 individuals have a lower level of education, are more often unemployed, and have less disposable income. Supposedly, those who invest more in education invest more in health, as well, both being aspects of human capital. By assumption, individuals invest in their human capital as a result of their consciousness. As group P_2 lacks consciousness, its members have lower socioeconomic status (its constituents are level of education, employment status, and income) and are less likely to be employed. At the same time, they are more likely to suffer from overweight and obesity. Therefore, the following empirical investigation examines whether systematic socioeconomic differences are related to an increased BMI.

5.2.1 Analytical Framework

If the hypothesis of significant differences between population groups were correct, mean BMI values must significantly differ for varying levels of education, employment statuses, and levels of income. The above hypothesis is examined for education and income applying Mann-Whitney U tests. For employment status, Pearson chi-square tests are conducted.

5.2.2 Empirical Implementation

The questions relevant to this analysis pertain to BMI value, education ("What is the highest grade or year of school you completed?", answers are subdivided into six categories, the lowest defined as 'never attended school' and the highest as 'college graduate'), annual household income ("Is your annual household income from all sources...?", answers are subdivided into eight categories ranging from 'less than US $ 10,000' to 'US $ 75,000 or more'), and employment ("Are you currently...?", answers can be chosen out of seven categories: employed for wages, self-employed, out of work for more than one year, out of work for less than one year, homemaker, student, retired). In Figure 5-1, BMI categories are denoted

- 1 for underweight
- 2 for normal weight
- 3 for pre-obese
- 4 for obese.

The column denoted '% share of total subsample' displays the fraction of subjects belonging to the respective level of education, employment status, or income bracket for the whole subsample. This column is not differentiated by weight level. Subjects who refused to provide information on the respective question constitute the percentage points that are missing to 100 per cent.

BMI categories are spread over levels of education, employment status, and income brackets as depicted in the following figure:

Figure 5-1: Socioeconomic Status by BMI Category [Per Cent]
(a) White Women (b) Black Women (c) Other Women
(d) White Men (e) Black Men (f) Other Men
(Reference: Own construction)

Socioeconomic Status by BMI Category: (a) White Women						
		% Share of BMI Category				% Share of Total Subsample
		1	2	3	4	
Level of Education	Never attended school	1.6	27.2	33.2	38.0	0.1
	Elementary education	2.6	28.5	33.7	35.2	2.4
	Some high school	2.4	30.9	33.4	33.2	5.9
	High school graduate	1.8	34.5	34.7	28.9	31.3
	Some College	1.7	37.5	33.3	27.5	27.8
	College graduate	1.7	47.5	30.5	20.3	32.3
Employment Status	Wage earner	1.3	39.9	32.0	26.7	41.6
	Self-employed	1.7	46.3	31.7	20.2	6.8
	Out of work > 1 year	2.6	34.3	29.4	33.6	1.4
	Out of work < 1 year	1.7	37.5	31.5	29.3	1.7
	Homemaker	2.1	42.6	32.3	23.1	13.0
	Student	3.2	53.4	23.1	20.3	1.5
	Retired	2.1	37.4	36.8	23.7	27.7
	Unable to work	2.5	24.9	27.3	45.3	6.2
Family Income [US $]	Income < 10,000	2.9	30.1	30.0	37.1	4.2
	10,000 ≤ income < 15,000	2.1	31.0	32.5	34.4	5.3
	15,000 ≤ income < 20,000	2.2	32.7	33.4	31.7	6.7
	20,000 ≤ income < 25,000	2.0	33.5	33.7	30.9	8.5
	25,000 ≤ income < 35,000	1.7	35.2	34.5	28.6	10.9
	35,000 ≤ income < 50,000	1.6	36.3	33.9	28.1	13.9
	50,000 ≤ income < 75,000	1.2	39.7	33.0	26.0	14.6
	Income ≥ 75,000	1.4	48.7	31.1	18.8	21.3

Socioeconomic Status by BMI Category: (b) Black Women						
		% Share of BMI Category				% Share of Total Subsample
		1	2	3	4	
Level of Education	Never attended school	0.0	37.5	28.1	34.4	0.1
	Elementary education	1.2	18.3	28.4	52.1	4.4
	Some high school	1.4	18.3	27.7	52.6	12.6
	High school graduate	1.2	19.7	31.5	47.6	33.7
	Some College	1.1	20.1	31.7	47.2	26.3
	College graduate	0.7	24.5	35.2	39.7	22.6
Employment Status	Wage earner	0.7	21.1	32.8	45.4	46.9
	Self-employed	0.8	26.7	33.7	38.8	3.9
	Out of work > 1 year	1.6	21.4	29.0	48.0	3.0
	Out of work < 1 year	0.7	21.6	29.7	47.9	3.6
	Homemaker	1.3	21.4	32.7	44.6	5.6
	Student	2.5	33.4	29.0	35.1	3.1
	Retired	1.3	19.9	35.4	43.4	20.0
	Unable to work	1.4	15.2	23.3	60.0	13.5
Family Income [US $]	Income < 10,000	1.3	20.2	26.5	52.1	11.3
	10,000 ≤ income < 15,000	1.4	16.0	29.9	52.7	8.6
	15,000 ≤ income < 20,000	1.4	17.7	30.2	50.7	11.9
	20,000 ≤ income < 25,000	1.1	20.3	31.0	47.6	11.0
	25,000 ≤ income < 35,000	0.7	20.3	33.2	45.7	13.4
	35,000 ≤ income < 50,000	1.1	20.7	32.7	45.4	12.7
	50,000 ≤ income < 75,000	0.5	22.0	34.0	43.4	9.5
	Income ≥ 75,000	0.5	26.0	36.7	36.8	8.8

Socioeconomic Status by BMI Category: (c) Other Women						
		% Share of BMI Category				% Share of Total Subsample
		1	2	3	4	
Level of Education	Never attended school	1.5	23.5	36.4	38.6	0.7
	Elementary education	1.3	21.4	34.2	43.0	8.7
	Some high school	1.7	26.3	34.4	37.6	10.1
	High school graduate	1.9	32.8	34.7	30.7	27.9
	Some College	1.7	33.9	32.8	31.7	25.4
	College graduate	2.5	48.6	30.1	18.7	27.0
Employment Status	Wage earner	1.3	36.3	33.8	28.6	45.0
	Self-employed	3.0	41.8	32.7	22.5	6.1
	Out of work > 1 year	2.6	30.8	29.1	37.5	2.7
	Out of work < 1 year	1.8	32.6	33.6	31.9	3.0
	Homemaker	2.1	35.1	33.7	29.1	15.4
	Student	3.6	52.0	25.3	19.1	3.5
	Retired	2.4	38.0	34.5	25.1	15.0
	Unable to work	2.4	20.7	29.1	47.8	8.9
Family Income [US $]	Income < 10,000	3.0	25.8	32.3	38.9	9.3
	10,000 ≤ income < 15,000	1.7	26.9	33.6	37.8	7.6
	15,000 ≤ income < 20,000	1.9	27.8	33.8	36.4	9.4
	20,000 ≤ income < 25,000	0.9	30.5	35.1	33.4	10.3
	25,000 ≤ income < 35,000	1.4	33.1	33.7	31.7	11.3
	35,000 ≤ income < 50,000	1.3	37.5	31.9	29.4	12.1
	50,000 ≤ income < 75,000	2.2	40.2	33.7	23.9	10.4
	Income ≥ 75,000	2.5	49.6	30.7	17.3	14.5

Socioeconomic Status by BMI Category: (d) White Men						
		% Share of BMI Category				% Share of Total Subsample
		1	2	3	4	
Level of Education	Never attended school	3.4	28.8	45.2	22.6	0.1
	Elementary education	1.1	28.3	41.9	28.6	2.7
	Some high school	1.3	28.9	40.9	28.9	5.5
	High school graduate	0.7	24.8	44.8	29.7	29.1
	Some College	0.5	24.2	45.2	30.1	24.4
	College graduate	0.3	28.5	48.0	23.1	38.0
Employment Status	Wage earner	0.4	24.8	46.2	28.6	47.2
	Self-employed	0.4	26.4	48.4	24.8	13.2
	Out of work > 1 year	1.6	29.4	36.0	33.0	1.2
	Out of work < 1 year	1.1	29.7	39.6	29.6	1.8
	Homemaker	1.2	32.0	40.8	25.9	0.3
	Student	2.1	50.1	31.1	16.7	1.3
	Retired	0.7	28.1	47.4	23.8	29.3
	Unable to work	1.5	22.8	35.8	39.9	5.4
Family Income [US $]	Income < 10,000	1.8	31.2	37.2	29.8	2.6
	10,000 ≤ income < 15,000	1.7	29.8	38.1	30.4	3.5
	15,000 ≤ income < 20,000	1.2	29.3	42.3	27.2	4.8
	20,000 ≤ income < 25,000	0.9	29.0	42.1	28.1	7.1
	25,000 ≤ income < 35,000	0.7	27.5	44.2	27.7	10.7
	35,000 ≤ income < 50,000	0.5	25.5	46.2	27.9	15.4
	50,000 ≤ income < 75,000	0.3	23.8	47.2	28.7	17.2
	Income ≥ 75,000	0.2	24.6	49.1	26.1	29.3

Socioeconomic Status by BMI Category: (e) Black Men						
		% Share of BMI Category				% Share of Total Subsample
		1	2	3	4	
Level of Education	Never attended school	7.4	33.3	25.9	33.3	0.3
	Elementary education	1.4	34.1	36.1	28.4	6.2
	Some high school	2.1	34.8	33.6	29.5	12.4
	High school graduate	1.1	29.5	36.9	32.6	35.6
	Some College	0.8	27.7	40.0	31.5	24.4
	College graduate	0.5	26.4	43.8	29.9	20.8
Employment Status	Wage earner	0.7	26.6	40.4	32.3	47.8
	Self-employed	1.1	32.7	37.6	28.6	7.8
	Out of work > 1 year	0.9	38.5	35.1	25.6	3.3
	Out of work < 1 year	0.7	37.5	35.1	26.7	4.0
	Homemaker	2.4	31.7	26.8	39.0	0.4
	Student	3.9	53.2	27.7	15.2	2.2
	Retired	1.0	28.2	41.0	29.8	22.7
	Unable to work	2.3	30.6	31.8	35.2	11.4
Family Income [US $]	Income $< 10{,}000$	3.3	35.2	33.3	28.2	7.2
	$10{,}000 \leq$ income $< 15{,}000$	1.5	33.8	34.6	30.1	6.7
	$15{,}000 \leq$ income $< 20{,}000$	1.3	32.1	37.2	29.4	10.0
	$20{,}000 \leq$ income $< 25{,}000$	1.2	30.9	35.4	32.5	10.2
	$25{,}000 \leq$ income $< 35{,}000$	0.7	30.1	38.3	30.9	14.2
	$35{,}000 \leq$ income $< 50{,}000$	0.3	25.2	41.0	33.5	14.0
	$50{,}000 \leq$ income $< 75{,}000$	0.4	24.5	42.9	32.2	11.8
	Income $\geq 75{,}000$	0.6	22.5	45.2	31.7	13.8

Socioeconomic Status by BMI Category: (f) Other Men						
		% Share of BMI Category				% Share of Total Subsample
		1	2	3	4	
Level of Education	**Never attended school**	4.2	27.1	33.3	35.4	0.7
	Elementary education	1.0	29.3	40.8	28.9	8.2
	Some high school	1.5	30.8	40.2	27.6	9.9
	High school graduate	1.4	28.5	41.4	28.7	29.3
	Some College	1.2	27.0	43.1	28.7	23.0
	College graduate	0.8	36.9	43.1	19.2	28.3
Employment Status	**Wage earner**	0.8	30.2	43.3	25.7	54.3
	Self-employed	0.9	30.2	44.7	24.2	10.7
	Out of work > 1 year	2.0	30.0	35.3	32.7	2.2
	Out of work < 1 year	2.2	30.1	41.1	26.6	3.6
	Homemaker	1.1	32.3	37.6	29.0	0.7
	Student	4.8	48.6	32.9	13.7	3.1
	Retired	1.2	33.1	41.4	24.2	17.4
	Unable to work	2.1	23.7	37.3	36.9	7.5
Family Income [US $]	**Income < 10,000**	2.4	29.6	37.7	30.2	6.0
	10,000 ≤ income < 15,000	3.1	32.3	38.6	25.9	6.0
	15,000 ≤ income < 20,000	1.7	29.3	41.1	27.9	8.6
	20,000 ≤ income < 25,000	0.9	30.3	41.1	27.6	10.1
	25,000 ≤ income < 35,000	1.1	28.4	43.1	27.5	12.2
	35,000 ≤ income < 50,000	0.7	28.2	43.1	28.0	13.6
	50,000 ≤ income < 75,000	0.5	27.4	45.7	26.3	12.7
	Income ≥ 75,000	0.6	32.8	44.2	22.4	18.5

The **White female** subsample displays the most clear-cut trends:

- BMI decreases with rising level of education. In the two lowest groups – consisting of those who never attended school and those with elementary education – most females are obese. The proportion of obese subjects continuously decreases with a rising level of education. Simultaneously, the proportion of those with normal bodyweight continuously rises
- Most White women who are unable to work are obese. In contrast, for all other employment statuses, most subjects are in the normal weight range
- White females suffer less from excess weight the higher their income. While the proportion of obese subjects continuously decreases with higher income, the proportion of those with normal bodyweight continuously increases.

Other females display similar, although less clear-cut patterns:

- Weight decreases with higher level of education
- Weight decreases with rising income. By income group, the same continuous trends as for White females can be observed. Most subjects in the three lowest income groups are obese, and most of those in the highest three income groups are in the normal weight range
- Most females who are unable to work are obese. In this subsample, those who are out of work are heavier than the other groups.

The picture is considerably different for **Black women**:

- The only category of the three measures of socioeconomic status in which most subjects are not obese is those who never attended school. In this category, most have normal bodyweight. In all other categories, most Black women are obese
- The proportion of obese Black women falls with rising income
- By employment status, the proportion of obese females is highest among those who are unable to work.

White and **Other men** display similar patterns:

- In both subsamples, most males are pre-obese

- Among Whites, the only exceptions are students (most students are in the normal weight category) and those unable to work (most are obese)
- Among those with other ethnic backgrounds, the only exceptions are men who never attended school (mostly obese) and students (mostly normal)
- Furthermore, the proportion of pre-obese men rises with higher income.

Black men display different patterns:

- Among Black males, the proportion of pre-obese tends to rise with level of education
- The proportion of pre-obese Black men rises with income. The lowest income group is the only group whose subjects mostly display normal bodyweight
- While students are mostly in the normal weight range, most homemakers and those unable to work are obese.

Taking a look at the mean diagrams for education, employment, and income group by BMI level for the respective subsamples further clarifies that women's BMI increases with decreasing income and decreasing education while the pattern is less clear-cut for men. This conclusion is consistent with a wealth of empirical literature finding a clearer picture for women than for men (compare studies nos. 5, 10, 25, 38, 42, and 55 of Appendix 8.2, studies nos. I and II of Appendix 8.3, or Figure 8-2). The respective figure visualising this finding using White women and men as examples is Figure 8-2 (mean diagrams for the other subsamples are not displayed but the main differences are explained in the following). Obviously, mean diagrams by employment status must be interpreted with caution as categories are not ranked as they are for education and income. The mean diagrams concerning education show that on average, White men who never attended school are the lightest group, while for women this group has the highest average BMI. Except for college graduates, the pattern is reversed for both genders: On average, White women become lighter with higher education, while White men tend to become heavier. For Black women, a notable difference could be detected: Those with the lowest level of education are lightest. For the other levels of education, weight decreases with higher education. Women of other ethnic origin exhibit a pattern consistent with White women. Like Black women and White men, Black men are also lightest in the least educated group. They are, on average, severely heavier in the top three groups. Among men with other ethnic background, college graduates are lightest. All other levels of education hardly differ by average weight.

The low average weight of students is likely to stem from their young age. By employment status, those unable to work are by far the heaviest group for both genders: On average, White women unable to work are obese. The average BMI of White men who are unable to work is hardly lower (above 29.5). In addition, employment status exhibits the largest spread of the considered variables (average values range between 25 and 31 compared to a range of 26 to 30 for education and employment). Those unable to work are also the heaviest group for Black and Other males and females, whereas students are always the lightest. Notably, for all three ethnic groups, women unable to work are obese on average (Black women display an average BMI of more than 33, women of other ethnic origin a BMI of more than 31, on average).

The mean diagram by family income again shows a clear-cut pattern for White women. Their average weight falls as income rises. In the income range between US $ 15,000 and 75,000, White men display the opposite pattern as their average weight rises with income. Still, this pattern is inconsistent. The highest income group has a severely lower average weight than the second-highest income group. The patterns displayed in the mean diagrams for Black and Other women are consistent with White women. On average, Black men are lightest in the lowest income group while Other men are lightest in the highest income group (their weight hardly changes by level of family income).

As a consequence, severe gender differences could be detected. The female patterns are consistent over the different ethnic groups with the exception of Black women who never attended school. Male patterns are more difficult to compare, and hardly comparable to female patterns.

As a consequence of their ordinal scale, education and income can be tested for equality of means using Mann-Whitney U tests. The null hypothesis states that the means of the two samples compared are equal. The samples are differentiated by subjects' level of weight. All tests are run twice: To start with, one sample consists of non-obese and the other of obese subjects (BMI categories 1, 2, and 3 vs. category 4). Thereafter, one sample consists of underweight and normal-weight individuals, and the other of pre-obese and obese subjects (BMI categories 1 and 2 vs. categories 3 and 4). The Mann-Whitney U tests then reveal whether mean level of education and mean family income differ for the samples described above, that is, whether they differ by level of weight. As employment status is a categorical variable, Pearson chi-square tests are conducted by BMI category, for obesity (BMI categories 1, 2, and 3 vs. category 4), and overweight (BMI categories 1 and 2 vs. categories 3 and 4). Here, the null states that employment status is independent of the level of weight. If the null is rejected, it can be assumed that overweight and obese persons averagely differ in their employment status from their normal-weight counterparts.

For education and income, the relevant significance values are one-sided as it is suspected that heavier subjects are less educated and receive a lower household income. Significance values for employment status are two-sided due to the categorical nature of employment as a variable.

The sample size of the two White subsamples is too large for SPSS to conduct Mann-Whitney U tests. As a result, SPSS draws a smaller sample (n = 112,420; subcommand: /SAMPLE) to process the data.

5.2.3 Results

In the subsequent tables, n denotes the number of processed cases which depends on the response ratio to questions on education and income. The asymptotic significance, given in the fifth column, denotes the probability that the given results are due to chance. By conventional significance values, a value below 0.05 (0.01) is necessary to claim that the described relationship is significant as this means that the probability the result is produced by chance is below 5 per cent (1 per cent). For example, in Figure 5-2 (a), all results but the one for

Black men are produced by chance with a probability below 0.1 per cent. Thus, White women's average level of education is significantly lower by 0.223 in obese individuals compared to non-obese persons (the mean difference measures the average absolute difference in education categories between obese and non-obese individuals). For Black men, the result hints at a level of education that is averagely 0.005 categories lower in obese individuals, but the error probability is 32.5 per cent. The test statistic is included for the sake of completeness.

Figure 5-3 provides the respective results for overweight compared to non-overweight individuals.

Figure 5-2: Test for Equality of Means: Obesity [One-sided Significance] (a) Education (b) Income

(Reference: Own construction)

Test for Equality of Means: (a) Education and Obesity					
		Mann-Whitney U Test			
	Subsample	**n**	**Test Statistic**	**Asymp. Sig.**	**Mean Difference**
Women	White	112,305	1,149,576,970.0	0.000	-0.223
	Black	22,432	57,327,335.500	0.000	-0.167
	Other	19,609	32,654,335.000	0.000	-0.415
Men	White	112,265	1,154,928,926.000	0.000	-0.128
	Black	10,552	11,840,738.500	0.325	-0.005
	Other	13,445	15,634,701.000	0.000	-0.211

Test for Equality of Means: (b) Income and Obesity					
		Mann-Whitney U Test			
	Subsample	n	Test Statistic	Asymp. Sig.	Mean Difference
Women	White	103,227	958,877,686.000	0.000	-0.545
	Black	19,640	43,268,245.000	0.000	-0.383
	Other	16,695	23,653,846.000	0.000	-0.757
Men	White	102,319	1,020,000,000.000	0.000	-0.075
	Black	9,312	9,073,507.000	0.016	0.109
	Other	11,865	12,980,970.000	0.000	-0.189

Figure 5-3: Test for Equality of Means: Overweight [One-sided Significance]
(a) Education (b) Income
(Reference: Own construction)

Test for Equality of Means: (a) Education and Overweight					
		Mann-Whitney U Test			
	Subsample	n	Test Statistic	Asymp. Sig.	Mean Difference
Women	White	112,293	1,332,427,653.000	0.000	-0.239
	Black	22,432	40,471,841.500	0.000	-0.106
	Other	19,609	35,907,989.000	0.000	-0.453
Men	White	112,261	1,222,548,361.500	0.000	-0.029
	Black	10,552	10,854,273.500	0.000	0.163
	Other	13,445	18,496,489.500	0.000	-0.120

Test for Equality of Means: (b) Income and Overweight					
		Mann-Whitney U Test			
	Subsample	n	Test Statistic	Asymp. Sig.	Mean Difference
Women	White	103,357	1,130,000,000.000	0.000	-0.468
	Black	19,640	30,552,906.000	0.000	-0.214
	Other	16,695	26,313,034.000	0.000	-0.746
Men	White	102,361	955,662,265.000	0.000	0.238
	Black	9,312	7,811,906.000	0.000	0.500
	Other	11,865	14,950,132.000	0.299	0.043

Running separate tests for equality of means for all six subsamples yields the following results: Except for Black men (concerning education and obesity) and Other men (concerning income and excess weight), all test statistics are asymptotically statistically significant. In all tables, females with other ethnic background display the largest mean difference in absolute terms, and Black men always have the highest (positive) value. Concerning obesity, all mean differences are negative except for Black men and income. Concerning excess weight, all mean differences of the female subsamples are also negative. Notably, male subsamples' mean differences concerning income and excess weight are all positive. Regarding education and excess weight, only Black males display a positive mean difference.

As a result, significant differences between population subgroups could be confirmed. Again, the picture is less clear-cut for males. Concerning education, females' mean differences are comparable for obese and overweight subjects. In contrast, women's income displays higher mean differences for obese subjects (between -0.757 and -0.383) than for those suffering from excess weight (values range from -0.746 to -0.214). Whether the penalty results from the labour or the marriage market remains unclear as the survey asks for 'household income from all sources'.

Figure 5-4: Test for Independence: Employment [Two-sided Significance]
(a) BMI Category (b) Obesity (c) Overweight
(Reference: Own construction)

Test for Independence: (a) Employment by BMI Category					
		Pearson Chi-Square			
	Subsample	n	Test Statistic	Degrees of Freedom	Sig.
Women	White	206,887	4,266.894	21	0.000
	Black	22,394	410.948	21	0.000
	Other	19,567	530.719	21	0.000
Men	White	133,216	1,939.966	21	0.000
	Black	10,541	198.264	21	0.000
	Other	13,451	237.307	21	0.000

Test for Independence: (b) Employment and Obesity					
		Pearson Chi-Square			
	Subsample	n	Test Statistic	Degrees of Freedom	Sig.
Women	White	206,887	3,174.036	7	0.000
	Black	22,394	305.616	7	0.000
	Other	19,567	394.073	7	0.000
Men	White	133,216	1,070.849	7	0.000
	Black	10,541	54.791	7	0.000
	Other	13,451	109.280	7	0.000

Test for Independence: (c) Employment and Overweight					
		Pearson Chi-Square			
	Subsample	**n**	**Test Statistic**	**Degrees of Freedom**	**Sig.**
Women	White	206,887	1,817.395	7	0.000
	Black	22,394	146.168	7	0.000
	Other	19,567	294.197	7	0.000
Men	White	133,216	802.002	7	0.000
	Black	10,541	137.330	7	0.000
	Other	13,451	115.382	7	0.000

Obese White and Other males also have a significantly lower level of education and lower household income. Black males' level of education is not significantly lower for obese subjects, but significantly higher for those with excess weight. Income rises for obese and overweight Black males, and even more for the latter. While obese White and Other men are slightly financially penalised for being obese, mere overweight leads to *higher* income. Here, the difference to the female subsamples is especially noteworthy.

The results of the Pearson chi-square test for independence are described in Figure 5-4. Again, n denotes the number of processed cases which depends on the response ratio to questions on employment status. Calculating a mean value for employment status does not make sense. Thus, the following figures can only state whether the employment status is independent of BMI category and obesity / overweightness, but cannot provide information on the kind or direction of this difference. The decisive information in Figure 5-4 is the significance value (given in the last column) which provides information on the probability of error in an analogue manner to the two preceding figures: A value below 0.05 (0.01) is necessary to claim that the described relationship is significant as this means that the probability the result is produced by chance is below 5 per cent (1 per cent). Test statistic and degrees of freedom are included for the sake of completeness.

below 5 per cent (1 per cent). Test statistic and degrees of freedom are included for the sake of completeness.

Across all subsamples and for each variable considered, the association with employment status is significant. Test statistics are by far largest for White females, and smallest for Black or Other males.

The key results of this paragraph are:

- Differentiating by obesity / non obesity and overweightness / non-overweightness, all female subsamples under consideration display significantly different (mean) values concerning education, employment, and income
- Overweight and obese females have a significantly lower level of education and receive significantly less household income
- Obese White and Other men's level of education and annual household income are significantly lower
- Black overweight males are significantly more educated. Overweight and obese Black men receive significantly more household income
- Overall, overweight men receive higher incomes, on average. This trend is most pronounced for Blacks
- All subsamples display a significant association between employment status and BMI category, obesity, and excess weight
- By employment status, those unable to work are the heaviest group in all subsamples. In addition, those out of work for more than one year are second-heaviest for Whites of both genders and for Other men.

Although the direction of causality remains unclear, the hypothesis that population subgroups systematically differ and that these differences can be detected by comparing BMI values is supported.

5.3 Differences between Health Habits Induced by Socioeconomic Status

The results presented in section 5.2 of this dissertation confirm significant differences in mean values of level of education, employment status, and income when samples are differentiated by obesity / non-obesity or overweight / normal weight and underweight. Now, the question remains as to whether such differences in socioeconomic status – pointing at differences in health consciousness – can be observed by adverse health behaviour other than sustained food overconsumption. In the present paragraph, systematic differences in education, employment status, and income between individuals displaying adverse health behaviour and those who do not are analysed.

5.3.1 Analytical Framework

The financial consequences of the adverse health habits examined in this analysis are comparable to those of obesity: The costs of self-inflicted low levels of health are paid by society as a whole, that is, also by those refraining from adverse health behaviour.

Questions relevant to the correlations examined as a preparatory work (results are depicted in Appendix 8.9) for this paragraph pertain to physical activity in general ("During the past month, other than your regular job, did you participate in any physical activities or exercises such as running, calisthenics, golf, gardening, or walking for exercise?"), moderate and vigorous physical activities ("Thinking about the moderate / vigorous activities you do in a usual week, do you do moderate activities for at least ten minutes at a time, such as brisk walking, bicycling, vacuuming, gardening, or anything else that causes some increase in breathing or heart rate? / vigorous activities for at least ten minutes at a time, such as running, aerobics, heavy yard work, or anything else that causes large increases in breathing or heart rate?"), immunisation ("A flu shot is an influenza vaccine injected into your arm. During the past twelve months, have you had a flu shot?"), smoking status ("Do you now smoke cigarettes every day, some days, or not at all?"), binge drinking ("Considering all types of alcoholic beverages, how many times during the past 30 days did you have four (women) / five (men) or more drinks on an occasion?" – the amount of alcohol equivalent to one drink is specified in the previous question), a proxy for quality of nutrition ("Not counting juice, how often do you eat fruit?"), and obesity (BMI ≥ 30). Subjects smoking every day or on some days are considered smokers. The data are recoded so favourable health behaviour is always represented by '1' (generally, moderately, and vigorously physically active, vaccinated, non-smoker, no binge drinking, at least daily fruit consumption, non-obesity), unfavourable health behaviour by '2'. The Pearson correlation coefficient is used to measure correlations of different aspects of health behaviour.

As in section 5.2, the subsamples contain 207,303 (White), 22,477 (Black), and 19,666 (Other) female subjects, respectively. The respective numbers for men are 133,477 (White), 10,584 (Black), and 13,515 (Other).

The key results are:

- Correlations are usually low but significant. A consistent pattern can hardly be detected
- Correlations are highest for the three physical activity measures: They range from 0.403 to 0.274 and are more variable for females than for male subjects
- The next-highest correlation is found between smoking and binge drinking: For all subsamples, this correlation is approximately 0.2 (between 0.245 and 0.185)
- Furthermore, obese subjects are less likely to smoke (compare Figure 8-2 for empirical literature confirming this result) in all subsamples and to have received a flu shot in the past twelve months. The exception is the White male subsample for which no correlation at all could be detected between these two aspects of health behaviour
- The correlation between obesity and a flu shot is stronger (i.e. more negative) for women than for men. For most subsamples, a flu shot is

negatively correlated with all three measures of activity, the only exceptions being men and women with other ethnic background

- Clear-cut gender differences cannot be detected.

All in all, the significant differences between obese and non-obese subjects cannot be transferred to other adverse health behaviour. The present results nevertheless do not contradict the division into a subpopulation that is aware of the health consequences of eating and, simultaneously, concerned with other aspects of human capital, and another subpopulation that lacks this awareness.

If the hypothesis of significant differences between population groups were correct, the prevalence of adverse health behaviour (smoking, binge drinking, less than daily fruit consumption, being physically inactive, not receiving a flu shot) may significantly differ for varying levels of education, employment statuses, and levels of income. In an analogue manner to paragraph 5.2, these hypotheses are examined applying Mann-Whitney U tests for education and income, and Pearson chi-square tests for employment status.

5.3.2 Empirical Implementation

The questions relevant to this analysis are specified in section 5.3.1. As only physical activity in general is considered in the following section, moderate and vigorous activity are neglected. Subjects who refused to provide information on their socioeconomic status are removed from the sample. As a result, there are 177,007 White, 19,569 Black, and 16,607 Other Women left in the sample. The respective numbers for men are 120,837 (White), 9,269 (Black), and 11,798 (Other). The prevalence of adverse health behaviour in per cent by level of education, employment status, and income is depicted in Figure 8-13.

The key observations for the **female subsamples** are:

- Except for not having received a flu shot, White and Other women with a high level of education are unlikely to display adverse health behaviour. In contrast, the least educated Black women tend to live most healthily

- For all female subsamples, smoking, binge drinking, and less than daily fruit consumption are most common for those with some high school education
- By employment status, employed females (either wage earners or self-employed persons) take great care of their health, again except for the flu shot. Retired females have the lowest rates of adverse health behaviour except for physical activity
- The highest female income group lives most healthily. The prevalence of adverse health behaviour is highest in the lowest income group. Again, the flu shot is an exception
- Smoking prevalence is distinctively lower among White than among Black and Other women, and White women are also physically most active and have the highest vaccination rate. Binge drinking is most prevalent among Other females.

The key observations for the **male subsamples** are:

- Concerning the level of education, male college graduates display the lowest rates of smoking, binge drinking, and physical inactivity. Those with some high school education are most likely to smoke (The same is true for the female subsamples)
- In all male subsamples, students are physically most active, and like retired females, retired men also have the lowest rates in all other categories of health behaviour
- Except for the flu shot, the highest income group tends to live most healthily, while the lowest income group is the most unhealthy
- In the White subsample, binge drinking is most prevalent among students. In contrast, in the other two subsamples, those out of work are most likely to participate in binge drinking
- Comparably to women, smoking prevalence is substantially lower among Whites. In addition, their vaccination coverage is considerably higher.

From those with some high school education to college graduates, **smoking prevalence** continuously decreases for all subsamples. White men and women and Black men display a continuous decrease in smoking prevalence from the lowest to the highest income group. For the other subsamples, the same can be observed for the four highest income groups.

Furthermore, there is a continuous decrease in **binge drinking** from 'some high school education' to 'college graduates' in all six subsamples. By trend, binge drinking decreases with rising income. This trend is more pronounced in some (Black and Other women) than in other subsamples (White and Other men).

In most subsamples, **fruit consumption** clearly increases with income (Whites of both genders, Black women, Other men). Although less clear-cut, the same tendency can be observed for the remaining subsamples. This finding highlights the role of prices in nutrition-related decisions.

In all subsamples, **physical activity** continuously rises with higher income. A continuous increase can also be observed by level of education: For White and Black subsamples beginning from elementary education, and for Other men and women even over the whole range.

For the **flu shot**, clear-cut patterns are missing. Vaccination seems incomparable with the other health behaviour analysed.

In the following, the same methodology as used in section 5.2 is applied to the behavioural patterns described in this paragraph. As a consequence of their scale, education and income can be tested for equality of means using Mann-Whitney U tests. For employment status, Pearson chi-square tests are conducted. For education and income, the relevant significance values are one-sided as it is suspected that those with a healthier lifestyle are more educated and receive a higher household income. Significance values for employment status are two-sided.

For both White subsamples, the sample size is too large for SPSS to conduct Mann-Whitney U tests. As a result, SPSS draws a smaller sample (n = 112,420; subcommand: /SAMPLE).

5.3.3 Results

In the subsequent tables, n denotes the number of processed cases which depends on the response ratio to questions on education and income. For example, in Figure 5-5 (a), White women who refrain from smoking have a level of education that is averagely 0.325 categories higher. The probability of error for this result is below 0.1 per cent (as given by the asymptotic significance of 0.000). Thus, the result is significant. The test statistic is included for the sake of completeness. Figure 5-6 provides the respective results for family income. Running separate tests for equality of means for all six subsamples yields the results described in Figure 5-5.

Except for White women and Black men receiving a flu shot, all test statistics are asymptotically statistically significant. With the exception of Blacks of both genders and vaccination, all mean differences are positive. Mean differences are comparably large for physical activity (ranging from 0.420 to 0.665) and small for the flu shot (between -0.083 and 0.171).

Consequently, those who smoke, participate in binge drinking, eat fruit less than daily, and are physically inactive have, on average, a lower level of education. Drawing conclusions on vaccination is more difficult due to the relatively low and frequently negative mean differences.

Except for women of other ethnic origin receiving a flu shot, all test statistics depicted in Figure 5-6 are asymptotically statistically significant. With the exception of Whites and Blacks of both genders and vaccination, all mean differences are positive. This finding supports the conclusion drawn from the tests on education: Having received a flu shot in the past twelve months differs from the other aspects of health behaviour considered. Again, mean differences are comparably large for physical activity (ranging from 0.918 to 1.288, so values are approximately twice as high as for education and physical activity) and small for the flu shot (between -0.193 and 0.126).

Figure 5-5: Test for Equality of Means: Education / Adverse Health Behaviour [One-sided Significance]
(a) Smoking (b) Binge Drinking
(c) Fruit Consumption (d) Physical Activity (e) Flu Shot
(Reference: Own construction)

Test for Equality of Means: (a) Education and Smoking					
		Mann-Whitney U Test			
	Subsample	n	Test Statistic	Asymp. Sig.	Mean Difference
Women	White	52,180	276,647,287.000	0.000	0.325
	Black	6,779	5,038,279.000	0.000	0.207
	Other	5,788	3,694,479.500	0.000	0.202
Men	White	62,851	363,377,379.500	0.000	0.326
	Black	4,551	2,336,409.500	0.000	0.175
	Other	6,057	3,830,786.500	0.000	0.308

Test for Equality of Means: (b) Education and Binge Drinking					
		Mann-Whitney U Test			
	Subsample	n	Test Statistic	Asymp. Sig.	Mean Difference
Women	White	49,586	176,111,063.000	0.000	0.130
	Black	5,886	2,204,352.000	0.000	0.400
	Other	5,474	2,373,294.000	0.000	0.328
Men	White	66,644	395,994,158.000	0.000	0.259
	Black	4,179	1,576,074.000	0.000	0.265
	Other	5,873	3,142,213.500	0.000	0.464

Test for Equality of Means: (c) Education and Fruit Consumption					
		Mann-Whitney U Test			
	Subsample	n	Test Statistic	Asymp. Sig.	Mean Difference
Women	White	109,685	1,307,118,126.500	0.000	0.240
	Black	18,696	40,407,475.000	0.000	0.082
	Other	16,055	29,657,858.500	0.000	0.144
Men	White	109,141	1,248,365,665.500	0.000	0.188
	Black	8,728	8,157,042.000	0.001	0.067
	Other	11,260	13,732,260.000	0.000	0.177

Test for Equality of Means: (d) Education and Physical Activity					
		Mann-Whitney U Test			
	Subsample	n	Test Statistic	Asymp. Sig.	Mean Difference
Women	White	112,339	880,534,744.500	0.000	0.568
	Black	19,551	34,328,617.500	0.000	0.420
	Other	16,597	22,430,724.000	0.000	0.545
Men	White	112,306	758,240,222.500	0.000	0.586
	Black	9,258	6,570,600.500	0.000	0.480
	Other	11,786	9,597,431.500	0.000	0.665

Test for Equality of Means: (e) Education and Flu Shot						
		Mann-Whitney U Test				
	Subsample	**n**	**Test Statistic**	**Asymp. Sig.**	**Mean Difference**
Women	White	112,186	1,568,980,332.500	0.401	0.012
	Black	19,522	40,663,349.500	0.000	-0.083
	Other	16,556	31,684,126.000	0.007	0.037
Men	White	112,100	1,436,959,251.500	0.000	0.112
	Black	9,235	9,662,681.000	0.185	-0.034
	Other	11,731	14,552,450.500	0.000	0.171

As a consequence of the results described in the following figure, those who smoke, participate in binge drinking, eat fruit less than daily, and are physically inactive have, on average, a lower family income. Notably, the exact same conclusions apply to education. Again, drawing conclusions on vaccination is difficult: Mean differences are relatively low, and four out of six are negative.

Again, calculating a mean value for employment status does not make sense. Therefore, Figure 5-7 can only state whether the employment status is independent of the prevalence of adverse health behaviour, but cannot provide information on the kind or direction of this difference. The probability of error is provided in the last column. A value below 0.05 (0.01) is necessary to claim that the described relationship is significant. Test statistic and degrees of freedom are included for the sake of completeness. The Pearson chi-square test applied to employment status by adverse health behaviour delivers the results depicted in Figure 5-7 (the number of processed cases which depends on the response ratio is denoted by n). The association between employment status and the respective health behaviour is significant across all subsamples and for each variable considered.

Figure 5-6: Test for Equality of Means: Income / Adverse Health Behaviour [One-sided Significance]
(a) Smoking (b) Binge Drinking
(c) Fruit Consumption (d) Physical Activity (e) Flu Shot
(Reference: Own construction)

Test for Equality of Means: (a) Income and Smoking					
		Mann-Whitney U Test			
	Subsample	n	Test Statistic	Asymp. Sig.	Mean Difference
Women	White	52,137	271,412,954.000	0.000	0.716
	Black	6,779	4,988,514.500	0.000	0.492
	Other	5,788	3,476,216.500	0.000	0.666
Men	White	62,910	370,537,285.000	0.000	0.600
	Black	4,551	2,153,959.000	0.000	0.629
	Other	6,057	3,845,995.000	0.000	0.572

Test for Equality of Means: (b) Income and Binge Drinking					
		Mann-Whitney U Test			
	Subsample	n	Test Statistic	Asymp. Sig.	Mean Difference
Women	White	49,525	183,456,979.000	0.000	0.136
	Black	5,886	2,177,059.500	0.000	0.884
	Other	5,474	2,338,267.000	0.000	0.743
Men	White	66,725	445,417,894.000	0.000	0.164
	Black	4,179	1,549,877.500	0.000	0.588
	Other	5,873	3,326,438.000	0.000	0.667

Test for Equality of Means: (c) Income and Fruit Consumption					
		Mann-Whitney U Test			
	Subsample	**n**	**Test Statistic**	**Asymp. Sig.**	**Mean Difference**
Women	White	109,725	1,370,000,000.000	0.000	0.342
	Black	18,696	38,669,157.000	0.000	0.339
	Other	16,055	29,133,268.000	0.000	0.375
Men	White	109,107	1,320,000,000.000	0.000	0.200
	Black	8,728	8,016,213.500	0.000	0.211
	Other	11,260	14206233.000	0.000	0.238

Test for Equality of Means: (d) Income and Physical Activity					
		Mann-Whitney U Test			
	Subsample	**n**	**Test Statistic**	**Asymp. Sig.**	**Mean Difference**
Women	White	112,338	833,979,151.000	0.000	1.288
	Black	19,551	33,254,447.000	0.000	0.918
	Other	16,597	21,480,405.000	0.000	1.107
Men	White	112,306	731,808,128.000	0.000	1.113
	Black	9,258	6,344,893.500	0.000	0.986
	Other	11,786	9,538,571.500	0.000	1.096

Test for Equality of Means: (e) Income and Flu Shot					
		Mann-Whitney U Test			
	Subsample	n	Test Statistic	Asymp. Sig.	Mean Difference
Women	White	112,205	1,510,000,000.000	0.000	-0.156
	Black	19,522	40,735,115.000	0.000	-0.130
	Other	16,556	32,186,178.000	0.241	0.025
Men	White	112,100	1,520,000,000.000	0.000	-0.063
	Black	9,235	9,274,681.000	0.000	-0.193
	Other	11,731	15,197,574.000	0.000	0.126

Figure 5-7: Test for Equality of Means: Employment / Adverse Health Behaviour [Two-sided Significance]
(a) Smoking (b) Binge Drinking
(c) Fruit Consumption (d) Physical Activity (e) Flu Shot
(Reference: Own construction)

Test for Independence: (a) Employment and Smoking					
		Pearson Chi-Square			
	Subsample	n	Test Statistic	Degrees of Freedom	Sig.
Women	White	80,378	4,183.675	7	0.000
	Black	6,779	478.723	7	0.000
	Other	5,788	252.284	7	0.000
Men	White	67,552	5,146.235	7	0.000
	Black	4,551	382.344	7	0.000
	Other	6,057	352.658	7	0.000

Test for Independence: (b) Employment and Binge Drinking					
		Pearson Chi-Square			
	Subsample	n	Test Statistic	Degrees of Freedom	Sig.
Women	White	83,834	1,976.485	7	0.000
	Black	5,886	104.433	7	0.000
	Other	5,474	116.275	7	0.000
Men	White	71,821	2,530.012	7	0.000
	Black	4,179	53.361	7	0.000
	Other	5,873	152.133	7	0.000

Test for Independence: (c) Employment and Fruit Consumption					
		Pearson Chi-Square			
	Subsample	n	Test Statistic	Degrees of Freedom	Sig.
Women	White	173,020	2,551.231	7	0.000
	Black	18,696	252.451	7	0.000
	Other	16,055	247.434	7	0.000
Men	White	117,312	1,336.598	7	0.000
	Black	8,728	51.667	7	0.000
	Other	11,260	93.521	7	0.000

Test for Independence: (d) Employment and Physical Activity					
		Pearson Chi-Square			
	Subsample	n	Test Statistic	Degrees of Freedom	Sig.
Women	White	176,886	8,921.878	7	0.000
	Black	19,551	639.483	7	0.000
	Other	16,597	530.991	7	0.000
Men	White	120,715	4,805.827	7	0.000
	Black	9,258	316.945	7	0.000
	Other	11,786	396.411	7	0.000

Test for Independence: (e) Employment and Flu Shot					
		Pearson Chi-Square			
	Subsample	n	Test Statistic	Degrees of Freedom	Sig.
Women	White	176,647	13,231.435	7	0.000
	Black	19,522	897.682	7	0.000
	Other	16,556	947.042	7	0.000
Men	White	120,500	13,176.725	7	0.000
	Black	6,057	352.658	7	0.000
	Other	11,731	771.590	7	0.000

Thus, the key results are:

- All six subsamples under consideration display significant differences concerning education and income by the health behaviour considered except for the flu shot
- Those who live healthier are more educated
- Adverse health behaviour is displayed less frequently with rising income. This relation is even more apparent for income than for education as the respective mean differences are higher (with the exception of the flu shot)

- The employment status is related with all adverse health behaviour, even with the flu shot
- Vaccination apparently differs from the other health behaviour.

Thus, this paragraph confirms that population subgroups also systematically differ with respect to adverse health behaviour other than excess weight.

Comparing paragraphs 5.2 and 5.3 yields the following conclusions:

- More educated individuals and those with a higher income tend to live healthier (for overweight and obesity, this trend is more pronounced for females than for males)
- The employment status is associated with overweight, obesity, and all other kinds of adverse health behaviour considered
- Still, correlations between the single patterns of adverse health behaviour remain low. This result also holds when individuals with high socioeconomic status are removed from the subsamples.[145]

As a result, health behaviour in general is associated with education, employment, and income. Prevalence of adverse health behaviour is low in individuals with a high socioeconomic status. Nevertheless, the individual types of health behaviour are hardly interrelated. These results are summarised in Figure 5-8.

What seems most surprising about the above findings is the low correlation between the types of adverse health behaviour. Still, this result is supported by previous analyses.[146] Their authors suspect the results may be due to measurement problems (Fuchs), or that variation in health behaviour is caused by genetic or behaviour-specific individual differences (Cutler and Glaeser).

145 Results available from the author on request.

146 Fuchs (1982) investigates whether there is a causal relationship between time preference and health-related behaviour and mostly finds significant but low correlation coefficients. Cutler and Glaeser (2005) investigate the correlations between various aspects of health behaviour, as well as between their year-to-year changes, also finding low correlations.

Figure 5-8: Summary of Results
(Reference: Own construction)

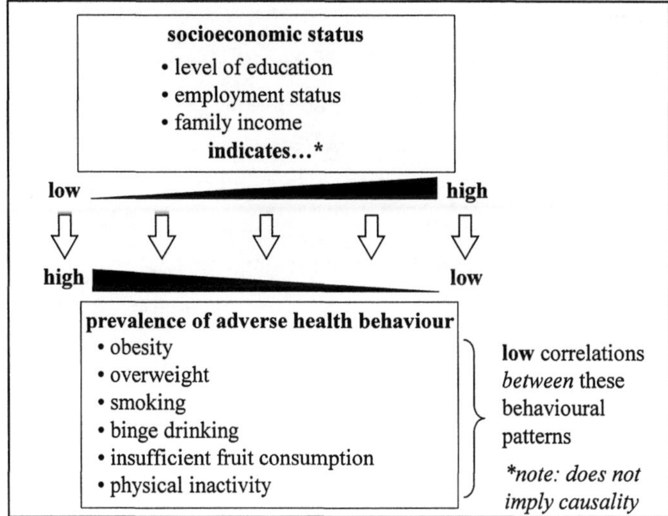

Alternative explanations may be:

- As correlations measure the linear relationship between variables, the actual relationship between patterns of adverse health behaviour may be non-linear
- A third underlying variable may cause the above findings and independently influence them, for example health consciousness
- The individual health habits may be substitutes. For example, smoking suppresses appetite. This substitutability may also occur for financial reasons (i.e. those who spend money on cigarettes cannot pay for a gym membership or afford high-quality food) or due to the underlying addictive pattern (one addiction may be sufficient)
- The results may be due to the (non-linear) pattern of risk awareness: While individuals think they can safely live with one bad habit and underestimate its consequences for health, numerous adverse health habits are perceived as severely harmful

- The fact that adverse behaviours are hardly associated with physical inactivity may stem from a compensation for harmful health behaviour by performing physical activities.

Assuming that a general attitude towards life (denoted consciousness in this dissertation) causes the results illustrated in Figure 5-8, taking educational measures against adverse health habits will be ineffective. In this case, financial incentives must be provided to influence health habits, either through a tax on harmful health habits (i.e. a fat tax), a subsidy on favourable health behaviour, or a health insurance scheme as described in the following chapter.

Chapter 6. Consequences for Insurance Design

Section 3.1 substantiates that individual eating habits influence the probability that a diet-related condition occurs, and in section 4.1 it is shown that eating habits depend on health-consciousness. If those with adverse health habits are not charged with the costs resulting from their behaviour, they will lack an incentive to change their attitude towards health-consciousness. As a consequence, society as a whole must bear the burden of self-inflicted conditions of those putting their health at risk due to private consumption behaviour: They do not pay for the costs resulting from the adverse health behaviour. In such cases, the design of the health insurance scheme is decisive: Under a system where equal health insurance premiums for all insured is the norm, healthy individuals subsidise those with a worse state of health, irrespective of the self-inflicted high or low level of health care. For this reason, the present section investigates how an insurance scheme should be designed to provide a disincentive for harmful health behaviour. Based on the assumption that a healthy diet is more costly, expenditures on health food are interpreted as preventive expenditures. However, as a starting point, moral hazard and adverse selection are clarified in the context of obesity.

6.1 Externalities, Moral Hazard, and Adverse Selection

On insurance markets, external effects are related to the diversification of risk, which can involve moral hazard and, as a consequence, adverse selection. Both are defined in the following (Note that in the following paragraph, only the costs resulting from increased health care contributions are considered, not the indirect costs due to productivity losses).

Due to the fact that in compulsory health insurance, the insured are obliged to pay the same rates despite differing degrees of health care utilisation, the insured lack an incentive to act health-consciously.[147]

Health habits lead to a change in the likelihood that a person becomes sick and needs health services. Unfortunately, the insurance does not distinguish between individuals who take care of their health and those who put their health at risk, for example due to unhealthy eating habits. Therefore, all insured pay the same premium although their health care utilisation differs. Those with adverse health habits have an incentive to hide their risky behaviour from the insurance as with equal premiums, they can consume health services without paying the full costs arising from their behaviour.

This special case of asymmetric information – the insured lacking a sufficient incentive to inform the insurer of her individual health risk – is also known as 'hidden information' or 'hidden characteristics'.[148]

The above incentive problems are referred to as **moral hazard**. They represent a rational response to economic incentives which is induced by the elasticity of demand to the price of health services. Moral hazard can either refer to the increased usage of services when the pooling of risks leads to decreased marginal costs for these services, or it may refer to the disincentives created by the insurance for the insured to reduce the probability of a loss.[149] Both problems are relevant to the case of obesity.

Kenneth J. Arrow, describing moral hazard as "perhaps the most important" limitation of insurance, explains that "the insurance policy might itself change incentives and therefore the probabilities upon which the insurance company has relied".[150] As a result, full coverage is suboptimal when the insurance influences the demand for the services the insurer provides. As the amount of insurance

147 See Zdrowomyslaw, Dürig 1997, pp. 52/53.

148 See Fritsch et al. 2003, p. 280.

149 See Folland et al. 2001, p. 154.

150 Arrow 1974, p. 142.

payment depends not only on a state of nature but also on a decision made by the insured, the outcome will be suboptimal under full coverage.[151]

Arrow defines insurance as an exchange of money at the present time for money which is payable contingent on the occurrence of certain events. The essence of insurance is the shifting of risk. Consequently, it allows individuals to take risks which they wouldn't take without the possibility of insurance. As a solution, Arrow suggests risks should not be fully but rather partially shifted.[152] Alternatively, he proposes detailed examination by the insurance company whether the cost items that the insurance company has had to pay in the past can be regarded as normal, or trusting either the professional ethics of physicians or the willingness of the individual.[153] Obviously, the two latter propositions do not sufficiently discipline the insured.

As a consequence of moral hazard, the market for health insurance suffers from **adverse selection**. Although each individual knows her risk of becoming ill, this information is not available to the insurance company. Consequently, the insurer treats every person alike and offers the same cover at the same premium to everyone despite the heterogenous distribution of risks. Based on statistics, the insurer has expectations on the average risk of illness and on the arising costs. The premium must be calculated to at least cover the costs for health services that occur in a period. It is thus an average value of the expected costs divided by the number of insured persons.[154]

As a result, those caring for their health who have a low risk of illness subsidise those who do not act health-consciously. In Germany, the health-conscious may, as a consequence, choose private instead of compulsory health insurance (Under private insurance, the correspondence between premium and risk is closer).

In contrast, those at higher risk of catching a disease will remain with the compulsory health insurance. The ratio of those with relatively high risk of illness is

151 See Arrow 1974, pp. 220/221.

152 See Arrow 1974, pp. 134-143.

153 See Arrow 1974, pp. 220/221.

154 See Breyer, Zweifel 1999, pp. 161/162.

then higher among the compulsorily insured than among all individuals who could potentially be in compulsory health insurance. Thus, health expenditures are raised, in turn raising insurance premiums. Due to the higher insurance premiums, more and more individuals quit the compulsory insurance, and the premiums have to be raised further. Theoretically, this process continues until only those with a very high risk of illness remain compulsorily insured. This process is called adverse selection.[155]

The process of adverse selection can theoretically continue until the market breaks down and must, therefore, be considered a crucial barrier to an efficient insurance market. Adverse selection and moral hazard are possible reasons why the government may have to intervene in a market.[156]

The concepts of moral hazard, adverse selection, and the resulting consequences have been described by Akerlof (1970). Not only does he realise the danger of bad risks driving the good out of the market, but he also notices that this process can continue until the market ceases to exist under the assumption that different quality grades – or in this context, different states of health – exist. In markets where statistics are used to make quality judgements, social and private returns differ. Furthermore, Akerlof (1970) finds that on the market for health insurance, the average medical condition of those applying for coverage deteriorates with a rising price level. Insurance companies simply cannot afford to offer attractive risk coverage at appropriate premiums as these will attract too many bad risks.[157] In fact, insurance companies are only willing to offer a fair health insurance plan under very restrictive assumptions.[158]

155 See Fritsch et al. 2003, pp. 280-284.

156 See Rosen 2005, pp. 216/217.

157 See Akerlof 1970, pp. 488-494.

158 See Bergstrom 1982, pp. 305/306. Bergstrom explains that in a decentralised economy, an optimal health insurance plan will only be offered if transaction costs to the insurer are negligible, if the number of identical consumers in the economy is large enough so the variance in the proportion of the population with a given condition is irrelevant, and if there is symmetrical information. Under these restrictive conditions, neither moral hazard nor adverse selection occur.

In the case of obesity, every person can influence her probability of becoming ill by healthy eating. The individual acts *before* a disease occurs. Therefore, the relevant type of moral hazard is "ex-ante" moral hazard.[159]

The existence of adverse selection on the German health insurance market has been proven by a study analysing morbidity as a criterion for choosing compulsory or private health insurance. Five indicators are chosen to proxy morbidity: Indispositions in the first quarter of 2006, chronic diseases, the number of nights spent in hospital in 2006, general practitioner visits in the same year, and regular taking of medicines. The author comes to the conclusion that, on average, the compulsorily insured have a worse state of health than privately insured individuals and make use of health services more often. This result is supported by previous studies.[160]

Investigating data from approximately 1.5 million insured, a study conducted by German health insurance GEK (Gmünder Ersatzkasse) found that Germany has the highest number of annual patient visits per capita in an international comparison. The results from the GEK study were compared to OECD data from Australia, Austria, Belgium, Canada, Denmark, France, Italy, Japan, Luxemburg, Slovakia, the Czech Republic, and the US (in the listed countries, the number of patient visits ranged between 3.7 in the US and fifteen in Slovakia in the year 2000). On average, German citizens consulted their practitioner sixteen times in the year 2004.[161]

As a result of the compulsory health insurance system, the described externalities are internalised. Unfortunately, the internalisation does not take place on an individual, but on a collective level. As a result, every individual has to pay for the collective health risk and the personal incentive to care for one's health is lowered.

---

159 See Breyer, Zweifel 1999, p. 186.
160 See Jacobs et al. 2006, pp. 68-75.
161 See Grobe et al. 2006, pp. 30-49.

This internalisation was originally intended to guarantee a minimum level of health services independent of personal income. It is thus a conscious political decision.[162]

6.2 The Influence of Preventive Expenditures

The relationship between preventive expenditures, premiums, and indemnification payments is analysed here. To start with, optimal preventive expenditures are determined without the possibility of insurance. Thereafter, insurance contracts can be closed, and the cases of observable and unobservable preventive expenditures are illustrated.

The following elaborations are based on Breyer and Zweifel (1999).[163] It is assumed that the individual can influence the probability distribution of health care costs, but once the condition has occurred, the resulting costs are definitely determined. Health-conscious behaviour causes costs, but raises the utility of health-conscious individuals. These costs are borne by the individual, not by the insurance. In the case of excess weight, preventive expenditures can be interpreted as the higher costs of healthy food.

The probability of illness, η, is a function of the expenditure for prevention, PE:

$$\eta = \eta(PE) \tag{6.1}$$

$$\eta > 0; \eta'(PE) < 0; \eta''(PE) > 0$$

162 See Hajen et al. 2006, p. 61.

163 See Breyer, Zweifel 1999, pp. 206-212.

As Figure 6-1 illustrates, PE is convex, and prevention has decreasing marginal productivity. The probability of illness, η, never becomes zero. Thus, it cannot be completely eliminated, not even with very high expenditures for prevention.

Figure 6-1: The Probability of Illness as a Function of Preventive Expenditures

(Reference: Own construction)

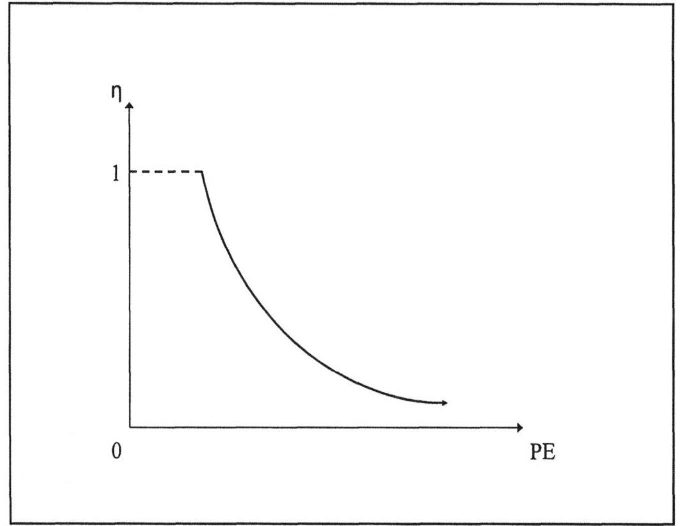

To start with, the case of optimal prevention expenditures without insurance coverage is considered. In this case, expected utility, EU, is an average of disposable income, d, in the case of illness and without the occurrence of illness, respectively, which is weighted by the probability of becoming ill. Obviously, the amount of disposable income depends on the expenditure for prevention:

$$EU(PE) = E[U(d(PE))] \tag{6.2}$$

Disposable income is further specified: In case of illness, disposable income d_s equals gross income Y less expenditures for prevention PE and the costs of illness CD:

$$d_s = Y - PE - CD \tag{6.3}$$

Disposable income without the occurrence of illness, d_h, equals gross income less expenditures for prevention:

$$d_h = Y - PE \tag{6.4}$$

Thus, equation (6.2) becomes:

$$EU(PE) = \eta(PE) \cdot U[d_s] + (1 - \eta(PE)) \cdot U[d_h] \tag{6.5}$$

As expected utility depends on disposable income, it is dependent on gross income, Y, the costs of illness, CD, and PE. U(d) represents individual utility.

In order to maximise expected utility, equation (6.5) is differentiated by PE and set equal to zero. Optimal prevention expenditures are denoted PE*. As $\eta(PE^*) \cdot U'(d_s) + (1 - \eta(PE^*)) \cdot U'(d_h)$ represents the expected value of marginal utility, $EU'(d)$, the first-order condition for optimal prevention expenditures is:

$$\eta'(PE^*) \cdot (U(d_s) - U(d_h)) = EU'(d) \tag{6.6}$$

On the left hand side of the equation, additional utility from decreasing the probability of illness by increasing prevention expenditures by one monetary unit is depicted. The right hand side represents the expected utility loss due to the lowered disposable income (for both states of health: with and without the actual occurrence of illness). If both terms are equal, expenditure for prevention will be optimal.

Now, the individual is offered insurance coverage. In the case of illness, the insurance pays an amount of indemnification payments IP, which can range from zero to CD (obviously, if IP equals CD, the costs of illness will be completely covered). The insured is free to choose the value of IP. Assume the insurer can observe the amount of preventive expenditures the insured spends and takes this observation into account when deciding on the premium PM:

$$PM(PE, IP) = (1+\omega)\cdot\eta(PE)\cdot IP \tag{6.7}$$

PM is proportional to the expected payment. ω represents the percentage of mark-up. The individual maximises expected utility, which is now subject to prevention expenditures and indemnification payments:

$$\begin{aligned} EU(PE, IP) = E(U(d)) &= \eta(PE)\cdot U[Y - PM(PE, IP) - PE - CD + IP] \\ &+ (1-\eta(PE))\cdot U[Y - PM(PE, IP) - PE] \end{aligned} \tag{6.8}$$

Again, expected utility is an average of disposable income d in the case of illness and without the occurrence of illness, respectively, which is weighted by the probability of becoming ill: In contrast to (6.5), premium and indemnification payments appear in the equation. Differentiating the above expression by IP and by PE, it can be shown that, given the above assumptions, the customer will choose the following insurance coverage:

- full insurance coverage if ω, the percentage of mark-up, equals zero (the premium then equals $\eta(PE^*)\cdot IP$)
- less than full insurance coverage if ω is positive

- no insurance coverage at all if $1-(1+\omega)\cdot\eta(PE^*)$ approaches zero (the premium then approaches IP).

On the one hand, a person will decrease the amount spent on preventive measures if an insurance contract is closed. On the other hand, the insurer can observe this amount and take this piece of information into account when determining the premium.

Figure 6-2: The Case of Observable Preventive Expenditures
(Reference: Own Construction)

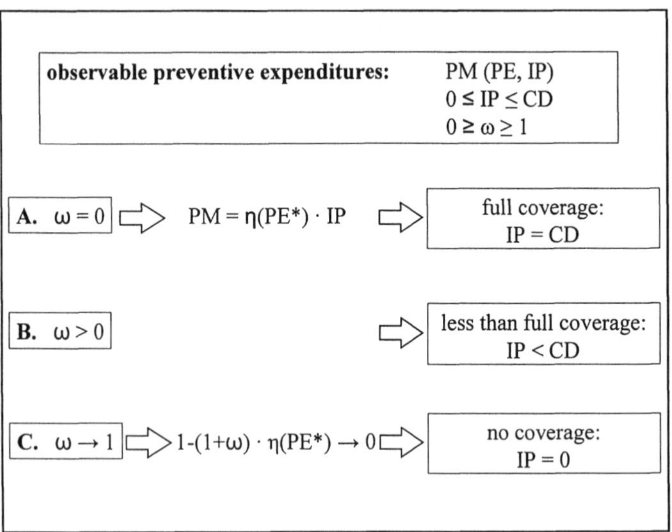

However, if PE is unobservable, the premium cannot be adjusted. In the case of an actuarially fair insurance, namely when ω equals zero and the insured pays a premium equal to the expected amount of her future claims, the insured will pay for preventive measures until the expected value of disposable income is maximised. The individual will only refrain from prevention expenditures if, starting from the first unit, it does not increase expected disposable income.

In the more realistic case, it is assumed that expenditures for preventive measures cannot be observed by the insurance company. As a result, the premium is independent of PE and solely depends on IP:

$$PM = PM(IP) \tag{6.9}$$

As a result, the premium cannot provide an incentive for the insured to invest in prevention. To reward the individual for investments in preventive measures despite the hidden information, the insurance company can progressively increase the premium with IP, as opposed to linearly. Full insurance coverage is then disproportionately high. The individual will neither choose full coverage nor completely refrain from investing in preventive measures. This case is depicted in panel A of Figure 6-3.

If the insurance company offers premiums as a linear function of the insurance sum, and the insurance is fair, the insured will completely lack an incentive to invest in prevention. She will choose full coverage. This case is depicted in panel B of Figure 6-3.

If the insurer offers a premium which progressively increases with IP, and the insurance is fair, the insured will choose less than full coverage. In this case, the characteristics of the two functions η(PE) and PE(IP) must be known and customers must be prevented from buying several policies at lower insurance sums because thus, they could avoid the progressive increase in premiums. Therefore, information requirements will be remarkably high if prevention expenditures cannot be observed.[164] Unfortunately, the case of unobservable preventive expenditures is the most realistic.

164 See Breyer, Zweifel 1999, pp. 213-219.

Figure 6-3: The Case of Unobservable Preventive Expenditures
(Reference: Own construction)

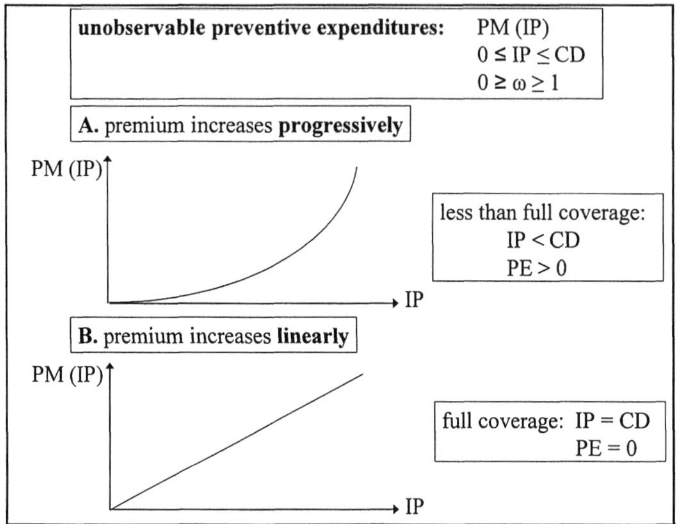

When preventive expenditures cannot be observed, policy holders lack an incentive to invest in prevention to decrease their probability of illness, thus potentially worsening their state of health. Preventive expenditures will be suboptimal, and disposable income will be spent on commodities other than health.

6.3 Differentiation of Premiums by Risk

Commonly, one of the characteristics of private insurance is the payment of fortuitous losses. By definition, a fortuitous event involves the element of chance and is not influenced by probabilities. Thus, the loss is unexpected.[165] If

165 See Rejda 2008, p. 20.

a person's behavioural pattern is harmful to health, the condition will not be unexpected but likely to occur. In such cases, illnesses do not randomly appear.

Under the assumption that those seeking insurance are risk-averse, insurance is more valuable to the insured the greater the uncertainty involved. In order to retain the full social benefit, the insurance market must provide maximum possible discrimination of risk. Thus, the higher the proneness to illness, the higher the premium should be. The actual practice in most countries – at least in Germany – is to equalise premiums. Therefore, a redistribution of income from those with low to those with high probability of illness takes place. If the market were truly competitive, premiums could not be equalised, and those with low risk of becoming ill would be charged with low premiums.[166]

Insurance companies can use information on individual health behaviour to set premiums. This procedure is called "experience rating". While risk-adjusted premiums are more efficient, the risk is spread over fewer individuals. Experience rating may lead to welfare losses, but can easily be justified for conditions occurring as a result of individual health behaviour.[167]

As the previous paragraph has already shown, the premium should be linked to the risk to an individual's health in order to provide an incentive for health-conscious behaviour.[168] In the case of obesity, this means linking the premium to the BMI. This procedure may lower the overall costs for conditions related to excess weight – provided individuals recognise the incentive – or at least the costs are paid by those with risky private behaviour.

A premium will be differentiated if the expected value of costs is based on (objective or subjective) individual risk factors that are taken into consideration when risk premiums are determined. Differentiated premiums require a sufficiently exact estimation of the costs expected from the relevant risk factors. The correlation between risk factors and the expected value of damages must be significant, constant, and plausible in order to be accepted on the market. The deci-

166 See Arrow 1974, pp. 204/205.

167 See Cutler, Zeckhauser 2000, pp. 626-628.

168 See Breyer, Zweifel 1999, p. 190.

sive consequence of differentiated premiums is the avoidance of adverse selection as premiums are calculated independently of the pool of insured risks. In addition, those responsible for costs are more likely to pay their way, thus providing an incentive for loss prevention.[169]

Moral hazard is avoided as premiums can be adjusted once an individual enters a risk group with higher proneness to illness. In order to prevent higher expenditures on insurance premiums, individuals prefer a high level of health, thus reducing their probability of illness. Obviously, the described health care scheme must be compulsory. If it were optional, those with a worse state of health would choose an insurance design that is more favourable to them. Their freedom of choice would result in moral hazard and adverse selection.

The risk groups can either be differentiated depending on one specific factor (i.e. BMI), or on several factors, comparable to motor insurance. Weight, tobacco and alcohol consumption, physical activity, and eating habits are appropriate factors for such a classification within the framework of a health insurance scheme. In order to calculate an individual risk premium, morbidity and mortality figures must be known, possibly depending on age and gender. However, the more precise the differentiation into specific groups, the higher information requirements may be (notably, finding out a patient's BMI is by no means difficult), but the more direct the allocation of the burden of disease.

As a result of premiums that are tailored to specific risk groups, premiums will not remain equal. The possibility to differentiate risk premiums can be justified under the imperative of equal treatment of policy holders that is applied in Germany (German: "Gleichbehandlungsgebot"). Accordingly, premiums and indemnification payments must be equal if the same premises apply to all policy holders. Therefore, if certain premises are unequal, premiums and / or indemnification payments should be differentiated. Noteworthy, differentiated premiums do not contradict the basic principle of insurance: As a result of differentiated premiums, policy holders pay the expected value of damages of their risk group

169 See Farny 1995, pp. 55/56.

as opposed to paying the costs actually incurring to the individual.[170] Thus, risk is diversified despite differentiated premiums.

170 See Farny 1995, pp. 57/58.

Glossary

CD:	costs of illness
d:	disposable income
dh:	disposable income without the occurrence of illness
ds:	disposable income in case of illness
EU:	expected utility
IP:	indemnification payments
PE*:	optimal preventive expenditures
PE:	preventive expenditures
PM:	premium
U:	utility function
Y:	gross income
η:	probability of illness
ω:	percentage of mark-up on the insurance premium

Chapter 7. Conclusion

7.1 Summary

This dissertation is concerned with the economic consequences of the rising obesity prevalence in affluent societies.

After discussing medical and socioeconomic aspects of excess weight in the second chapter, the dissertation continues with the repercussions of overweight and obesity for health and the resulting economic implications. Thereafter, the theoretical concepts relevant to the precedent paragraphs are explained in the third chapter.

Chapter four concentrates on a model describing food consumption and its health consequences from the perspective of the individual consumer. Here, the differentiation between health-conscious individuals and those lacking consciousness – the central hypothesis of this dissertation – is introduced. By this assumption, education and health are interrelated aspects of human capital. Thus, those who insufficiently invest in their education also pay little attention to their health. The dynamic model yields conditions for utility-maximising consumption over time: The marginal costs of food consumption must be adapted to the level of prices and to variations in the BMR. This result holds independently of the weight status category and of the level of health-consciousness. In addition, underweight and overweight individuals' marginal costs of food consumption converge to an equilibrium state (which is already reached by individuals with physically optimal weight). The chapter closes with extensions relevant to food overconsumption, namely the influence of diet composition and the rate of time preference, as well as the incorporation of addictive aspects and dynamic inconsistency. These extensions deliver conditions under which instability can occur: Either the assumption of a concave utility function, a stable rate of time preference or discounting, or the assumption of standard goods must be abandoned.

Chapter five presents empirical work on systematic differences between obese and non-obese individuals (as well as overweight and non-overweight persons, respectively) and those who display other adverse health behaviour, each by socioeconomic status. The analyses make clear that obese and overweight individuals generally have a lower level of education and receive less annual household income than their normal-weight counterparts. These results are consistent over all female as well as the White and Other male subsamples. In addition, all subsamples display a significant association between employment status and BMI category, obesity, and excess weight: Those unable to work represent the group with the highest average weight in all cases considered. Persons out of work for more than one year have the second-heaviest average bodyweight for Whites of both genders and for Other men. Furthermore, all six subsamples under consideration display significant differences concerning education and income by smoking, alcohol and fruit consumption, and physical inactivity. Generally, more educated individuals live healthier, and harmful health behaviour is displayed less frequently with rising income. Employment status is related with all adverse health behaviour including the flu shot. By contrast, vaccination apparently differs from the other aspects of health behaviour regarding education and income. Notably, as a consequence of the empirical examinations, the fundamental assumption of this dissertation – the differentiation between health-conscious subgroup P_1 and unconscious subgroup P_2 – could not be rejected.

In chapter six, the implications of chapters two to five are used as a basis to analyse modifications of the existing health insurance schemes that are required due to current trends in bodyweight. As a result, premiums of compulsory health insurance should be differentiated by key aspects of adverse health behaviour, such as excess weight, smoking, alcohol consumption, or physical inactivity in order to avoid redistribution of income from individuals with a health-conscious lifestyle to those with a self-inflicted low state of health.

7.2 Future Research

This dissertation leads to several issues that should be intensively researched in the future: To begin with, with respect to excess weight and numerous other health habits, the role of time preference in individual decision making should be clarified.

Furthermore, the question whether consumption decisions are dynamically consistent or inconsistent should be illuminated. This issue can be clarified as soon as an appropriate empirical framework is developed which is applicable to existing data sources.

The empirical work presented in this dissertation is confined to the situation in the United States as a wealth of health-related data is readily available from US sources. In contrast, the German Federal Statistics Office ('Bundesamt für Statistik') could not even supply information on the fraction of obese individuals who are currently unemployed. Obviously, there is wide scope for improvement of health-related data collection in Germany.

To successfully tackle the problem of obesity, political solutions to other health-related issues provide helpful information. The most promising analogies are found in tobacco consumption (male smoking patterns, for example, clearly differ from female ones). Still, the case of smoking is different: Here, a policy mix must be found that induces individuals to quit smoking. By contrast, eating habits must be changed towards healthier alternatives despite the human evolutionary heritage that makes us crave for fat and sugar. Still, a lot can be learned from smoking: Smoking prevalence in industrialised countries has been decreasing for some time.

The above paragraph leads to the next important question that should be addressed in future research: In both empirical analyses related to socioeconomic status that are included in this dissertation, patterns are more clear-cut for women than for men. Why is this the case, and which conclusions can be drawn from it apart from the fact that policy implications may also differ by gender?

The empirical investigation in section 5.3 shows that vaccination differs from other health habits. In contrast to the other aspects of health behaviour considered, correlations of the flu shot with other habits are frequently negative. In addition, it is less closely related to socioeconomic status. Finding the reason for these observations may shed light on vaccination-related problems and on health behaviour in general.

In summary, is important to learn from related problems which have, at least partly, already been successfully tackled, and to transfer the consolidated findings to the problems raised by obesity. This holds for other wealth-related diseases, such as caries, tooth decay, or alcohol consumption, as well as for health issues in countries with lower stages of development.

7.3 Implications for Health Care and Health Policy

Obesity, so it appears, will become the dominant aspect of personal and public health. In the present context, an important insight is that achieving and maintaining health is costly. This fact is stressed by the results of the dynamic model in chapter four stating that to attain maximal lifetime utility, the marginal costs of food consumption must not only be adapted to physical processes (variations to the basal metabolic rate), but also to the level of prices. Those suffering from self-inflicted unfavourable states of health should bear the resulting financial responsibility. In this respect, all health habits considered in this dissertation are comparable: Private behaviour, such as the decision to overconsume food over a long period, but also the decision to smoke, to overconsume alcohol, or to refrain from being physically active or receiving adequate vaccination, increases the probability of illness and thus, induces costs. In such cases, the idea of personal responsibility is usually inadequately interpreted: Those who demand freedom of choice must also accept the costs they have caused precisely *because* they were free to choose an unhealthy way of living. If personal responsibility excluded the consequences of one's action, the costs of other people's actions would have to be borne by society as a whole, and members of society would be unable to choose whether they wish to solidarise with others or not. Both ideas – health is costly and freedom of choice includes accepting responsibility for the consequences – are essential to designing a stable and sustainable public health scheme and health insurance system.

The elaborations concerning the health and financial consequences of obesity clearly show that for the time being, personal responsibility as it is commonly understood does not suffice to solve the problems at hand. Furthermore, the German government is concerned with educational measures to tackle the problem of obesity. This strategy has not proven successful so far. In addition, despite the enormous financial burden imposed by excess weight, overweight and obese people can order any amount of fatty food while smokers have to leave public places or restaurants to indulge in their habit. Obviously, the public attitude towards private risky behaviour is inconsistent.

To design a sustainable health insurance scheme, premiums must be differentiated by risk. This does not mean the solidarity principle will be abandoned, but solidarity must be interpreted in a different way: If solidarity is to be based on equality, then those who deliberately choose a higher risk to their health must pay higher premiums. Still, premiums should be equal for those in the same risk class. The German 'Gesundheitsfonds' (health fund) which sets equal contributions irrespective of private behaviour is clearly a step in the wrong direction.

In order to enforce a comprehensive policy mix, not only the existing health insurance scheme, but also the attitude towards self-inflicted health problems must change so more drastic policy measures against the prevalence of obesity, such as nutrient-specific taxation (on fat or carbohydrates), restructured agricultural subsidies, or advertisement bans for sweetened foods and beverages become enforceable (The policy mix aimed at smoking could be used as a blueprint for policy measures against other adverse health habits). Still, a modified health insurance scheme is a promising starting point that may, in addition to the shifting of the external costs to those who have caused them, lead to immediate behavioural changes.

Chapter 8. Appendix

8.1 The Determinants of the Basal Metabolic Rate

Figure 8-1: Determinants of the Basal Metabolic Rate
(Reference: Own construction following Whitney and Rolfes 2005, p. 257 and Insel et al. 2007, p. 337)

Factor	Effect on BMR	Comments
Caffeine	positive	Caffeine increases energy expenditure.
Fever	positive	Fever raises the BMR by seven per cent for each degree Fahrenheit.
Growth	positive	BMR is higher in pregnant women and children.
Height	positive	BMR is higher in tall, thin people as a greater skin surface radiates more heat.
Hyperthyroidism	positive	Excess thyroxine production can increase energy expenditure.
Pregnancy and lactation	positive	Both factors temporarily increase women's energy expenditure.
Smoking	positive	Nicotine increases energy expenditure.
Stresses	positive	Stresses, such as diseases and certain drugs, raise the BMR.
Body composition (gender)	mixed	Males usually have a higher BMR than females as they have more lean tissue. Conversely, the more fat tissue, the lower the BMR.
Environmental temperature	mixed	Both extreme heat and cold raise the BMR.
Hormones (gender)	mixed	Depending on the specific hormone, the BMR can be raised or lowered. For women, the BMR also varies during the menstrual cycle.
Age	negative	Due to a reduction in lean body mass with age. The decrease starts in early adulthood, after growth and development cease.
Fasting and starvation	negative	Both circumstances lower BMR.
Hypothyroidism	negative	Inadequate thyroxine production can slow energy expenditure.
Malnutrition	negative	Malnutrition lowers BMR.
Sleep	negative	BMR decreases during sleep.

8.2 Selected Empirical Studies on Overweight and Obesity

Within the last two decades, obesity as a topic has come to the attention of economic, medical, and social researchers. As a result, a vast amount of literature has been published. In this section, selected studies are presented. They have been chosen so a broad picture of the possible determinants of habits leading to excess weight is provided. The following tables show which variables have a (statistically significant) impact on excess bodyweight. The Arabian numbers refer to the alphabetically ordered list explaining the studies in more detail which follows the tables. The relation to BMI depicts the direction of the influence attributable to the independent variable. Mentionable aspects are quoted in the last column. While the first table deals with economic factors, the second and third table provide the social determinants of excess bodyweight. In addition, the third table includes the influence of information. The fourth table is concerned with environmental factors, and the last one with health behaviour and the influence of genes.

Figure 8-2: Determinants of Obesity
(a) Economic Factors (b) Social Determinants
(c) Social Determinants and Information
(d) Environmental Factors (e) Health Behaviour and Genes
(Reference: Own construction)

(a) Economic factors

Independent variable	Study showing this impact	Relation to BMI	Comments
Income	3, 6, 8, 12, 15, 16, 17, 24, 28, 37, 38, 40, 43, 44, 52	negative / quadratic / inverse U-shaped	Effect differs by gender (42 refers to women, 43 refers to men) and by development stage of the country (51). In developing countries, progressively less traditional foods and more animal products are consumed. According to (39), more individuals tend to be in the healthiest weight range during recessions than during periods of economic upswing.
Prices of or taxes on snack foods, soft drinks	6, 11, 12, 24	negative	The trends observed in the US are: more calories, more refined carbohydrates, more added sugars, more total fats – all in all, energy-dense food is more cost-effective. As a result, Americans are becoming more obese while spending a progressively lower proportion of their disposable income on food. Results differ for developing countries (12).
Socioeconomic Status	2, 3, 10, 11, 14, 20, 25, 26, 31, 39, 43, 49, 54, 55, 58	negative	Usually computed as an index consisting of education, occupation, and income. The relationship in developing countries may be inverse U-shaped. The socioeconomic status attained in adulthood may not override the consequences of a low socio-economic status in childhood. The relationship between family socioeconomic status and weight gain is more pronounced among children from lower-income countries.
Cigarette Price	6	positive	(-)

	Independent variable	Study showing this impact	Relation to BMI	Comments
(b) Social determinants	**Age**	5, 6, 7, 8, 22, 24, 28, 30, 31, 37, 38, 41, 44, 45, 56	positive / inverse U-shaped / quadratic	Most studies find that age first increases obesity, but beyond a certain point starts decreasing it.
	Education	6, 16, 17, 22, 24, 28, 31, 32, 33, 34, 37, 38, 41, 44, 52, 53, 56	negative	Not only the heads of the household, but also children from families with low educational attainment are more likely to be obese.
	Other demographic variables (i.e. family structure, race / ethnicity, gender, residence)	3, 6, 7, 8, 15, 16, 17, 23, 24, 26, 28, 31, 32, 34, 37, 38, 39, 41, 44, 49, 52, 53, 57	mixed	Blacks tend to be heavier and gain weight at a faster rate. Many studies explain racial differences with socioeconomic position. On average, married persons (especially males) usually display a higher BMI. In most studies, males have a higher bodyweight, while women obviously gain weight at a faster rate.
	Food stamp participation	5	positive	Low-income women are more likely to be obese and have a higher bodyweight.

	Independent variable	Study showing this impact	Relation to BMI	Comments
(c) Social determinants	**Family food insecurity or insufficiency**	13, 51	positive	(-)
	Insurance status	17	negative	Uninsured or publicly insured adolescents are more likely to be obese.
	Immigration status	31, 49, 50, 54	mixed	For immigrants, the probability of being overweight or obese appears to be lower on arrival than for native-born individuals, but the incidence of gaining excess weight increases with additional years in the immigration country. Children of immigrants from higher-income countries gain more weight than children from lower-income countries.
	Neighbourhood collective efficacy	7	negative	For adolescents, neighbourhood collective efficacy influences both overweight and the risk of being overweight.
(c) Information	**Health information / health knowledge**	18, 19, 22, 33, 34, 53	negative	Results differ by gender (i.e. in 22, the effect is only found for women). Still, even the most educated seem to benefit from additional health information.
	Pro-advertising	1, 18	positive	Effect is only found for adolescents with an overweight parent (1).

	Independent variable	Study showing this impact	Relation to BMI	Comments
(d) Environmental factors	**Food processing technology**	9, 48	positive	Obviously, a larger variety of foods is consumed during the day due to the reduced time costs of food preparation – countries in which more time is spent on food preparation tend to have lower levels of obesity.
	Availability of energy-dense foods	1, 48	positive	Influence is detectable for adolescents with an overweight parent. Away-from-home foods are energy-denser. Portion sizes have increased.
	Urban sprawl	28, 31	positive	Effect is probably due to increased automobile use leading to decreased physical activity.
	Urban environment	10, 45	positive	Effect in one of the studies evident for girls, not for boys, and particularly for those with low socioeconomic status. Urban environment may be associated with decreased physical activity and changed dietary habits.
	Walkable environment	15, 46	negative	Influence is only detected for those preferring walkability. Like in the case of urban sprawl, the effect may be due to slightly higher levels of physical activity which are induced by lower levels of driving.
	Number of restaurants	6	positive	(-)

	Independent variable	Study showing this impact	Relation to BMI	Comments
(e) Health behaviour	**Television watching**	7, 22, 34, 36, 41, 48	positive	Among the range of sedentary behaviour, television viewing seems to play a decisive role as it is common to enjoy snacks while watching TV.
	Smoking status	21, 37, 38, 39, 49, 56	negative	Some studies find a positive association between BMI and smoking cessation. Those who quit smoking exhibit a larger increase in BMI than those who have never smoked. Some time after quitting, bodyweight converges to its usual level.
	Alcohol consumption	4, 5, 14, 56	mixed	According to (4), increased alcohol consumption has led to a dramatic increase in weight among Chinese men.
	Consumption of sugar-sweetened beverages	14, 29, 36	positive	Increased diet-soda consumption seems to be negatively related to obesity incidence.
	Physical activity	4, 30, 32, 35, 39, 45, 48, 49, 56	negative	Magnitude of effect differs by age group and gender.
(e) Genes	**Genes**	27, 47	mixed	Correlation between parental bodyweight and their adult offspring is well-established, results of studies indicate influence from twenty to 60 per cent. Recent research suggests that genetic influences on children's bodyweight may be independent of those that influence BMI in adults (47).

(1) Anderson and Butcher (2006) examine whether students' BMI is higher in schools under financial pressure as these may raise funds through contracts with soft drink or snack food companies, thus offering energy-dense foods. They find a positive effect of availability and advertising of snack foods and soft drinks on adolescent BMI for pupils with an overweight parent, while school food policies do not affect the weight of students whose parents are not overweight. The results thus point at the importance of shared genetics, or shared environment, or both.

(2) Ball and Mishra (2006) investigate the associations of mother's, father's, and own socioeconomic status, as well as intergenerational social mobility, with BMI and weight change in young women. The results suggest that both childhood and adult socioeconomic status are independently inversely related to obesity risk, but the associations differ for different indices of status and weight.

(3) Baltrus et al. (2005) analyse whether race differences in weight gain can be traced back to differences in socioeconomic position and psychosocial and behavioural factors, such as physical activity, cigarette smoking, alcohol consumption, depression, marital status, and the number of children. The authors observe that Black women are heavier and gain more weight than White women while Black males weigh significantly more but do not gain weight at a higher rate than White men. Most of the above racial differences can be explained by a cumulative measure of socioeconomic position. Of the individual factors, only income displays a sizeable effect.

(4) Bell et al. (2001) describe a population-based cohort study of weight change among Chinese adults and analyse its predictors. The authors find that low physical activity is a strong predictor of weight gain. Alcohol consumption is associated with drastic weight gain in men. For males, smoking is inversely, but not significantly, related to weight. The results for socioeconomic status are mixed.

(5) Chen et al. (2005) analyse whether food stamp participation is positively related to obesity. The authors find that food stamp participation is positively associated with bodyweight and the likelihood of being obese among low-income women. Alcohol and beer consumption are negatively related to bodyweight and the likelihood of being obese, while consumption of carbonated beverages and sugar, spending more time watching TV or playing video games and being Black exhibit a positive relation. Bodyweight increases with age before the age of 40 and declines afterwards.

(6) Chou et al. (2004) empirically test a list of possible determinants of overweight and obesity: In addition to genetic factors, bodyweight is determined by gender (on average, males have a higher BMI while females are more likely to be obese) and marital status (married and widowed persons have a higher average BMI). Age shows an inverted U-shaped influence on bodyweight. Furthermore, BMI is negatively influenced by years of schooling, income, and the prices of alcohol and food. It is positively influenced by the number of restaurants and the real cigarette price.

(7) Cohen et al. (2006) examine whether neighbourhood collective efficacy (the norms and networks that enable collective action, the willingness of people to intervene for the good of a community, and the linkage of mutual trust within a community) is associated with BMI and overweight in adolescents. The authors find that adolescents in neighbourhoods with low efficacy exhibit 64 per cent higher odds of being at risk for overweight. Residents in such neighbourhoods are 52 per cent more likely to be overweight than those in average neighbourhoods. Age, gender, and hours of television watching per week are also significant.

(8) In their study on social interactions and the determinants of bodyweight, Costa-Font and Gil (2004) find that males have higher bodyweight, with affluent middle-aged men displaying the highest BMI. Age and income both have a quadratic effect, thus displaying non-linear effects. Those that have been mar-

ried at some point in their lives and those currently married are likely to have a higher bodyweight than those who have never been married. The authors conclude that individuals compare themselves when interacting socially, thus encouraging behavioural patterns that prevent obesity and overweight.

(9) Cutler et al. (2003) empirically support the positive impact of new food processing technology on obesity rates. The authors find that the reduced time costs of preparing food result in consumption of a larger variety of foods at more times during the day, such as snacks. In addition, individuals increasingly consume food items with a high degree of commercial preparation. Countries in which individuals spend more time on food preparation seem to display lower rates of obesity.

(10) Dollman and Pilgrim (2005) attempt to compare the influence of urban or rural residence and low, medium or high socioeconomic status on rates of change in Australian children's relative weight, fatness and fat distribution. They find that the most rapid increase in body fatness is evident among girls, particularly those with low socioeconomic status and those living in an urban environment.

(11) Drewnowski (2004) examines the relationship between household purchasing power, diet quality, and diet costs. Taking price developments into account, he examines US trends in certain food groups and comes to the conclusion that the major trends are: more calories, more refined carbohydrates, more added sugars, and more total fats. Fresh fruits and vegetables, which are relatively costly, do not contribute to the rising energy consumption. The author concludes that diet quality is a function of socioeconomic status, education, and income. The impact of socioeconomic variables on obesity may be mediated by the low cost of energy-dense foods.

(12) Du et al. (2004) analyse public health consequences of income growth on nutrition-related decisions in China. The authors find that total energy intake

is decreasing, while more high-fat and animal products, as well as edible oil, and less traditional foods are consumed. Flour and rice products have apparently become inferior goods, whereas animal food intakes increase with rising income. High-fat diets have obviously become superior goods at all income levels.

(13) Dubois et al. (2006) examine the relationship between family food insufficiency and being overweight in a cohort of pre-school children. They find that family food insufficiency is positively related to mean BMI. Being born with a low birth weight, maternal smoking during pregnancy, and having overweight or obese parents also significantly increases the odds for obesity.

(14) Fernald (2007) explores the association of BMI with socioeconomic status and beverage consumption (sweetened carbonated soda and alcoholic beverages) among low-income Mexican adults. She finds that BMI is positively associated with socioeconomic status: Those with the highest BMI are the most educated, with the best occupations and the best-equipped houses. In contrast, across Mexico as a whole, the prevalence of overweight and obesity is negatively related to socioeconomic status. In addition, she finds a significant positive association between the consumption of soda and alcoholic beverages and BMI.

(15) Frank et al. (2007) examine the effect of the built environment on walking, car use, and obesity. They find that creating walkable environments may result in higher levels of physical activity and less driving and in slightly lower obesity prevalence, but only for those preferring walkability. Gender, race, and household income are also significant predictors of obesity.

(16) Goodman (1999) explores whether socioeconomic status gradients exist for obesity among US adolescents. She finds that males are more likely to be obese, and that obesity is significantly and independently associated with household income and all indicators of education.

(17) Haas et al. (2003) examine the association of race / ethnicity, socioeconomic status, and health insurance status with the prevalence of overweight among children and adolescents. The results show that boys, Black and Latino children, as well as children from families with low educational attainment and low income are more likely to be overweight. Receipt of support is found to be negatively related to excess weight among children. For adolescents, males, Asian / Pacific Islanders and Latinos are more likely to be overweight, as well as those with a low household income and uninsured or publicly insured adolescents.

(18) Ippolito and Mathios (1994) analyse food consumption data in order to determine which food categories are involved in overall reductions in fat, saturated fat, and cholesterol consumption and whether producer health claims make a difference. They find that between 1975 and 1985, reductions in fat were mostly concentrated in the meat category, while post-1985, fat reduction occurred in a wider range of food categories. The authors conclude that information and advertising both affect consumer choices, that the effects are largest in food categories in which general statements can be made, and that producer-provided information is likely to be effective across a wide range of food groups.

(19) Ippolito and Mathios (1995) examine whether information and advertising can influence fat consumption. They find that providing information on the risk of cancer and heart diseases due to increased fat intake lowers the consumption of both fat and saturated fatty acids in the sample.

(20) James et al. (2006) examine the relationship between childhood and adulthood socioeconomic position and prevalence of obesity in adulthood, taking the possible influence of women's relative access to socioeconomic resources into account. As a result, women who grew up in the most economically disadvantaged households are twice as likely to be obese than those with a less

impoverished background, independently of the socioeconomic position attained during adulthood, marital status, and health behaviour.

(21) Kahn et al. (1997) identify behaviour associated with change in BMI or weight gain at the waist. They find BMI is positively associated with meat consumption and smoking cessation and negatively associated with vegetable consumption, vitamin E supplementation, continued smoking, and some vigorous activities, such as running.

(22) Kan and Tsai (2004) investigate the relationship between BMI and the individuals' knowledge on health risks of obesity. The authors find that television news watching is statistically significant for men, while newspaper reading is statistically significant for women. In addition, males with increased health risk knowledge are less likely to be underweight. While mildly overweight males do not seem to be responsive to health knowledge, males close to the conventional definition of being obese well heed health risk knowledge. Age has a quadratic effect while years of education display a significantly negative impact. For females, no statistically significant relationship between health knowledge and BMI can be found. The effect of age is quadratic, and education has a statistically negative impact.

(23) Kuchler et al. (2005) examine price elasticities on snack foods. They find that, in general, demand for snack food is inelastic. Household size is significant, as are presence of children, ethnicity and regional differences: Households with children, those situated in the central US regions, and non-Hispanic households consume more chips. The own-price elasticity estimates are similar in magnitude to estimates for cigarettes and alcohol.

(24) Lakdawalla and Philipson (2002) find that technological change has induced weight growth by making home and market production of food less strenuous, which is associated with declining physical activity, and by lowering food prices through agricultural innovation. The former accounts for 60, the lat-

ter for approximately 40 per cent of the change in weight. The authors also reason that additional years of schooling have a negative effect on BMI, that both Black and Hispanic women tend to be heavier than Whites, and that income and age have an inverted U-shaped effect on BMI.

(25) Langenberg et al. (2003) investigate the influence of six social classes in childhood, young adulthood, and middle age on obesity at 53 years of age. The results indicate that father's social class is inversely related to all measures of obesity in both genders. For women, both adult social classes are inversely associated with obesity.

(26) Lawlor et al. (2005) assess the association of childhood socioeconomic status with risk factors for cardiovascular disease. The authors find that men are more likely to be overweight, and that low socioeconomic status at birth is associated with a higher risk of being overweight, independent of adult social class and income.

(27) As obesity involves both environmental and genetic influences, Li et al. (2006) attempt to evaluate genetic influences on BMI and other obesity traits in the study population. The genetic correlations range from 0.36 to 0.71 in obesity-related trait pairs, with the highest correlation for BMI and body surface area. The results largely correspond to results of other studies on genetic influences of obesity with estimates usually ranging from 20 to 60 per cent.

(28) Lopez (2004) demonstrates that urban sprawl contributes to the rise in bodyweight. Blacks, Hispanics, males, those who are older, and those with less household income and less education are more likely to be overweight or obese. The sample consists of 104,084 US-American men and women.

(29) Ludwig et al. (2001) examine the association between baseline consumption and change in consumption of sugar-sweetened drinks, and measures of obesity. They find that the odds of becoming obese significantly

increase for each additional daily serving of sugar-sweetened drink. By contrast, increased diet-soda consumption is negatively related to obesity incidence.

(30) Using data from the German National Health Survey 1998, Maennig et al. (2008) find a significantly negative impact of physical activity and a significantly positive impact of age on BMI. Based on their results, the authors conclude that nine hours of physical activity per week is necessary to reduce the average BMI of the sample to a normal level of 25.

(31) McDonald and Kennedy (2005) compare the weight of recent immigrants to that of native-born Canadians and analyse the likelihood of gaining excess bodyweight with additional years in Canada. They find that the probability of being overweight or (for women) obese is lower on arrival than for comparable native-born Canadians. The incidence of gaining excess weight increases with additional years in Canada. Immigrants are less likely to be overweight or obese when they live in a neighbourhood with a relatively large ethnic community. Furthermore, individuals are more likely to be obese when they are older and married, and less likely to be obese when they are more educated and live in an urban area. Higher socioeconomic status is associated with less excess weight.

(32) Nayga (1999) investigates which socioeconomic factors are related to obesity. He concludes that a person is more likely to be obese when she has children, is Black, female, less educated, from the Midwest, and physically inactive in her spare time.

(33) Nayga (2000) examines the relationship between schooling, health knowledge, and obesity. The author finds that, although health knowledge is insignificant, those with higher education are less likely to be obese. Schooling has a negative effect on relative weight and the probability of being obese. It also appears that on average, males have a lower level of diet-disease knowledge, which has a positive effect on the probability of being obese.

(34) According to Nayga (2001), schooling has a negative effect on the probability of both genders of being obese, while health knowledge only has a negative effect on the likelihood that a woman is obese. Blacks are found more likely to be obese. For men, household size and television watching (five hours per day) both have a positive and statistically significant impact.

(35) Parsons et al. (2006) measure the relation between physical activity at ages eleven and sixteen years and subsequent changes in BMI to mid-adulthood life. The results show that physical activity at age eleven neither has an effect on BMI at age 33 nor on the slope of the BMI trajectory. In contrast, physical activity at the age of sixteen has significant effects on both BMI at age 33 and on the slope of the BMI trajectory.

(36) Phillips et al. (2004) examine the longitudinal relationship of energy-dense snack food intake to relative weight status and percentage of body fat, as well as its relationship to television viewing. They find that soda is the only item in the food group that shows a significant relationship to relative weight status. Despite the absence of a significant relationship between snacking and overall sedentary behaviour, the authors find a positive and significant relationship between energy-dense snack food intake and television viewing.

(37) Rashad (2006) empirically examines the contribution of caloric intake, smoking, and exercise to the rise in obesity. As a result, those with higher caloric intake and individuals who are older, Blacks, Hispanics, females, and married males are likely to have a higher BMI. Smokers, those with a college education, and females with a higher household income are likely to weigh less.

(38) Rashad et al. (2006) test the implication whether the United States have experienced a rapid increase in obesity rates due to economic changes (i.e. the per capita number of restaurants, the number of women in the labour force, technological changes) that have, in turn, induced behavioural changes leading to weight gains in the population. The authors model obesity as a function of

caloric intake, caloric expenditure, smoking, and predisposition. As a result, the per capita number of cigarettes affects females more than males. A higher cigarette tax increases female BMI but not obesity rates. Blacks, Hispanics, older people, and those who are married or widowed are more likely to have a higher BMI, while those with higher income and college education tend to have a lower BMI.

(39) Robert and Reither (2004) examine the impact of socioeconomic status and community disadvantage (defined as an index consisting of the percentage of households receiving public assistance, the percentage of families receiving incomes higher than US $ 30,000, and the percentage of adult unemployment) on the BMI of Black adults. For women, they demonstrate that race and low individual socioeconomic status are each independent risk factors for a higher BMI. Community socioeconomic disadvantage and community income inequality are each independently associated with BMI. Furthermore, physical activity and smoking are predictors of a low BMI.

(40) Ruhm (2000) demonstrates that mortality is procyclical. As possible explanations, the author mentions the fact that individuals are more likely to be in the healthiest weight range under unfavourable economic conditions. He can prove this relation in an econometric analysis.

(41) Salmon et al. (2000) investigate whether physical activity modifies the association between television viewing and overweight. The authors find that age, gender, and education are all significantly associated with overweight. The likelihood of being overweight rises with increased television viewing. Apart from the respondents in the inactive category, increased hours of television viewing are significantly related to overweight within each level of physical activity.

(42) Salmon et al. (2005) examine trends in active transport to and from school, in school sports and physical education, and in weight status in a sample

comprising 557 male and female Australian children aged nine to thirteen years. The authors attempt to identify a possible influence of socioeconomic status and find that there have been declines in the mean frequency of physical activity and walking or cycling to school. Simultaneously, the frequency of school sports and the proportion of children that is overweight or obese have increased. These trends appear stronger among children attending schools in areas with low socioeconomic status.

(43) Sarlio-Lähteenkorva and Lahelma (1999) examine whether overweight is associated with economic and social disadvantage. For men, they fail to detect any associations between excess bodyweight and social or economic disadvantage. Thin men are more likely to be unemployed and earn a lower wage. Among women, obesity is associated with unemployment and low income. Thin women are also more likely to earn little.

(44) Sobal et al. (1992) examine the association between marital status, fatness, and obesity. The authors find that married men are significantly fatter and more likely to be obese than never married or previously married men. A comparable (significant) association cannot be established for women. For females, age, race and education show especially strong significant associations with BMI. Living alone, having children, age, and income are significantly associated with male BMI.

(45) Sobngwi et al. (2004) investigate the association between lifetime exposure to urban environment and obesity, diabetes, and hypertension. The authors find a significantly positive correlation between BMI and lifetime exposure to an urban environment, as well as a significantly negative relationship between BMI and time spent in a rural environment. Furthermore, age and physical inactivity are associated with overweight and obesity.

(46) Stafford et al. (2007) analyse which local, social, and physical environmental characteristics make an impact on physical activity and diet. They find

significant associations between obesity and neighbourhood disorder (defined as an index consisting of five items concerning trust in the neighbourhood and neighbours, litter and vandalism) and access to local high street facilities: While neighbourhood disorder is positively associated with obesity, access to local high street facilities, proximity to a post office, and population density (indicating proximity of places that people can walk to) are associated with lower levels of obesity.

(47) Stunkard et al. (1999) assess the relationship between measures of bodyweight of parents with those of their children during the first two years of life, half of them born to obese and half born to lean mothers. Each infant is weighed at ages three, twelve and 24 months. As neither maternal or paternal BMI nor maternal or paternal bodyweight turn out to be predictors of bodyweight at twelve or 24 months, while the correlation between parental bodyweight and their adult offspring is well-established, their results suggest that genetic influences on the bodyweight of children may be independent of those that influence BMI in adults.

(48) A study by Sturm (2004) on the allocation of time between sleep, leisure, occupation, transportation, and home-based activities (SLOTH) suggests that while sleep does not exhibit any trend that could have contributed to obesity, and the total amount of leisure time has remained stable, leisure time is increasingly spent on sedentary rather than physical activities. TV watching displays the largest increase. Time spent in occupational activities has declined. The value of time spent in home production has been reduced as a result of demographic and technological changes. In addition, away-from-home foods tend to be energy-denser, and portion sizes have increased.

(49) Sundquist and Johansson (1998) investigate the effects of ethnicity / country of birth and socioeconomic status on BMI. The authors find that socioeconomic status and ethnicity are two separate independent factors related to an increased BMI. Not exercising is also related to a higher BMI for both genders.

Men and women who quit smoking exhibit a larger increase in BMI than never smokers.

(50) Sundquist and Winkleby (2000) analyse the relation between acculturation status and abdominal obesity for Mexican-Americans. The authors find that waist circumference is significantly larger among US-born women and men than among those born in Mexico, indicating an influence of country of birth. Among women, larger waist circumference of those speaking Spanish than of English-speaking women is also significant.

(51) Townsend et al. (2001) examine the relationship between food insecurity and overweight. They find that food insecurity remains a significant predictor of overweight status, even after adjustment for potentially confounding demographic and lifestyle variables.

(52) Truong and Sturm (2005) empirically examine weight gain trends across several sociodemographic groups. The authors find that in general, lower educational attainment is associated with a higher BMI, but considering weight gain, only college graduates gain weight at a significantly smaller rate. BMI is higher for the lowest-income than for the highest-income group. Non-Hispanic Blacks gain weight faster than other ethnic groups. On average, women have a lower BMI than men, but they gain weight at a faster rate.

(53) Tsou and Liu (2006) analyse the impact of schooling and health knowledge on the level of obesity. The authors find that schooling has a statistically significant negative effect on obesity that is independent of individual differences in health knowledge, which is consistent with evidence from developed countries. In addition, older and married women and those with lower levels of education, obesity-disease knowledge, and fiber intake are more likely to suffer from excess bodyweight.

(54) Van Hook and Stamper Balistreri (2007) examine whether socioeconomic status and economic development of the emigration country influence children's BMI. They find that children of immigrants from higher-income countries gain more weight than children from lower-income countries, that the relationship between family socioeconomic status and weight gain is significantly more positive among children from lower-income countries, and that weight gain is only positively associated with generation among children with lower socioeconomic status from low-income countries.

(55) Wang (2001) examines the relationship between factors determining socioeconomic status and obesity in male and female children and adolescents. As a result of the analyses, Wang concludes that national socioeconomic development levels influence the prevalence of obesity: In the US and Russia, prevalence of obesity and overweight is highest among low-income groups, whereas in China, high-income groups have the highest obesity levels. In Russia, prevalence of obesity is higher in rural areas but in China, the same is true for urban areas.

(56) Wilsgaard et al. (2005) investigate the relationship between lifestyle factors and BMI. The authors find that baseline age, physical activity at work, and shift work or night work are positively associated with BMI. Alcohol consumption, leisure-time physical activity, level of education, and daily breakfast-eating are found to be negatively associated. While previous smokers display significantly higher baseline BMI values compared to non-smokers, current smokers have significantly lower BMI values.

(57) Winkleby et al. (1996) examine the effects of gender and socioeconomic factors on ethnic differences in BMI by applying a matched pairs design. The authors find that Hispanic women and men both have significantly higher BMI levels than White women and men with whom they are matched in accordance with gender, age group, level of education, city of residence, and survey time

period. These differences persist across every level of education and cannot be explained by any of the sociodemographic factors included in the analysis.

(58) Applying the concentration index to assess the degree of socioeconomic inequality in the distribution of obesity among American adults, Zhang and Wang (2004) find that obesity is negatively related to socioeconomic status. While there are strong disparities among women, the obesity burden appears almost equally distributed among men across groups with different socioeconomic status. In addition, the degree of inequality varies across age groups.

8.3 Selected Empirical Studies on the Relationship between Wages, Academic and Economic Performance, and Excess Weight

(I) Averett and Korenman (1996) examine differentials concerning income, marriage status, and hourly wages by BMI. The authors find that females who suffered from excess weight at ages sixteen to 24 seven years later obtain lower family income and lower hourly wages, are less likely to be married, and have lower spousal income compared to their normal-weight counterparts. Both marriage and labour markets contribute to this outcome. The penalty is larger for White than for Black women. Results for men are less clear-cut. Still, there is evidence of wage penalties for obese and underweight men.

(II) Baum and Ford (2004) examine the effects of obesity on male and female employees' wages. The authors find that the resulting wage penalty is almost twice as large for females (6.1 per cent and 3.4 per cent compared to normal-weight counterparts for females and males, respectively). Nevertheless, a wage penalty can be detected over the first two decades of a career for both genders. Furthermore, overweight only decreases wages for females, not for males.

(III) Based on OLS estimates, Cawley (2004) finds that for females, BMI and weight in pounds are negatively statistically significant for wages. The wage gap is highest for Whites and lowest for Blacks. For males, results are mixed. The influence of weight is statistically insignificant for White males, negatively statistically significant for Hispanic males, and reversed for Black males: Their wages rise with higher bodyweight.

(IV) Crosnoe and Muller (2004) find evidence that adolescents at risk of obesity attain lower academic achievement. This correlation is stronger in schools with high rates of romantic activity, and in those with lower average weight. It is weaker in schools with higher athletic participation.

(V) Grossman (1975) develops a recursive system of demand equations into which the possible causal relationships between schooling and health can be incorporated. Empirically testing their relevance, the author finds that schooling significantly increases current health. In addition, current health is significantly increased by past health and by years of formal schooling completed. A decomposition analysis shows that the effect of education on health is mainly conveyed by wives' schooling, job satisfaction, and weight difference.

(VI) Gortmaker et al. (1993) investigate the impact of overweight on subsequent educational attainment, marital status, household income, and self-esteem. The authors come to the conclusion that women who had been overweight at the beginning of the survey completed fewer years of schooling, were less likely to be married, earned lower household incomes, and suffered from higher rates of household poverty seven years thereafter. Males were only less likely to be married.

(VII) Pagán and Dávila (1997) examine the relationship between occupational attainment, earnings, and obesity. The authors find that obese women are indeed penalised. Their penalty varies little across occupations. Females compensate very little via occupational sorting, and they may be obese for employment-related reasons. In contrast, men sort themselves into jobs that offset the wage penalty. Furthermore, men can even gain from their excess weight, either through a productivity advantage or by accepting a premium for higher job-related risk. In addition, the analysis reveals that the probability of labour force participation is unaffected for obese men but lower for obese women, at least in the employment categories selected for this study.

(VIII) Sabia (2007) investigates the relationship between adolescent bodyweight and academic achievement. The author largely follows Cawley (2004) in his methodology. For women, he finds a negative statistically significant relationship between weight and academic performance: A weight increase by 50 pounds leads to a 0.15 to 0.2 point difference in GPA. For White males, a significant relationship cannot be detected. For non-White males, a nonlinear effect is observed: Underweight and obese individuals display lower GPA.

8.4 Utility Maximisation: Diet Composition

The objective functional is denoted by Q:

$$U_t(f_t^C, f_t^F, H_t(D_t); L_t) - \lambda e^{-rt}(BW_t^F(o_t\delta_t^F + \frac{l_t\delta_t^F}{0.8}) + \dot{BW}_t^F(o_t + \frac{l_t}{0.8}) - \frac{l_t J_t^F}{0.8} - 0.8 \cdot o_t J_t^C + n_t K_t + W_t TL_t) = Q \qquad (8.1)$$

Therefore, the Euler Equation to determine the optimal path of bodyweight becomes:

$$\frac{\partial Q}{\partial BW_t^F} - \frac{d}{dt} \cdot \frac{\partial Q}{\partial \dot{BW}_t^F} = 0 \qquad (8.2)$$

The individual terms of the Euler Equation are:

$$\frac{\partial Q}{\partial BW_t^F} = \frac{\partial U_t}{\partial H_t} \cdot \frac{\partial H_t}{\partial D_t} \cdot \frac{\partial D_t}{\partial BW_t^F} - \lambda e^{-rt}(o_t\delta_t^F + \frac{l_t\delta_t^F}{0.8})$$

$$-\lambda e^{-rt}W_t \cdot \frac{\partial TL_t}{\partial H_t} \cdot \frac{\partial H_t}{\partial D_t} \cdot \frac{\partial D_t}{\partial BW_t^F} \tag{8.3}$$

$$\frac{\partial Q}{\partial \dot{B}W_t^F} = -\lambda e^{-rt}(o_t + \frac{l_t}{0.8}) \tag{8.4}$$

$$\frac{d}{dt} \cdot \frac{\partial Q}{\partial \dot{B}W_t^F} - -\lambda e^{-rt}(\dot{o}_t + \frac{\dot{l}_t}{0.8}) + \lambda e^{-rt}r(o_t + \frac{l_t}{0.8}) \tag{8.5}$$

As the utility function is assumed to be continuous, twice differentiable, and concave, the extremum is a maximum.

8.5 The Basic BRFSS 2007 Sample

8.5.1 Descriptive Statistics

Figure 8-3: Descriptive Statistics of the Basic BRFSS 2007 Sample by Gender and Ethnic Group
(a) White Women (b) Black Women (c) Other Women
(d) White Men (e) Black Men (f) Other Men
(Reference: Own construction)

Descriptive Statistics: (a) White Women					
Variable	**Mean**	**Standard Deviation**	**Minimum Value**	**Maximum Value**	**Number of Observations**
Reported Weight [lb]	158.37	37.49	50.00	650.00	207,489
Reported Weight [kg]	71.84	17.00	22.68	294.84	207,489
Reported Height [in]	64.33	2.78	24.00	90.00	207,489
Reported Height [m]	1.63	0.07	0.61	2.29	207,489
BMI Value	26.90	6.14	8.51	122.73	207,489

Descriptive Statistics: (b) Black Women					
Variable	Mean	Standard Deviation	Minimum Value	Maximum Value	Number of Observations
Reported Weight [lb]	178.05	44.05	60.00	600.00	22,496
Reported Weight [kg]	80.76	19.98	27.22	272.16	22,496
Reported Height [in]	64.52	2.98	27.00	86.00	22,496
Reported Height [m]	1.64	0.08	0.69	2.18	22,496
BMI Value	30.09	7.35	11.34	221.82	22,496

Descriptive Statistics: (c) Other Women					
Variable	Mean	Standard Deviation	Minimum Value	Maximum Value	Number of Observations
Reported Weight [lb]	154.99	38.67	60.00	500.00	19,694
Reported Weight [kg]	70.30	17.54	27.22	226.80	19,694
Reported Height [in]	63.11	3.14	36.00	95.00	19,694
Reported Height [m]	1.60	0.08	0.91	2.41	19,694
BMI Value	27.37	6.64	10.97	115.13	19,694

Descriptive Statistics: (d) White Men					
Variable	Mean	Standard Deviation	Minimum Value	Maximum Value	Number of Observations
Reported Weight [lb]	196.28	39.14	59.00	660.00	133,574
Reported Weight [kg]	89.03	17.75	26.76	299.37	133,574
Reported Height [in]	70.27	2.92	24.00	93.00	133,574
Reported Height [m]	1.78	0.07	0.61	2.36	133,574
BMI Value	27.90	5.11	8.71	183.09	133,574

Descriptive Statistics: (e) Black Men					
Variable	**Mean**	**Standard Deviation**	**Minimum Value**	**Maximum Value**	**Number of Observations**
Reported Weight [lb]	198.49	43.85	77.00	562.00	10,594
Reported Weight [kg]	90.03	19.89	34.93	254.92	10,594
Reported Height [in]	69.92	3.36	47.00	91.00	10,594
Reported Height [m]	1.78	0.09	1.19	2.31	10,594
BMI Value	28.50	5.75	9.37	71.13	10,594

Descriptive Statistics: (f) Other Men					
Variable	**Mean**	**Standard Deviation**	**Minimum Value**	**Maximum Value**	**Number of Observations**
Reported Weight [lb]	185.70	41.44	65.00	555.00	13,537
Reported Weight [kg]	84.23	18.80	29.48	251.74	13,537
Reported Height [in]	68.52	3.43	41.00	90.00	13,537
Reported Height [m]	1.74	0.09	1.04	2.29	13,537
BMI Value	27.75	5.50	9.63	92.36	13,537

Figure 8-4: BMI Category by Gender and Ethnic Group [Per Cent]
(Reference: Own construction)

Calculated BMI Category by Gender and Ethnic Group [%]				
Subsample	**Underweight**	**Normal**	**Pre-Obese**	**Obese**
All Women	2.3	40.2	31.1	26.4
White	2.4	42.2	31.0	24.4
Black	1.4	23.0	31.9	43.6
Other	2.7	38.9	30.8	27.6
All Men	0.8	27.0	45.2	26.9
White	0.7	26.9	45.8	26.6
Black	1.1	25.8	40.8	32.3
Other	1.3	29.4	43.2	26.0

8.5.2 Histograms

Figure 8-5: Histograms of the Basic BRFSS 2007 Sample by Gender and Ethnic Group
(a) White Women (b) Black Women (c) Other Women
(d) White Men (e) Black Men (f) Other Men
(Reference: Own construction)

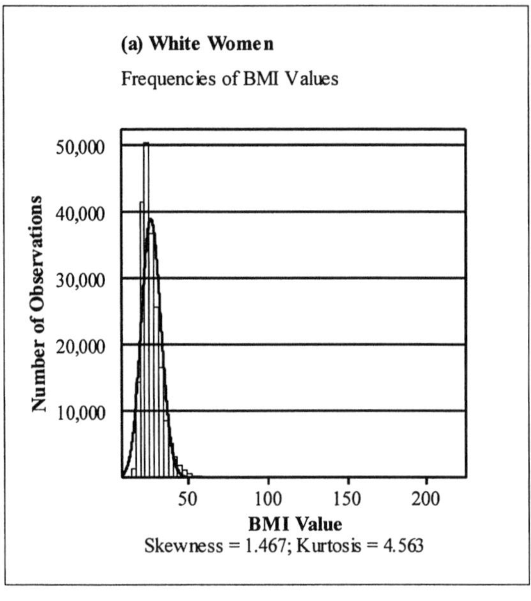

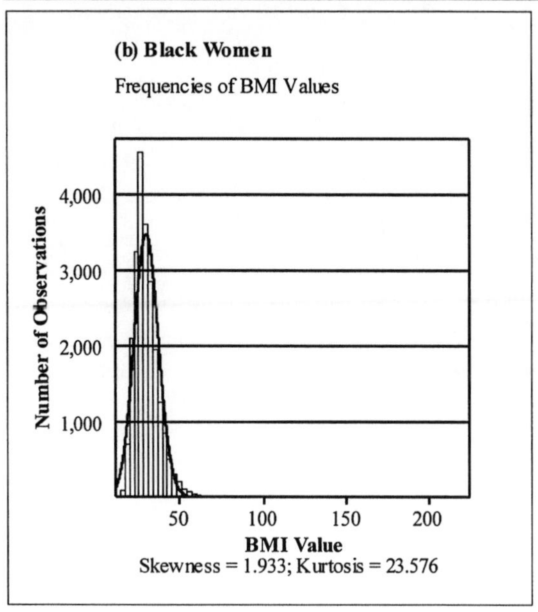
(b) Black Women
Frequencies of BMI Values
Number of Observations
4,000
3,000
2,000
1,000
50
100
150
200
BMI Value
Skewness = 1.933; Kurtosis = 23.576

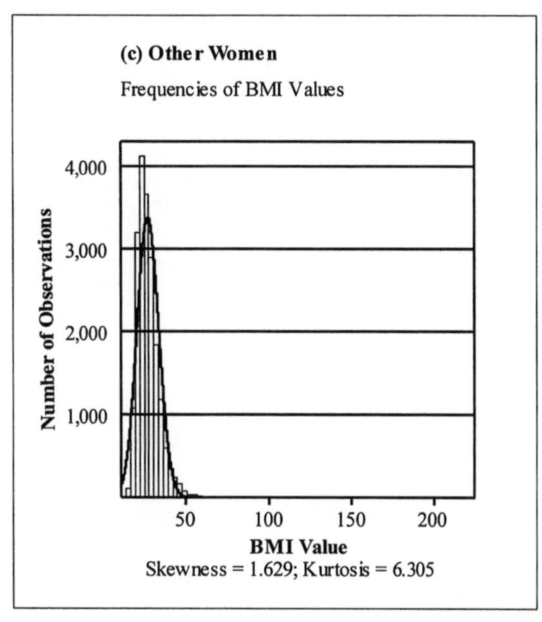
(c) Other Women
Frequencies of BMI Values
Number of Observations
4,000
3,000
2,000
1,000
50
100
150
200
BMI Value
Skewness = 1.629; Kurtosis = 6.305

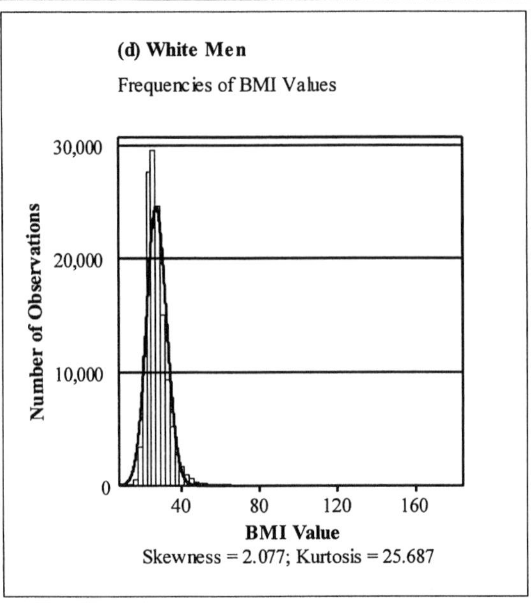
(d) White Men
Frequencies of BMI Values
30,000
20,000
10,000
0
Number of Observations
40
80
120
160
BMI Value
Skewness = 2.077; Kurtosis = 25.687

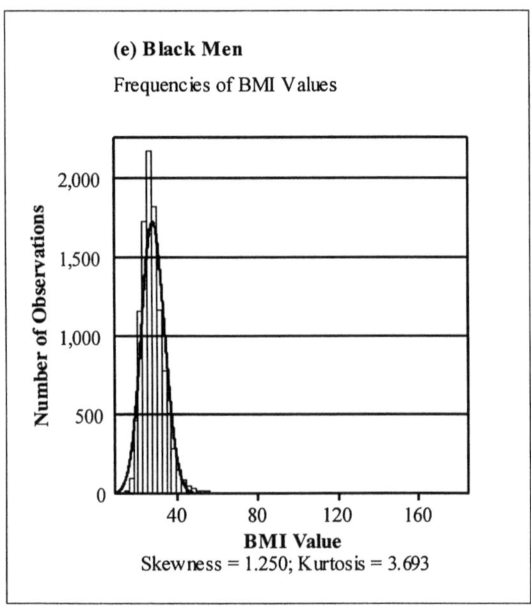
(e) Black Men
Frequencies of BMI Values
2,000
1,500
1,000
500
0
Number of Observations
40
80
120
160
BMI Value
Skewness = 1.250; Kurtosis = 3.693

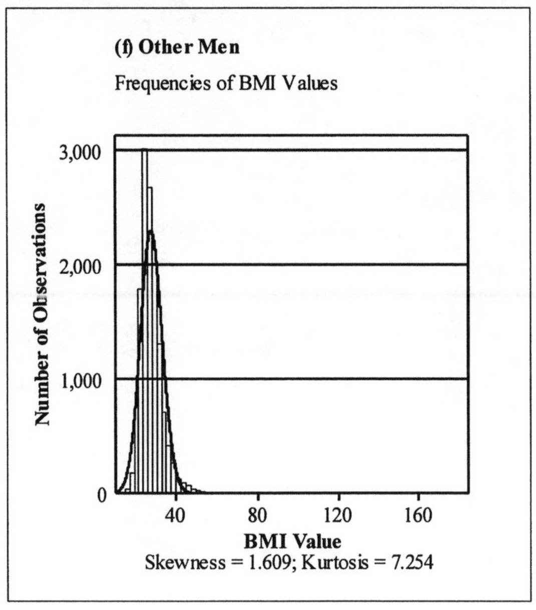
(f) Other Men
Frequencies of BMI Values
3,000
2,000
1,000
0
Number of Observations
40
80
120
160
BMI Value
Skewness = 1.609; Kurtosis = 7.254

8.6 Reporting Error in BMI, Weight, and Height

Figure 8-6: Reporting Error in
(a) BMI by Gender [Per Cent]
(b) Weight by Gender [Per Cent]
(c) Height by Gender [Per Cent]
(Reference: Own construction [Data obtained from Cawley 1999])

(a) Per Cent Reporting Error in BMI Women (NHANES III, Age 17 to 40)				
Group		**Average Error [%]**	**Standard Deviation**	**Number of Observations**
All Women		-1.50	6.26	3,854
	White	-1.47	5.90	2,257
	Black	-1.59	7.57	1,457
	Other	-1.63	7.75	139
Measured BMI	**BMI < 20**	1.89	5.15	548
	20 ≤ BMI < 25	-0.80	5.07	1,478
	25 ≤ BMI < 30	-2.23	6.09	901
	30 ≥ BMI	-5.70	7.41	927
Reported BMI	**BMI < 20**	-0.86	5.26	509
	20 ≤ BMI < 25	-0.86	5.51	1,658
	25 ≤ BMI < 30	-2.49	7.46	919
	30 ≥ BMI	-2.93	7.33	768

(a) Per Cent Reporting Error in BMI Men (NHANES III, Age 17 to 40)				
Group		**Average Error [%]**	**Standard Deviation**	**Number of Observations**
All Men		0.02	5.49	3,547
	White	-0.16	5.33	2,154
	Black	1.08	6.49	1,239
	Other	0.30	5.15	151
Measured BMI	**BMI < 20**	3.99	6.18	262
	20 ≤ BMI < 25	1.16	5.30	1,533
	25 ≤ BMI < 30	-0.71	4.38	1,177
	30 ≥ BMI	-3.69	5.66	575
Reported BMI	**BMI < 20**	-0.57	6.34	183
	20 ≤ BMI < 25	0.50	5.10	1,505
	25 ≤ BMI < 30	0.08	5.53	1,344
	30 ≥ BMI	-1.48	5.95	515

(b) Per Cent Reporting Error in Weight Women (NHANES III, Age 17 to 40)				
Group		**Average Error [%]**	**Standard Deviation**	**Number of Observations**
All Women		-1.58	5.14	3,854
	White	-1.67	4.79	2,257
	Black	-1.62	6.31	1,457
	Other	0.02	6.57	139
Measured Weight [lb]	**Weight < 160**	1.03	4.27	783
	160 ≤ Weight < 190	-0.92	3.77	1,262
	190 ≤ Weight < 220	-2.39	4.68	931
	220 ≥ Weight	-5.16	6.59	878
Reported Weight [lb]	**Weight < 160**	-0.14	4.34	706
	160 ≤ Weight < 190	-1.17	4.64	1,370
	190 ≤ Weight < 220	-2.10	5.31	1,006
	220 ≥ Weight	-3.75	6.13	772

(b) Per Cent Reporting Error in Weight Men (NHANES III, Age 17 to 40)				
Group		**Average Error [%]**	**Standard Deviation**	**Number of Observations**
All Men		1.04	4.62	3,547
	White	0.92	4.47	2,154
	Black	1.97	5.48	1,239
	Other	0.81	4.45	151
Measured Weight [lb]	**Weight < 160**	2.74	5.08	1,402
	160 ≤ Weight < 190	0.86	3.86	1,206
	190 ≤ Weight < 220	-0.29	3.74	572
	220 ≥ Weight	-1.83	4.28	367
Reported Weight [lb]	**Weight < 160**	1.60	5.16	1,157
	160 ≤ Weight < 190	1.31	4.20	1,365
	190 ≤ Weight < 220	0.73	4.39	625
	220 ≥ Weight	-0.70	4.45	400

(c) Per Cent Reporting Error in Height Women (NHANES III, Age 17 to 40)				
Group		**Average Error [%]**	**Standard Deviation**	**Number of Observations**
All Women		0.01	1.79	3,854
	White	-0.05	1.71	2,257
	Black	0.04	1.95	1,457
	Other	0.91	2.27	139
Measured Height [in]	**Height < 61**	0.72	3.37	570
	61 ≤ Height < 64	-0.11	1.58	1,472
	64 ≤ Height < 67	-0.09	1.41	1,345
	67 ≥ Height	0.03	1.46	467
Reported Height [in]	**Height < 61**	-1.08	2.55	437
	61 ≤ Height < 64	-0.32	1.56	1,314
	64 ≤ Height < 67	0.12	1.50	1,375
	67 ≥ Height	0.69	1.90	728

(c) Per Cent Reporting Error in Height Men (NHANES III, Age 17 to 40)				
Group		**Average Error [%]**	**Standard Deviation**	**Number of Observations**
All Men		0.55	1.70	3,547
	White	0.57	1.70	2,154
	Black	0.49	1.81	1,239
	Other	0.28	1.44	151
Measured Height [in]	**Height < 67**	0.47	2.41	937
	67 ≤ Height < 70	0.64	1.66	1,425
	70 ≤ Height < 73	0.47	1.33	867
	73 ≥ Height	0.56	1.26	318
Reported Height [in]	**Height < 67**	-0.68	2.05	764
	67 ≤ Height < 70	0.35	1.32	1,193
	70 ≤ Height < 73	0.88	1.32	1,062
	73 ≥ Height	1.09	2.14	528

8.7 The BRFSS 2007 Sample (Corrected for Reporting Error): Descriptive Statistics

Figure 8-7: Descriptive Statistics of the BRFSS 2007 Sample by Gender and Ethnic Group [Corrected for Reporting Error]
(a) White Women (b) Black Women (c) Other Women
(d) White Men (e) Black Men (f) Other Men
(Reference: Own construction)

Descriptive Statistics: (a) White Women					
Variable	**Mean**	**Standard Deviation**	**Minimum Value**	**Maximum Value**	**Number of Observations**
Weight [lb]	161.02	38.11	50.84	660.86	207,489
Weight [kg]	73.04	17.29	23.06	299.76	207,489
Height [in]	64.37	2.78	24.01	90.05	207,489
Height [m]	1.63	0.07	0.61	2.29	207,489
BMI Value	27.32	6.24	8.65	124.65	207,489

Descriptive Statistics: (b) Black Women					
Variable	**Mean**	**Standard Deviation**	**Minimum Value**	**Maximum Value**	**Number of Observations**
Weight [lb]	180.93	44.76	60.97	609.72	22,496
Weight [kg]	82.07	20.30	27.66	276.56	22,496
Height [in]	64.49	2.98	26.99	85.97	22,496
Height [m]	1.64	0.08	0.69	2.18	22,496
BMI Value	30.60	7.47	11.53	225.59	22,496

Descriptive Statistics: (c) Other Women					
Variable	**Mean**	**Standard Deviation**	**Minimum Value**	**Maximum Value**	**Number of Observations**
Weight [lb]	155.02	38.68	60.01	500.10	19,694
Weight [kg]	70.31	17.54	27.22	226.84	19,694
Height [in]	62.53	3.11	35.67	94.14	19,694
Height [m]	1.59	0.08	0.91	2.39	19,694
BMI Value	27.88	6.76	11.18	117.28	19,694

Descriptive Statistics: (d) White Men					
Variable	**Mean**	**Standard Deviation**	**Minimum Value**	**Maximum Value**	**Number of Observations**
Weight [lb]	194.48	38.78	58.46	653.93	133,574
Weight [kg]	88.21	17.59	26.52	296.62	133,574
Height [in]	69.87	2.90	23.86	92.47	133,574
Height [m]	1.77	0.07	0.61	2.35	133,574
BMI Value	27.96	5.12	8.73	183.49	133,574

Descriptive Statistics: (e) Black Men					
Variable	**Mean**	**Standard Deviation**	**Minimum Value**	**Maximum Value**	**Number of Observations**
Weight [lb]	194.58	42.98	75.48	550.93	10,594
Weight [kg]	88.26	19.50	34.24	249.90	10,594
Height [in]	69.58	3.34	46.77	90.55	10,594
Height [m]	1.77	0.08	1.19	2.30	10,594
BMI Value	28.22	5.70	9.28	70.42	10,594

Descriptive Statistics: (f) Other Men					
Variable	**Mean**	**Standard Deviation**	**Minimum Value**	**Maximum Value**	**Number of Observations**
Weight [lb]	184.20	41.10	64.47	550.50	13,537
Weight [kg]	83.55	18.64	29.24	249.70	13,537
Height [in]	68.33	3.42	40.89	89.75	13,537
Height [m]	1.74	0.09	1.04	2.28	13,537
BMI Value	27.68	5.49	9.61	92.12	13,537

Figure 8-8: BMI Category by Gender and Ethnic Group [Corrected for Reporting Error, Per Cent]

(Reference: Own construction)

Calculated BMI Category by Gender and Ethnic Group [%] Corrected for Reporting Error				
Subsample	**Underweight**	**Normal**	**Pre-Obese**	**Obese**
All Women	1.8	37.3	32.7	28.2
White	1.9	39.2	32.8	26.1
Black	1.1	20.7	31.7	46.5
Other	2.0	35.6	32.9	29.5
All Men	0.7	27.0	45.0	27.3
White	0.6	26.4	45.8	27.2
Black	1.2	29.4	38.6	30.9
Other	1.3	30.8	42.0	25.9

8.8 The BRFSS 2007 Sample (Corrected for Reporting Error, Outliers Removed)

8.8.1 Descriptive Statistics

Figure 8-9: Descriptive Statistics of the 2007 BRFSS Sample by Gender and Ethnic Group [Corrected for Reporting Error, Outliers Removed]
(a) White Women (b) Black Women (c) Other Women
(d) White Men (e) Black Men (f) Other Men
(Reference: Own construction)

Descriptive Statistics – Outliers Removed: (a) White Women					
Variable	Mean	Standard Deviation	Minimum Value	Maximum Value	Number of Observations
Weight [lb]	161.04	37.93	50.84	505.30	207,303
Weight [kg]	73.05	17.20	23.06	229.20	207,303
Height [in]	64.37	2.77	24.01	90.05	207,303
Height [m]	1.63	0.07	0.61	2.29	207,303
BMI Value	27.32	6.19	15.00	73.77	207,303

Descriptive Statistics – Outliers Removed: (b) Black Women					
Variable	Mean	Standard Deviation	Minimum Value	Maximum Value	Number of Observations
Weight [lb]	180.93	44.48	71.13	523.34	22,477
Weight [kg]	82.07	20.18	32.27	237.38	22,477
Height [in]	64.49	2.95	47.98	85.97	22,477
Height [m]	1.64	0.08	1.22	2.18	22,477
BMI Value	30.59	7.30	15.02	78.13	22,477

Descriptive Statistics – Outliers Removed: (c) Other Women					
Variable	Mean	Standard Deviation	Minimum Value	Maximum Value	Number of Observations
Weight [lb]	155.05	38.43	75.02	500.10	19,666
Weight [kg]	70.33	17.43	34.03	226.84	19,666
Height [in]	62.54	3.09	35.67	94.14	19,666
Height [m]	1.59	0.08	0.91	2.39	19,666
BMI Value	27.88	6.66	15.04	77.69	19,666

Descriptive Statistics – Outliers Removed: (d) White Men					
Variable	Mean	Standard Deviation	Minimum Value	Maximum Value	Number of Observations
Weight [lb]	194.44	38.45	79.26	528.10	133,477
Weight [kg]	88.20	17.44	35.95	239.54	133,477
Height [in]	69.87	2.89	41.76	92.47	133,477
Height [m]	1.77	0.07	1.06	2.35	133,477
BMI Value	27.95	4.99	15.04	65.02	133,477

Descriptive Statistics – Outliers Removed: (e) Black Men					
Variable	Mean	Standard Deviation	Minimum Value	Maximum Value	Number of Observations
Weight [lb]	194.67	42.91	86.27	550.93	10,584
Weight [kg]	88.30	19.46	39.13	249.90	10,584
Height [in]	69.57	3.34	46.77	90.55	10,584
Height [m]	1.77	0.08	1.19	2.30	10,584
BMI Value	28.23	5.68	15.03	70.42	10,584

Descriptive Statistics – Outliers Removed: (f) Other Men					
Variable	**Mean**	**Standard Deviation**	**Minimum Value**	**Maximum Value**	**Number of Observations**
Weight [lb]	184.24	40.73	73.40	525.71	13,515
Weight [kg]	83.57	18.47	33.29	238.46	13,515
Height [in]	68.33	3.40	40.89	89.75	13,515
Height [m]	1.74	0.09	1.04	2.28	13,515
BMI Value	27.68	5.37	15.06	67.88	13,515

Figure 8-10: BMI Category by Gender and Ethnic Group [Corrected for Reporting Error, Outliers Removed, Per Cent]

(Reference: Own construction)

Calculated BMI Category by Gender and Ethnic Group [%] Corrected for Reporting Error – Outliers Removed				
Subsample	**Underweight**	**Normal**	**Pre-Obese**	**Obese**
All Women	1.7	37.3	32.8	28.3
White	1.8	39.2	32.9	26.2
Black	1.1	20.7	31.8	46.5
Other	1.9	35.6	32.9	29.5
All Men	0.7	27.0	45.0	27.3
White	0.6	26.4	45.8	27.2
Black	1.1	29.4	38.6	30.9
Other	1.2	30.8	42.1	25.9

8.8.2 Histograms

Figure 8-11: Histograms of the 2007 BRFSS Sample by Gender and Ethnic Group [Corrected for Reporting Error, Outliers Removed]
(a) White Women (b) Black Women (c) Other Women
(d) White Men (e) Black Men (f) Other Men
(Reference: Own construction)

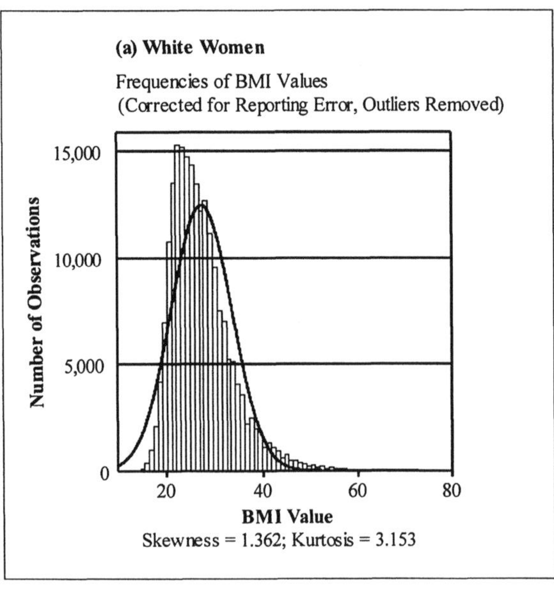

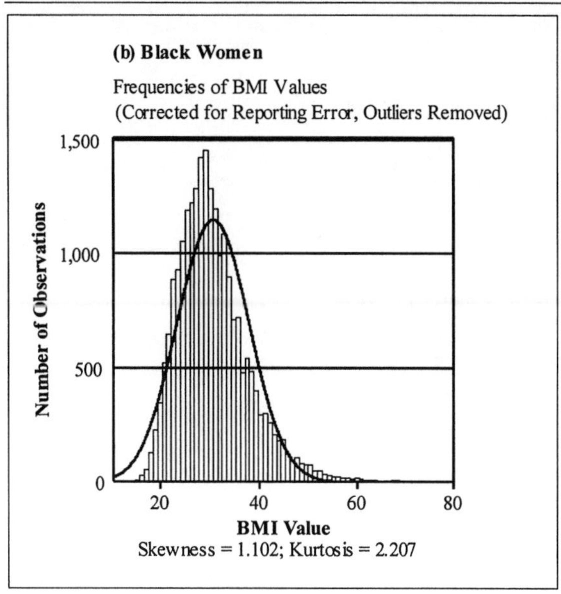
(b) Black Women
Frequencies of BMI Values
(Corrected for Reporting Error, Outliers Removed)
1,500
1,000
500
0
Number of Observations
20
40
60
80
BMI Value
Skewness = 1.102; Kurtosis = 2.207

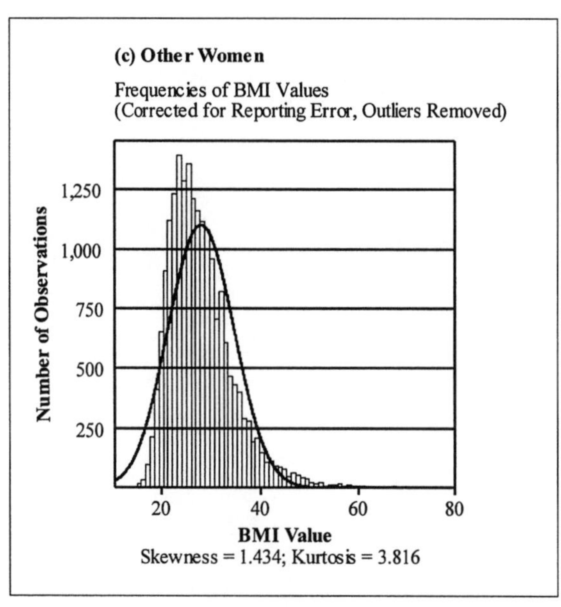
(c) Other Women
Frequencies of BMI Values
(Corrected for Reporting Error, Outliers Removed)
1,250
1,000
750
500
250
Number of Observations
20
40
60
80
BMI Value
Skewness = 1.434; Kurtosis = 3.816

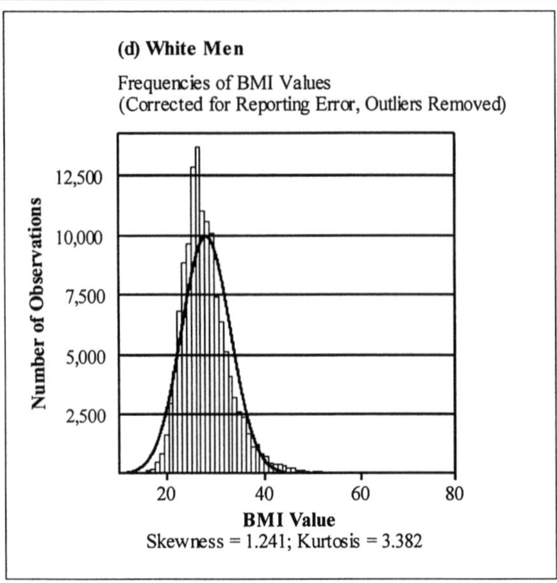
(d) White Men
Frequencies of BMI Values
(Corrected for Reporting Error, Outliers Removed)
Number of Observations
12,500
10,000
7,500
5,000
2,500
20
40
60
80
BMI Value
Skewness = 1.241; Kurtosis = 3.382

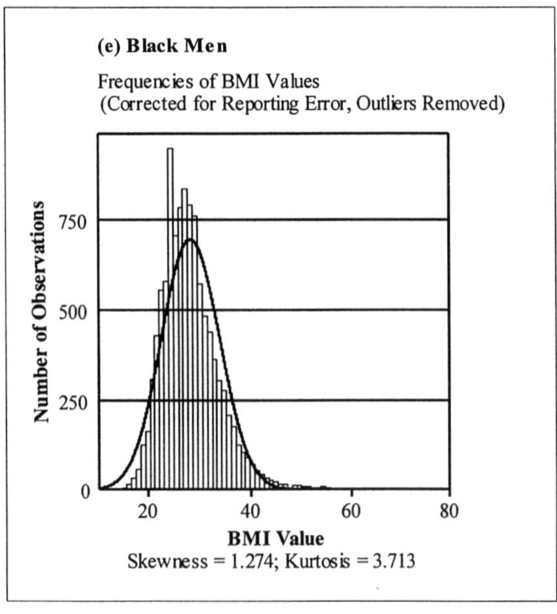
(e) Black Men
Frequencies of BMI Values
(Corrected for Reporting Error, Outliers Removed)
Number of Observations
750
500
250
0
20
40
60
80
BMI Value
Skewness = 1.274; Kurtosis = 3.713

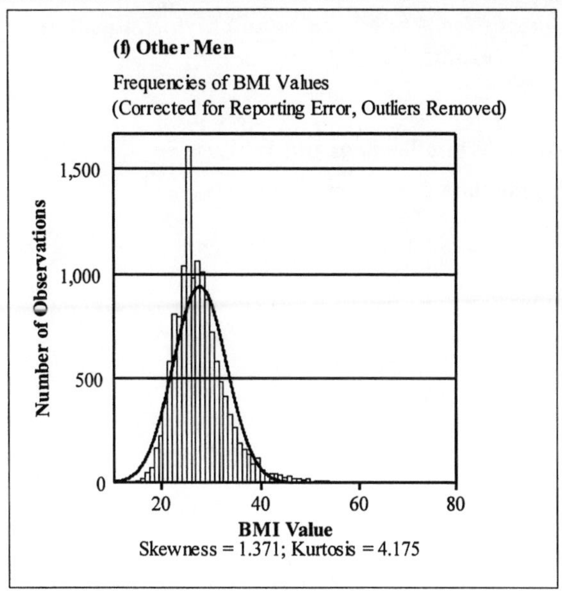
(f) Other Men
Frequencies of BMI Values
(Corrected for Reporting Error, Outliers Removed)
Number of Observations
1,500
1,000
500
0
20
40
60
80
BMI Value
Skewness = 1.371; Kurtosis = 4.175

8.8.3 Mean Diagrams for White Women and Men: Education, Employment, Income

Figure 8-12: Mean Diagrams: White Women and White Men
(a) Education (b) Employment (c) Income
(Reference: Own construction)

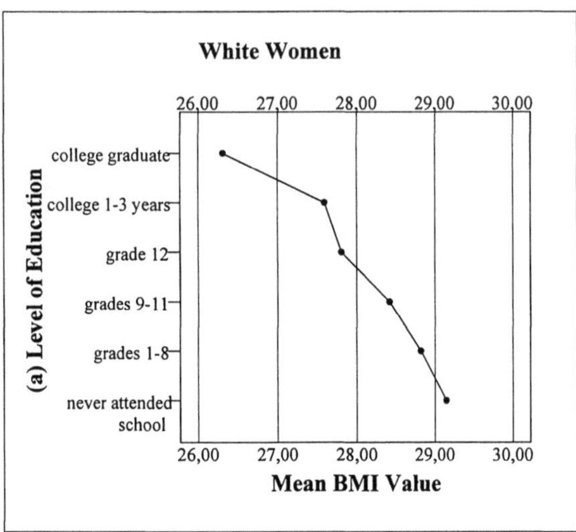

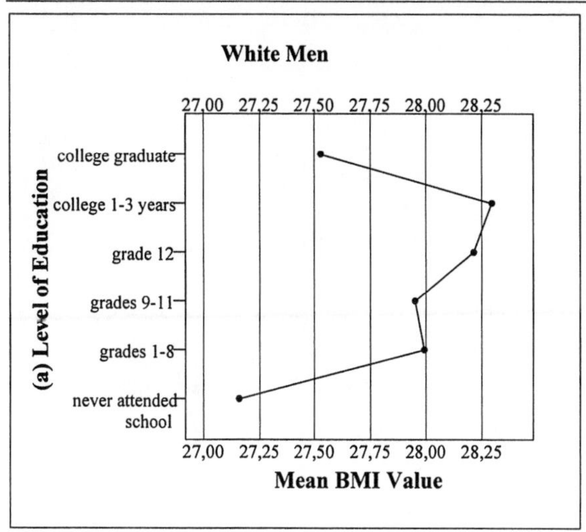
White Men
27,00 27,25 27,50 27,75 28,00 28,25
(a) Level of Education
college graduate
college 1-3 years
grade 12
grades 9-11
grades 1-8
never attended school
Mean BMI Value

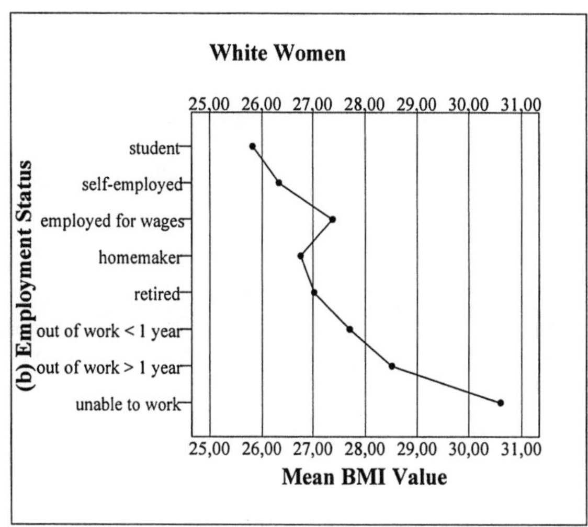
White Women
25,00 26,00 27,00 28,00 29,00 30,00 31,00
(b) Employment Status
student
self-employed
employed for wages
homemaker
retired
out of work < 1 year
out of work > 1 year
unable to work
Mean BMI Value

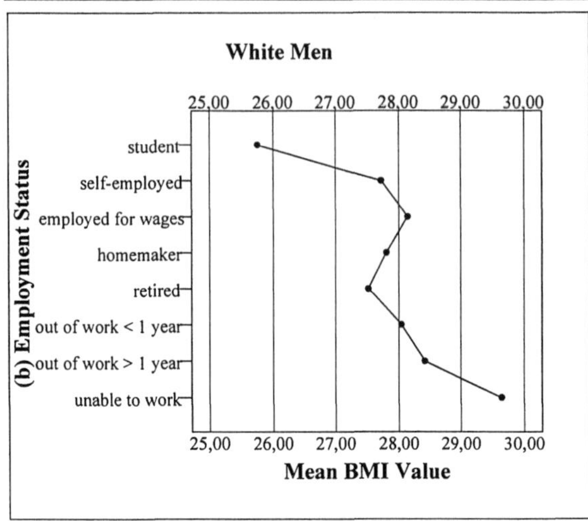
White Men
(b) Employment Status
student
self-employed
employed for wages
homemaker
retired
out of work < 1 year
out of work > 1 year
unable to work
25,00 26,00 27,00 28,00 29,00 30,00
Mean BMI Value

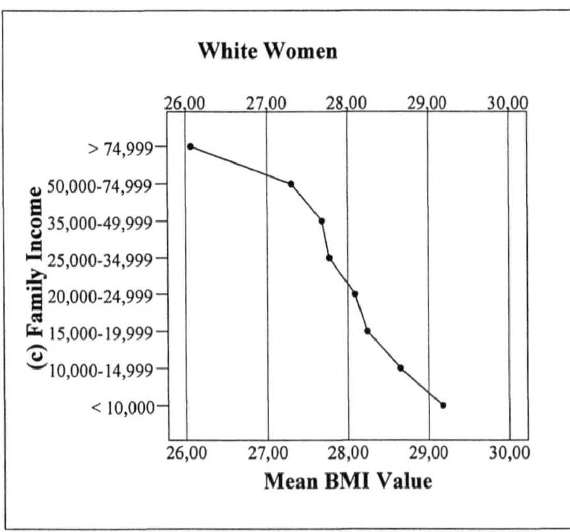
White Women
(c) Family Income
> 74,999
50,000-74,999
35,000-49,999
25,000-34,999
20,000-24,999
15,000-19,999
10,000-14,999
< 10,000
26,00 27,00 28,00 29,00 30,00
Mean BMI Value

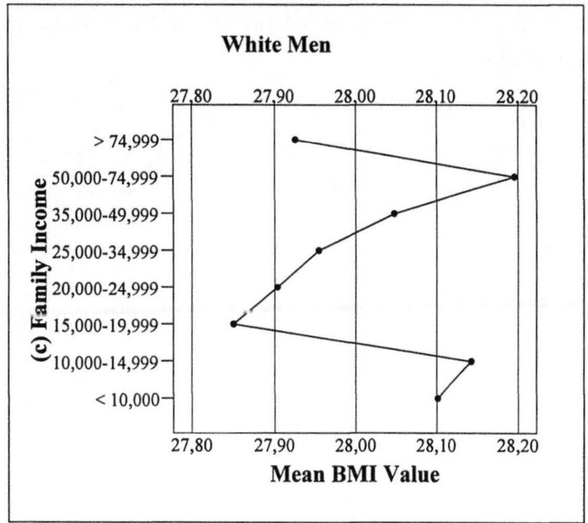

8.9 The Relationship between Different Aspects of Unhealthy Behaviour

Based on the idea that some individuals take their health into consideration when making consumption decisions while others neglect health consequences of their behaviour, it seems plausible that conscious health decisions not only pertain to food consumption and weight, but also to other health behaviour, such as physical activity, vaccination, smoking, or alcohol consumption. The present paragraph attempts to explain differences in health behaviour across individuals (Similar approaches are followed by David Cutler and Edward Glaeser (2005) and Victor R. Fuchs (1982). Both analyses find significant but low correlation coefficients).

The descriptive statistics of adverse health behaviour by gender and ethnic group are presented in Figure 8-13. Thereafter, Figure 8-14 depicts the correlations of the respective health behaviours. Correlations are significant but low for all subsamples.

Figure 8-13: Adverse Health Behaviour by Gender and Ethnic Group [Per Cent; Response Ratio in Parentheses]
(Reference: Own construction)

Subsample	Smoking	Binge Drinking	Obesity	Fruit Consumption	Physical Activity	Moderate Physical Activity	Vigorous Physical Activity	Flu Shot
All Women	41.7 (43.0)	18.8 (42.7)	28.3 (100.0)	49.3 (96.9)	27.5 (99.9)	16.3 (97.2)	62.1 (96.7)	53.4 (99.7)
White	40.0 (44.8)	18.3 (45.3)	26.2 (100.0)	48.2 (97.2)	26.1 (99.9)	15.0 (97.5)	61.3 (97.0)	51.3 (99.7)
Black	52.7 (34.3)	20.7 (28.2)	46.5 (100.0)	58.4 (94.8)	36.5 (99.9)	24.6 (95.6)	68.7 (94.9)	66.1 (99.7)
Other	51.5 (34.3)	25.6 (31.2)	29.5 (100.0)	50.6 (95.9)	32.6 (99.9)	20.4 (96.0)	63.1 (95.4)	61.1 (99.6)
All Men	35.6 (55.1)	30.4 (56.3)	27.3 (100.0)	62.2 (96.2)	23.1 (99.9)	16.1 (96.7)	47.2 (96.2)	57.2 (99.6)
White	33.7 (56.0)	29.6 (58.1)	27.2 (100.0)	62.1 (96.6)	22.3 (99.9)	15.0 (97.1)	46.9 (96.6)	55.9 (99.7)
Black	49.7 (49.2)	30.5 (43.5)	30.9 (100.0)	66.4 (93.1)	28.7 (99.8)	23.6 (94.8)	51.8 (94.2)	64.5 (99.5)
Other	45.7 (51.2)	39.2 (48.4)	25.9 (100.0)	60.5 (94.6)	26.6 (99.9)	21.4 (94.9)	47.1 (94.3)	64.0 (99.2)

Figure 8-14: Correlations of Health Behaviour by Gender and Ethnic Group

(a) White Women (b) Black Women (c) Other Women
(d) White Men (e) Black Men (f) Other Men

(Reference: Own construction)

Correlations of Health Behaviour: (a) White Women
(Significance at the 1 / 5 per cent level is denoted by * / **, respectively)

	Smoking	Binge Drinking	Obesity	Fruit Consumption	Physical Activity	Moderate Physical Activity	Vigorous Physical Activity	Flu Shot
Smoking	1.000							
Binge Drinking	0.212**	1.000						
Obesity	-0.051**	-0.009*	1.000					
Fruit Consumption	0.218**	0.121**	0.057**	1.000				
Physical Activity	0.102**	0.008*	0.152**	0.129**	1.000			
Moderate Physical Activity	0.011**	-0.009*	0.092**	0.060**	0.403**	1.000		
Vigorous Physical Activity	0.009*	-0.060**	0.142**	0.079**	0.329**	0.274**	1.000	
Flu Shot	0.203**	0.127**	-0.018**	0.100**	-0.035**	-0.058**	-0.099**	1.000

Correlations of Health Behaviour: (b) Black Women

(Significance at the 1 / 5 per cent level is denoted by * / **, respectively)

	Smoking	**Binge Drinking**	**Obesity**	**Fruit Consumption**	**Physical Activity**	**Moderate Physical Activity**	**Vigorous Physical Activity**	**Flu Shot**
Smoking	1.000							
Binge Drinking	0.188**	1.000						
Obesity	-0.102**	0.020	1.000					
Fruit Consumption	0.155**	0.081**	0.028**	1.000				
Physical Activity	0.047**	0.088**	0.085**	0.108**	1.000			
Moderate Physical Activity	-0.019	0.040**	0.044**	0.060**	0.368**	1.000		
Vigorous Physical Activity	-0.035**	0.030*	0.090**	0.068**	0.295**	0.274**	1.000	
Flu Shot	0.148**	0.047**	-0.026**	0.073**	-0.009	-0.025**	-0.060**	1.000

Correlations of Health Behaviour: (c) Other Women

(Significance at the 1 / 5 per cent level is denoted by * / **, respectively)

	Smoking	Binge Drinking	Obesity	Fruit Consumption	Physical Activity	Moderate Physical Activity	Vigorous Physical Activity	Flu Shot
Smoking	1.000							
Binge Drinking	0.255**	1.000						
Obesity	-0.051**	0.061**	1.000					
Fruit Consumption	0.185**	0.136**	0.076**	1.000				
Physical Activity	0.069**	0.044**	0.117**	0.113**	1.000			
Moderate Physical Activity	0.022	0.017	0.066**	0.055**	0.355**	1.000		
Vigorous Physical Activity	0.007	-0.019	0.101**	0.067**	0.315**	0.275**	1.000	
Flu Shot	0.134**	0.066**	-0.031**	0.095**	0.007	-0.007	-0.043**	1.000

Correlations of Health Behaviour: (d) White Men

(Significance at the 1 / 5 per cent level is denoted by * / **, respectively)

	Smoking	Binge Drinking	Obesity	Fruit Consumption	Physical Activity	Moderate Physical Activity	Vigorous Physical Activity	Flu Shot
Smoking	1.000							
Binge Drinking	0.245**	1.000						
Obesity	-0.067**	0.017**	1.000					
Fruit Consumption	0.170**	0.120**	0.051**	1.000				
Physical Activity	0.086**	0.015**	0.090**	0.093**	1.000			
Moderate Physical Activity	0.034**	0.000	0.057**	0.043**	0.382**	1.000		
Vigorous Physical Activity	-0.014**	-0.061**	0.095**	0.044**	0.313**	0.303**	1.000	
Flu Shot	0.243**	0.171**	0.000	0.106**	-0.008*	-0.027**	-0.101**	1.000

Correlations of Health Behaviour: (e) Black Men

(Significance at the 1 / 5 per cent level is denoted by * / **, respectively)

	Smoking	Binge Drinking	Obesity	Fruit Consumption	Physical Activity	Moderate Physical Activity	Vigorous Physical Activity	Flu Shot
Smoking	1.000							
Binge Drinking	0.185**	1.000						
Obesity	-0.131**	-0.045**	1.000					
Fruit Consumption	0.113**	0.070**	0.004	1.000				
Physical Activity	0.021	0.031**	0.050**	0.050**	1.000			
Moderate Physical Activity	-0.007	0.013	0.023*	0.037**	0.359**	1.000		
Vigorous Physical Activity	-0.038**	0.012	0.039**	0.025*	0.327**	0.298**	1.000	
Flu Shot	0.146**	0.044**	-0.003	0.074**	-0.12	-0.020*	-0.088**	1.000

Correlations of Health Behaviour: (f) Other Men

(Significance at the 1 / 5 per cent level is denoted by * / **, respectively)

	Smoking	Binge Drinking	Obesity	Fruit Consumption	Physical Activity	Moderate Physical Activity	Vigorous Physical Activity	Flu Shot
Smoking	1.000							
Binge Drinking	0.241**	1.000						
Obesity	-0.059**	0.038**	1.000					
Fruit Consumption	0.130**	0.101**	0.048**	1.000				
Physical Activity	0.058**	0.034**	0.075**	0.066**	1.000			
Moderate Physical Activity	0.027*	0.041**	0.026**	0.047**	0.353**	1.000		
Vigorous Physical Activity	-0.032**	-0.042**	0.066**	0.044**	0.354**	0.295**	1.000	
Flu Shot	0.183**	0.108**	-0.008	0.102**	0.018*	0.015	-0.049**	1.000

8.10 Socioeconomic Status by Adverse Health Behaviour

Figure 8-15: Socioeconomic Status by Adverse Health Behaviour [Per Cent]

(a) White Women (b) Black Women (c) Other Women

(d) White Men (e) Black Men (f) Other Men

(Reference: Own construction)

Socioeconomic Status by Adverse Health Behaviour [Prevalence in %]: (a) White Women			**Smoking**	**Binge drinking**	**Fruit consumption**	**Physical activity**	**Flu shot**
	Total		40.8	18.9	48.7	25.1	52.5
	Level of Education	**Never attended school**	47.9	21.2	50.8	45.5	53.4
		Elementary education	46.3	22.0	54.1	55.1	50.2
		Some high school	56.2	28.6	59.7	47.4	53.1
		High school graduate	46.5	20.8	54.5	33.4	52.5
		Some College	42.2	20.0	50.0	23.4	54.1
		College graduate	27.9	16.6	40.6	13.7	51.4
	Employment Status	**Wage earner**	45.8	22.0	52.2	19.6	58.9
		Self-employed	38.4	19.6	46.0	16.0	70.3
		Out of work > 1 year	60.0	24.9	59.9	35.6	66.4
		Out of work < 1 year	61.3	29.1	59.2	25.8	70.8
		Homemaker	40.0	17.0	46.4	23.2	59.6
		Student	54.2	36.8	56.4	15.0	72.3
		Retired	24.0	8.1	40.0	30.6	30.1
		Unable to work	57.8	19.6	59.4	57.7	49.5

Socioeconomic Status by Adverse Health Behaviour [Prevalence in %]: (a) White Women

		Smoking	Binge drinking	Fruit consumption	Physical activity	Flu shot
Total		40.8	18.9	48.7	25.1	52.5
Family Income [US $]	**Income < 10,000**	57.7	26.2	58.7	49.5	55.1
	10,000 ≤ income < 15,000	49.5	21.0	54.3	44.7	47.6
	15,000 ≤ income < 20,000	49.7	20.9	52.3	40.1	48.3
	20,000 ≤ income < 25,000	46.7	20.0	51.7	34.3	49.7
	25,000 ≤ income < 35,000	43.4	19.1	50.1	28.0	50.0
	35,000 ≤ income < 50,000	39.6	18.9	49.3	22.5	53.4
	50,000 ≤ income < 75,000	36.9	18.0	47.8	17.7	55.4
	Income ≥ 75,000	28.5	18.3	42.7	12.3	54.4

Socioeconomic Status by Adverse Health Behaviour [Prevalence in %]: (b) Black Women

		Smoking	Binge drinking	Fruit consumption	Physical activity	Flu shot
Total		53.7	20.6	58.6	35.5	67.0
Level of Education	**Never attended school**	14.3	0.0	47.6	52.4	52.4
	Elementary education	41.3	30.8	54.3	54.7	54.7
	Some high school	61.4	33.8	61.9	48.9	63.4
	High school graduate	58.2	25.3	60.2	40.9	67.8
	Some College	54.2	21.4	60.0	30.7	68.9
	College graduate	40.2	11.9	53.9	24.3	67.0
Employment Status	**Wage earner**	59.5	19.5	60.8	30.9	72.9
	Self-employed	54.5	20.2	51.7	23.2	78.8
	Out of work > 1 year	71.2	33.7	61.1	43.6	71.2
	Out of work < 1 year	75.0	31.5	69.3	35.5	76.1
	Homemaker	59.5	23.4	56.2	34.2	73.3
	Student	75.8	24.4	68.9	29.0	75.5
	Retired	30.2	10.7	48.3	36.6	49.2
	Unable to work	55.4	31.6	61.8	56.5	56.9
Family Income [US $]	**Income < 10,000**	59.1	34.0	63.9	49.4	64.4
	10,000 ≤ income < 15,000	56.7	30.2	62.7	46.2	62.6
	15,000 ≤ income < 20,000	59.4	26.9	60.5	43.5	67.4
	20,000 ≤ income < 25,000	57.1	23.1	60.4	37.3	67.3
	25,000 ≤ income < 35,000	53.7	22.3	58.0	34.1	69.1
	35,000 ≤ income < 50,000	49.5	16.7	57.6	27.9	68.0
	50,000 ≤ income < 75,000	45.7	13.5	54.2	23.5	68.6
	Income ≥ 75,000	37.5	12.6	50.5	20.4	66.8

Socioeconomic Status by Adverse Health Behaviour [Prevalence in %]: (c) Other Women

		Smoking	Binge drinking	Fruit consumption	Physical activity	Flu shot
Total		51.9	26.1	50.8	31.5	61.7
Level of Education	**Never attended school**	35.0	40.0	53.3	57.5	55.0
	Elementary education	45.8	33.1	47.7	49.2	61.0
	Some high school	63.7	40.1	56.7	45.6	63.2
	High school graduate	56.0	31.0	54.8	36.7	62.6
	Some College	52.5	28.4	53.0	27.6	62.9
	College graduate	40.4	18.3	43.7	20.5	59.5
Employment Status	**Wage earner**	53.3	26.4	52.3	28.7	64.8
	Self-employed	46.8	21.8	44.5	21.1	74.1
	Out of work > 1 year	67.3	36.0	60.5	43.6	67.2
	Out of work < 1 year	69.7	42.0	60.3	31.1	71.3
	Homemaker	53.9	24.6	50.3	31.1	70.1
	Student	64.2	36.3	59.1	22.6	72.7
	Retired	30.0	11.1	38.1	31.5	34.9
	Unable to work	61.8	37.9	59.0	56.6	54.8
Family Income [US $]	**Income < 10,000**	59.5	44.0	55.4	46.0	61.2
	10,000 ≤ income < 15,000	58.2	32.6	56.2	44.9	63.4
	15,000 ≤ income < 20,000	57.4	32.9	54.5	42.1	61.8
	20,000 ≤ income < 25,000	58.4	30.7	53.9	37.4	62.7
	25,000 ≤ income < 35,000	55.4	28.9	50.1	31.7	59.8
	35,000 ≤ income < 50,000	47.3	26.4	50.5	25.8	61.8
	50,000 ≤ income < 75,000	44.3	20.8	49.5	21.2	63.3
	Income ≥ 75,000	36.3	18.7	42.3	16.6	60.5

Socioeconomic Status by Adverse Health Behaviour [Prevalence in %]: (d) White Men

		Smoking	Binge drinking	Fruit consumption	Physical activity	Flu shot
Total		33.9	30.1	62.3	21.8	56.3
Level of Education	Never attended school	45.6	30.8	50.9	30.0	55.8
	Elementary education	34.1	31.3	62.9	49.1	49.4
	Some high school	47.5	42.2	69.2	39.4	60.0
	High school graduate	39.3	36.8	67.0	29.6	60.1
	Some College	36.5	33.4	64.9	21.7	59.2
	College graduate	22.3	23.7	56.2	12.0	51.6
Employment Status	Wage earner	41.4	35.3	65.0	17.1	65.9
	Self-employed	35.3	30.8	63.6	20.6	71.4
	Out of work > 1 year	56.6	38.7	69.6	33.6	67.1
	Out of work < 1 year	60.8	39.4	72.7	24.0	75.0
	Homemaker	49.5	24.9	64.4	18.6	64.5
	Student	55.6	54.0	65.3	9.6	74.1
	Retired	17.0	15.7	54.4	24.8	30.9
	Unable to work	52.5	32.8	69.5	53.0	51.5
Family Income [US $]	Income < 10,000	54.8	40.1	70.3	44.0	62.0
	10,000 ≤ income < 15,000	45.3	35.3	66.6	42.8	53.6
	15,000 ≤ income < 20,000	42.5	33.8	64.9	37.1	53.2
	20,000 ≤ income < 25,000	37.7	30.4	63.9	33.7	52.2
	25,000 ≤ income < 35,000	35.5	31.9	63.9	28.3	54.3
	35,000 ≤ income < 50,000	34.9	31.3	63.2	23.1	57.0
	50,000 ≤ income < 75,000	31.4	30.0	62.7	17.7	58.6
	Income ≥ 75,000	25.5	28.2	58.9	11.3	56.5

Socioeconomic Status by Adverse Health Behaviour [Prevalence in %]: (e) Black Men

		Smoking	Binge drinking	Fruit consumption	Physical activity	Flu shot
Total		49.9	30.3	66.5	27.8	64.5
Level of Education	**Never attended school**	44.4	80.0	58.8	38.9	57.9
	Elementary education	41.8	28.0	65.3	44.6	57.7
	Some high school	55.8	36.7	67.1	40.4	63.3
	High school graduate	55.4	36.2	68.9	31.6	65.9
	Some College	50.0	29.7	66.4	23.0	65.0
	College graduate	35.6	21.3	63.1	16.5	63.8
Employment Status	**Wage earner**	55.2	31.2	67.6	22.4	71.7
	Self-employed	57.1	30.1	65.1	21.9	78.7
	Out of work > 1 year	70.9	42.5	73.4	35.2	70.7
	Out of work < 1 year	77.9	35.9	72.3	25.8	77.4
	Homemaker	61.1	25.0	60.6	29.4	57.1
	Student	63.9	33.8	70.4	18.4	74.2
	Retired	28.2	20.0	60.6	32.4	44.8
	Unable to work	58.7	36.4	70.5	47.8	53.6
Family Income [US $]	**Income < 10,000**	62.4	43.5	70.4	42.7	60.7
	10,000 ≤ income < 15,000	56.5	35.2	71.3	38.4	60.7
	15,000 ≤ income < 20,000	54.0	34.8	68.3	37.6	63.7
	20,000 ≤ income < 25,000	53.2	36.5	66.9	34.8	62.8
	25,000 ≤ income < 35,000	52.3	33.6	65.8	28.3	65.2
	35,000 ≤ income < 50,000	45.2	29.3	66.7	23.1	65.7
	50,000 ≤ income < 75,000	39.6	23.5	63.5	19.8	63.6
	Income ≥ 75,000	37.4	22.9	64.1	13.9	68.7

Socioeconomic Status by Adverse Health Behaviour [Prevalence in %]: (f)Other Men

		Smoking	Binge drinking	Fruit consumption	Physical activity	Flu shot
Total		45.6	36.7	60.6	26.2	64.2
Level of Education	**Never attended school**	37.1	53.8	50.0	52.7	68.9
	Elementary education	43.8	43.8	60.6	50.1	67.6
	Some high school	61.3	56.4	65.3	38.3	70.8
	High school graduate	50.0	49.4	64.6	29.1	65.5
	Some College	46.3	41.5	63.9	22.5	64.7
	College graduate	31.2	25.3	52.5	15.1	59.5
Employment Status	**Wage earner**	49.2	41.2	61.4	22.9	69.4
	Self-employed	48.0	38.6	59.7	23.9	75.8
	Out of work > 1 year	65.4	57.4	67.8	32.9	67.1
	Out of work < 1 year	63.9	59.5	68.1	24.2	73.7
	Homemaker	60.0	37.5	69.3	32.1	71.4
	Student	60.2	48.4	67.5	9.8	75.8
	Retired	23.0	22.7	51.8	29.3	38.6
	Unable to work	54.9	46.6	65.8	52.1	55.4
Family Income [US $]	**Income < 10,000**	53.8	51.3	67.9	43.0	64.7
	10,000 ≤ income < 15,000	50.5	48.6	64.3	40.6	61.4
	15,000 ≤ income < 20,000	55.3	51.0	62.2	34.5	67.1
	20,000 ≤ income < 25,000	48.0	50.2	58.9	33.9	68.8
	25,000 ≤ income < 35,000	50.2	44.2	60.8	28.9	64.8
	35,000 ≤ income < 50,000	44.8	41.2	61.9	24.2	64.5
	50,000 ≤ income < 75,000	39.5	35.7	61.9	19.4	64.2
	Income ≥ 75,000	33.5	28.7	55.1	12.3	60.6

Chapter 9. References

Ainslie, G.W. (1974): "Impulse Control in Pigeons", in: Journal of the Experimental Analysis of Behavior, Vol. 21, pp. 485-489.

Ainslie, G.W. (1975): "Specious Reward: A Behavioral Theory of Impulsiveness and Impulse Control", in: Psychological Bulletin, Vol. 82, Issue 4, pp. 463-496.

Akerlof, G.A. (1970): "The Market for 'Lemons': Quality Uncertainty and the Market Mechanism", in: Quarterly Journal of Economics, Vol. 84, Issue 3, pp. 488-500.

Allison, D.B., Zannolli, R., Narayan, K.M. Venkat (1999): "The Direct Health Care Costs of Obesity in the United States", in: American Journal of Public Health, Vol. 89, Issue 8, pp. 1194-1199.

Anderson, P.M., Butcher, K.F. (2006): "Reading, Writing, and Refreshments: Are School Finances Contributing to Children's Obesity?", in: Journal of Human Resources, Vol. 41, Issue 3, pp. 467-494.

Arrow, K.J. (1963): "Uncertainty and the welfare economics of medical care", in: American Economic Review, Vol. 53, Issue 5, pp. 941–973.

Arrow, K.J. (1974): "Essays in the Theory of Risk-Bearing", 2nd edition, North-Holland Publishing Company, Amsterdam.

Averett, S., Korenman, S. (1996): "The Economic Reality of the Beauty Myth", in: Journal of Human Resources, Vol. 31, Issue 2, pp. 304-330.

Ball, K., Mishra, G.D. (2006): "Whose Socioeconomic Status Influences a Woman's Obesity Risk: Her Mother's, Her Father's, or Her Own?", in: International Journal of Epidemiology, Vol. 35, Issue 1, pp. 131-138.

Baltrus, P.T., Lynch, J.W., Everson-Rose, S., Raghunathan, T.E., Kaplan, G.A. (2005): "Race / Ethnicity, Life-Course Socioeconomic Position, and Body Weight Trajectories Over 34 Years: The Alameda County Study", in: American Journal of Public Health, Vol. 95, Issue 9, pp. 1595-1601.

Bardsley, P., Olekalns, N. (1999): "Cigarette and Tobacco Consumption: Have Anti-Smoking Policies Made a Difference?", in: Economic Record, Vol. 75, Issue 230, pp. 225-240.

Bask, M., Melkersson, M. (2004): "Rationally addicted to drinking and smoking?", in: Applied Economics, Vol. 36, Issue 4, pp. 373-381.

Baum II, C.L., Ford, W.F. (2004): "The wage effects of obesity: a longitudinal study", in: Health Economics, Vol. 13, Issue 9, pp. 885-899.

Becker, G.S. (1962): "Irrational Behaviour and Economic Theory", in: Journal of Political Economy, Vol. 70, Issue 1, pp. 1-13.

Becker, G.S. (1992): "Habits, Addictions, and Traditions", in: Kyklos, Vol. 45, Issue 3, pp. 327-346.

Becker, G.S., Grossman, M., Murphy, K.M. (1991): "Rational Addiction and the Effect of Price on Consumption", in: American Economic Review, Vol. 81, Issue 2, pp. 237-241.

Becker, G.S., Mulligan, C.B. (1997): "The Endogenous Determination of Time Preference", in: Quarterly Journal of Economics, Vol. 112, Issue 3, pp. 729-758.

Becker, G.S., Murphy, K.M. (1988): "A Theory of Rational Addiction", in: Journal of Political Economy, Vol. 96, Issue 4, pp. 675-700.

Bell, A.C., Ge, K., Popkin, B.M. (2001): "Weight Gain and its Predictors in Chinese Adults", in: International Journal of Obesity, Vol. 25, Issue 7, pp. 1079-1086.

Benecke, A., Vogel, H. (2003): "Übergewicht und Adipositas", Gesundheitsberichterstattung des Bundes, Themenheft 16, Robert Koch-Institut, Berlin.

Bentzen, J., Eriksson, T., Smith, V. (1999): "Rational Addiction and Alcohol Consumption: Evidence from the Nordic Countries", in: Journal of Consumer Policy, Vol. 22, Issue 3, pp. 257-279.

Bergstrom, T.C. (1982): "Medical Care, Medical Insurance, and Survival Probability: The True Cost of Living", in: Economic Aspects of Health, Victor R. Fuchs (ed.), University of Chicago Press, Chicago (IL).

Böhm-Bawerk, E. von (1891). "The Positive Theory of Capital", http://www.econlib.org/library/BohmBawerk/bbPTC.html, download April 28th, 2008, 11:45.

Bretteville-Jensen, A.L. (1999): "Addiction and Discounting", in: Journal of Health Economics, Vol. 18, Issue 4, pp. 393-407.

Breyer, F., Zweifel, P. (1999): "Gesundheitsökonomie", 3rd edition, Springer-Verlag, Berlin Heidelberg.

Brown, C.D., Higgins, M., Donato, K.A., Rohde, F.C., Garrison, R., Obarzanek, E., Ernst, N.D., Horan, M. (2000): "Body Mass Index and the Prevalence of Hypertension and Dyslipidemia", in: Obesity Research, Vol. 8, Issue 9, pp. 605-619.

Brownell, K. (2005): "Does a 'Toxic' Environment Make Obesity Inevitable?", in: Obesity Management, Vol. 1, Issue 2, pp. 52-55.

Cameron, S. (1997): "Are Greek Smokers Rational Addicts?", in: Applied Economics Letters, Vol. 4, Issue 7, pp. 401-402.

Cawley, J.H. (1999): "Rational Addiction, the Consumption of Calories, and Body Weight", PhD Dissertation, Department of Economics, University of Chicago.

Cawley, J.H. (2004): "The Impact of Obesity on Wages", in: Journal of Human Resources, Vol. 39, Issue 2, pp. 451-474.

Centers for Disease Control and Prevention (2006): "U.S. Obesity Trends 1985-2006", http://www.cdc.gov/nccdphp/dnpa/obesity/trend/maps/obesity_trends_2006.ppt, download November 21st, 2007, 11:38 h.

Centers for Disease Control and Prevention (2007): "Overview: BRFSS 2007", http://www.cdc.gov/brfss/technical_infodata/surveydata/2007/overview_07.rtf, download August 27th, 2008, 11:12 h.

Chaloupka, F.J. (1991): "Rational Addictive Behaviour and Cigarette Smoking", in: Journal of Political Economy, Vol. 99, Issue 4, pp. 722-742.

Chen, Z., Yen, S.T., Eastwood, D.B. (2005): "Effects of Food Stamp Participation on Body Weight and Obesity", in: American Journal of Agricultural Economics, Vol. 87, Issue 5, pp. 1167-1173.

Chou, S., Grossman, M., Saffer, H. (2004): "An Economic Analysis of Adult Obesity: Results from the Behavioral Risk Factor Surveillance System", in: Journal of Health Economics, Vol. 23, Issue 3, pp. 565-587.

Chung, S., Herrnstein, R.J. (1967): "Choice and Delay of Reinforcement", in: Journal of the Experimental Analysis of Behavior, Vol. 10, Issue 1, pp. 67-74.

Cohen, D.A., Finch, B.K., Bower, A., Sastry, N. (2006): "Collective Efficacy and Obesity: The Potential Influence of Social Factors on Health", in: Social Science and Medicine, Vol. 62, Issue 3, pp. 769-778.

Colditz, G.A. (1992): "Economic costs of obesity", in: American Journal of Clinical Nutrition, Vol. 55, Issue 2, pp. 503S-507S.

Comptroller and Auditor General (2001): "Tackling Obesity in England", Stationery Office, London.

Connolly, S., Munro, A. (1999): "Economics of the Public Sector", Prentice Hall Europe, London.

Cornes, R., Sandler, T. (1996): "The Theory of Externalities, Public Goods and Club Goods", 2nd edition, Cambridge University Press, New York (NY).

Costa-Font, J., Gil, J. (2004): "Social Interactions and the Contemporaneous Determinants of Individuals' Weight", in: Applied Economics, Vol. 36, Issue 20, pp. 2253-2263.

Crosnoe, R., Muller, C. (2004): "Body Mass Index, Academic Achievement, and School Context: Examining the Educational Experiences of Adolescents at Risk of Obesity", in: Journal of Health and Social Behavior, Vol. 45, Issue 4, pp. 393-407.

Cutler, D.M., Glaeser, E. (2005): "What Explains Differences in Smoking, Drinking, and Other Health-Related Behaviors?", in: American Economic Review, Vol. 95, Issue 2, pp. 238-242.

Cutler, D.M., Zeckhauser, R.J. (2000): "The Anatomy of Health Insurance", in: Handbook of Health Economics, Volume 1A, edited by Culyer, A.J., Newhouse, J.P., Elsevier, Amsterdam.

Diamond, P., Köszegi, B. (2003): "Quasi-hyperbolic discounting and retirement", in: Journal of Public Economics, Vol. 87, Issues 9-10, pp. 1839-1872.

Dockner, E.J., Feichtinger, G. (1993): "Cyclical Consumption Patterns and Rational Addiction", in: American Economic Review, Vol. 83, Issue1, pp. 256-263.

Dollman, J., Pilgrim, A. (2005): "Changes in Body Composition between 1997 and 2002 among South Australian Children: Influences of Socioeconomic Status and Location of Residence", in: Australian and New Zealand Journal of Public Health, Vol. 29, Issue 2, pp. 166-170.

Drewnowski, A. (2004): "Obesity and the Food Environment: Dietary Energy Density and Diet Costs", in: American Journal of Preventive Medicine, Vol. 27, Issue 3, Supplement 1, pp. 154-162.

Du, S., Mroz, T.A., Zhai, F., Popkin, B.M. (2004): "Rapid Income Growth Adversely Affects Diet Quality in China – Particularly for the Poor!", in: Social Science and Medicine, Vol. 59, Issue 7, pp. 1505-1515.

Dubois, L., Farmer, A., Girard, M., Porcherie, M. (2006): "Family Food Insufficiency is Related to Overweight among Preschoolers", in: Social Science and Medicine, Vol. 63, Issue 6, pp. 1503-1516.

Farny, D. (1995): "Versicherungsbetriebslehre", 2nd edition, Verlag Versicherungswirtschaft e.V., Karlsruhe.

Fernald, L.C.H. (2007): "Socio-Economic Status and Body Mass Index in Low-Income Mexican Adults", in: Social Science and Medicine, Vol. 64, Issue 10, pp. 2030-2042.

Folland, S., Goodman, A.C., Stano, M. (2001): "The Economics of Health and Health Care", 3rd edition, Prentice Hall, Upper Saddle River (NJ).

Forbes, G.B. (1987): "Human Body Composition: Growth, Aging, Nutrition, and Activity", Springer-Verlag, New York (NY).

Frank, D.L., Saelens, B.E., Powell, K.E., Chapman, J.E. (2007): "Stepping Towards Causation: Do Built Environments or Neighbourhood and Travel Preferences explain Physical Activity, Driving, and Obesity?", in: Social Science and Medicine, doi:10.1016/j.socscimed.2007.05.053, download October 24th, 2007, 15:14 h.

Fritsch, M., Wein, T., Ewers, H.J. (2003): "Marktversagen und Wirtschaftspolitik – Mikroökonomische Grundlagen staatlichen Handelns", 3rd edition, Vahlen, München.

Fry, J., Finley, W. (2005): "The prevalence and costs of obesity in the EU", in: Proceedings of the Nutrition Society, Vol. 64, Issue 3, pp. 359-362.

Fuchs, V.R. (1982): "Time Preference and Health: An Explanatory Study", in: Economic Aspects of Health, V.R. Fuchs (ed.), University of Chicago Press, Chicago (IL).

Fuchs, V.R., Zeckhauser, R. (1987): "Valuing Health – A 'Priceless' Commodity", in: American Economic Review, Vol. 77, Issue 2, pp. 263-268.

Goodman, E. (1999): "The Role of Socioeconomic Status Gradients in Explaining Differences in US Adolescents' Health Status", in: American Journal of Public Health, Vol. 89, Issue 10, pp. 1522-1528.

Gortmaker, S.L., Must, A., Perrin, J.M., Sobol, A.M., Dietz, W.H. (1993): "Social and Economic Consequences of Overweight in Adolescence and Young Adulthood", in: New England Journal of Medicine, Vol. 329, Issue 14, pp. 1008-1012.

Grobe, T.G., Dörning, H., Schwartz, F.W. / Institut für Sozialmedizin, Epidemiologie und Gesundheitssystemforschung [IMEG] (2006): "GEK-Report ambulant-ärztliche Versorgung 2006: Auswertungen der GEK-Gesundheitsberichterstattung", Gmünder Ersatzkasse (ed.), http://www.gek.de/presse/news/pressemeldungen/artikel.html?id=1101336, download December 7th, 2007, 15:22 h.

Grossman, M. (1972): "The Demand for Health: A Theoretical and Empirical Investigation", National Bureau of Economic Research, Occasional Paper 119, Columbia University Press, New York (NY).

Grossman, M. (1975): "The Correlation between Health and Schooling", in: Household Production and Consumption, Terleckyj, N.E. (ed.), Columbia University Press, New York (NY), pp. 147-211.

Grossman, M. (1995): "The Economic Approach to Addictive Behaviour", in: The New Economics of Human Behaviour, Tomassi, M., and Ierulli, K. (eds.), Cambridge University Press, New York (NY).

Grossman, M., Chaloupka, F.J. (1998): "The demand for cocaine by young adults: a rational addiction approach", in: Journal of Health Economics, Vol. 17, Issue 4, pp. 427-474.

Gruber, J., Köszegi, B. (2001): "Is Addiction 'Rational'? Theory and Evidence", in: Quarterly Journal of Economics, Vol. 116, Issue 4, pp. 1261-1303.

Gruber, J., Köszegi, B. (2004): "Tax incidence when individuals are time-inconsistent: the case of cigarette excise taxes", in: Journal of Public Economics, Volume 88, Issues 9-10, pp. 1959-1987.

Haas, J.S., Lee, L.B., Kaplan, C.P., Sonneborn, D., Phillips, K.A., Liang, S. (2003): "The Association of Race, Socioeconomic Status, and Health Insurance Status with the Prevalence of Overweight among Children and Adolescents", in: American Journal of Public Health, Vol. 93, Issue 12, pp. 2105-2110.

Haenle, M.M., Brockmann, S.O., Kron, M., Bertling, U., Mason, R.A., Steinbach, G., Boehm, B.O., Koenig, W., Kern, P., Piechotowski, I., Kratzer, W. (2006): "Overweight, physical activity, tobacco and alcohol consumption in a cross-sectional random sample of German adults", in: BMC Public Health, Vol. 6:233.

Hajen, L., Paetow, H., Schumacher, H. (2006): "Gesundheitsökonomie: Strukturen – Methoden – Praxisbeispiele", 3rd edition, Kohlhammer, Stuttgart.

Herrnstein, R.J. (1970): "On the Law of Effect", in: Journal of the Experimental Analysis of Behavior, Vol. 13, Issue 3, pp. 243-266.

Hodgson, T.A., Cohen, A.J. (1999): "Medical Expenditures for Major Diseases, 1995", in: Health Care Financing Review, Vol. 21, Issue 2, pp. 119-164.

Huang, K.X.D., Liu, Z., Zhu, J.Q. (2006): "Temptation and Self-Control: Some Evidence and Applications", Staff Report No. 367, Federal Reserve Bank of Minneapolis (MN).

Hyman, D.N. (1996): "Public Finance – A Contemporary Application of Theory to Policy", 5th edition, Dryden Press, Fort Worth (TX).

Iannaccone, L.R. (1986): "Addiction and Satiation", in: Economics Letters, Vol. 21, Issue 1, pp. 95-99.

Insel, P., Turner, R.E., Ross, D. (2007): "Nutrition", 3rd edition, Jones and Bartlett Publishers, Sudbury (MA).

International Association for the Study of Obesity (2008): "Adult overweight and obesity in the European Union (EU27)", http://www.iotf.org /database/documents/AdultEU27updatedJan08v2.pdf, download March 3rd, 2008, 15:32 h.

Ippolito, P.M., Mathios, A.D. (1994): "Information, Policy, and the Sources of Fat and Cholesterol in the US Diet", in: Journal of Public Policy and Marketing, Vol. 13, Issue 2, pp. 200-217.

Ippolito, P.M., Mathios, A.D. (1995): "Information and Advertising: The Case of Fat Consumption in the United States", in: American Economic Review, Vol. 85, Issue 2, pp. 91-95.

Jacobs, K., Klauber, J., Leinert, J. (2006): "Fairer Wettbewerb oder Risikoselektion? Analysen zur gesetzlichen und privaten Krankenversicherung", Wissenschaftliches Institut der AOK, Bonn.

James, S.A., Fowler-Brown, A., Raghunathan, T.E., Van Hoewyk, J. (2006): "Life-Course Socioeconomic Position and Obesity in African-American Women: The Pitt County Study", in: American Journal of Public Health, Vol. 96, Issue 3, pp. 554-560.

Johansson, P. (1996): "On the value of changes in life expectancy", in: Journal of Health Economics, Vol. 15, Issue 1, pp. 105-113.

Johannesson, M., Johansson, P. (1997): "The value of life extension and the marginal rate of time preference: a pilot study", in: Applied Economics Letters, Vol. 4, Issue 1, pp. 53-55.

Johnson, E., McInnes, M.M., Shinogle, J.A. (2006): "What is the Economic Cost of Overweight Children?", in: Eastern Economic Journal, Vol. 32, Issue 1, pp. 171-187.

Kahn, H.S., Tatham, L.M., Rodriguez, C., Calle, E.E., Thun, M.J., Heath, C.W. (1997): "Stable Behaviors Associated with Adults' 10-Year Change in Body Mass Index and Likelihood of Gain at the Waist", in: American Journal of Public Health, Vol. 87, Issue 5, pp. 747-754.

Kan, K., Tsai, W. (2004): "Obesity and Risk Knowledge", in: Journal of Health Economics, Vol. 23, Issue 5, pp. 907-934.

Kandel, E.R. (ed.), Schwartz, J.H., Jessel, T.M. (1996): "Neurowissenschaften: Eine Einführung", Oxford: Spektrum, Akademischer Verlag, Heidelberg, Berlin.

Kirby, K.N. (1997): "Bidding on the Future: Evidence Against Normative Discounting of Delayed Rewards", in: Journal of Experimental Psychology, Vol. 126, Issue 1, pp. 54-70.

Kohlmeier, L., Kroke, A., Pötzsch, J. (1993): "Ernährungsabhängige Krankheiten und ihre Kosten", Bundesministerium für Gesundheit (ed.), Schriftenreihe, Band 27, Nomos, Baden-Baden.

Kuchler, F., Tegene, A., Harris, J.M. (2005): "Taxing Snack Foods: Manipulating Diet Quality or Financing Information Programs?", in: Review of Agricultural Economics, Vol. 27, Issue 1, pp. 4-20.

Laibson, D. (1997): "Golden Eggs and Hyperbolic Discounting", in: Quarterly Journal of Economics, Vol. 112, Issue 2, pp. 443-477.

Lakdawalla, D., Philipson, T. (2002): "The Growth of Obesity and Technological Change: A Theoretical and Empirical Examination", http://harrisschool.uchicago.edu/About/publications/working-papers/pdf/wp_02_03.pdf, download October 31st, 2007, 9:21 h.

Lancaster, K. (1966): "A New Approach to Consumer Theory", in: Journal of Political Economy, Vol. 74, Issue 2, pp. 132-157.

Lancaster, K. (1971): "Consumer Demand – A New Approach", Columbia University Press, New York (NY).

Lancaster, K. (1976): "The Pure Theory of Impure Public Goods", in: Public and Urban Economics, Lexington Books, Lexington (MA), pp. 127-140.

Langenberg, C., Hardy, R., Kuh, D., Brunner, E., Wadsworth, M. (2003): "Central and Total Obesity in Middle Aged Men and Women in Relation to Lifetime Socioeconomic Status: Evidence from a National Birth Cohort", in: Journal of Epidemiology and Community Health, Vol. 57, Issue 10, pp. 816-822.

Laux, F.L., Peck, R.M. (2007): "Economic Perspectives on Addiction: Hyperbolic Discounting and Internalities", Social Science Research Network, http://ssrn.com/abstract=1077613, download February 5th, 2008, 16:08 h.

Lawlor, D.A., Batty, D., Morton, S.M.B., Clark, H., Macintyre, S., Leon, D.A. (2005): "Childhood Socioeconomic Position, Educational Attainment, and Adult Cardiovascular Risk Factors: The Aberdeen Children of the 1950s Cohort Study", in: American Journal of Public Health, Vol. 95, Issue 7, pp. 1245-1251.

Li, X., Quinones, M.J., Wang, D., Bulnes-Enriquez, I., Jimenez, X., De La Rosa, R., Aurea, G.L., Taylor, K.D., Hsueh, W.A., Rotter, J.I., Yang, H. (2006): "Genetic Effects on Obesity Assessed by Bivariate Genome Scan: The Mexican-American Coronary Artery Disease Study", in: Obesity, Vol. 14, Issue 7, pp. 1192-1200.

Loewenstein, G., Prelec, D. (1992): "Anomalies in Intertemporal Choice: Evidence and an Interpretation", in: Quarterly Journal of Economics, Vol. 107, Issue 2, pp. 573-597.

Lopez, R. (2004): "Urban Sprawl and Risk for Being Overweight or Obese", in: American Journal of Public Health, Vol. 94, Issue 9, pp. 1574-1579.

Ludwig, D.S., Peterson, K.E., Gortmaker, S.L. (2001): "Relation Between Consumption of Sugar-Sweetened Drinks and Childhood Obesity: A Prospective, Observational Analysis", in: Lancet, Vol. 357, Issue 9255, pp. 505-508.

Maennig, W., Schicht, T., Sievers, T. (2008): "Determinants of obesity: The case of Germany", in: The Journal of Socio-Economics, Vol. 37, Issue 6, pp. 2523-2534.

Mas-Colell, A., Whinston, M.D., Green, J.R. (1995): "Microeconomic Theory", Oxford University Press, New York (NY).

Matthews, C.E., Chen, K.Y., Freedson, P.S., Buchowski, M.S., Beech, B.M., Pate, R.R., Troiano, R.P. (2008): "Amount of Time Spent in Sedentary Behaviors in the United States, 2003-2004", in: American Journal of Epidemiology, Vol. 167, Issue 7, pp. 875-881.

Max Rubner-Institut (2008): "Nationale Verzehrsstudie II", Ergebnisbericht, Teil 1, http://www.bfel.de/cln_045/ nn_784936/DE/aktuelles/nvs__ergebnisbericht__teil1,templateId=raw,property=publicationFile.pdf/nvs_ergebnisbericht_teil1.pdf, download March 3rd, 2008, 14:38 h.

McClure, S.M., Laibson, D.I., Loewenstein, G., Cohen, J.D. (2004): "Separate Neural Systems Value Immediate and Delayed Monetary Rewards", in: Science, Vol. 306, Issue 5695, pp. 503-507.

McDonald, J.T., Kennedy, S. (2005): "Is Migration to Canada Associated with Unhealthy Weight Gain? Overweight and Obesity among Canada's Immigrants", in: Social Science and Medicine, Vol. 61, Issue 12, pp. 2469-2481.

Meyer, R. (1999): "Entscheidungstheorie: Ein Lehr- und Arbeitsbuch", Gabler, Wiesbaden.

Morris, S. (2006): "Body mass index and occupational attainment", in: Journal of Health Economics, Vol. 25, Issue 2, pp. 347-364.

Musgrave, R.A., Musgrave, P.B., Kullmer, L. (1994): "Die öffentlichen Finanzen in Theorie und Praxis", 6th edition, J.C.B. Mohr (Paul Siebeck), Tübingen.

Nayga, R.M. (1999): "Sociodemographic Factors Associated with Obesity in the USA", in: Journal of Consumer Studies and Home Economics, Vol. 23, Issue 3, pp. 161-164.

Nayga, R.M. (2000): "Schooling, Health Knowledge and Obesity", in: Applied Economics, Vol. 32, Issue 7, pp. 815-822.

Nayga, R.M. (2001): "Effect of Schooling on Obesity: Is Health Knowledge a Moderating Factor?", in: Education Economics, Vol. 9, Issue 2, pp. 129-137.

Ogden, C.L., Carroll, M.D., Curtin, L.R., McDowell, M.A., Tabak, C.J., Flegal, K.M. (2006): "Prevalence of Overweight and Obesity in the United States, 1999-2004", in: Journal of the American Medical Association, Vol. 295, Issue 13, pp. 1549-1555.

Olekalns, N., Bardsley, P. (1996): "Rational Addiction to Caffeine: An Analysis of Coffee Consumption", in: Journal of Political Economy, Vol. 104, Issue 5, pp. 1100-1104.

Pagán, J.A., Dávila, A. (1997): "Obesity, Occupational Attainment, and Earnings", in: Social Science Quarterly, Vol. 78, Issue 3, pp.756-770.

Parsons, T.J., Manor, O., Power, C. (2006): "Physical Activity and Change in Body Mass Index from Adolescence to Mid-Adulthood in the 1958 British Cohort", in: International Journal of Epidemiology, Vol. 35, Issue 1, pp. 197-204.

Phelps, E.S., Pollak, R.A. (1968): "On Second-Best National Saving and Game-Equilibrium Growth", in: Review of Economic Studies, Vol. 35, Issue 102, pp. 185-199.

Phillips, S.M., Bandini, L.G., Naumova, E.N., Cyr, H., Colclough, S., Dietz, W.H., Must, A. (2004): "Energy-Dense Snack Food Intake in Adolescence: Longitudinal Relationship to Weight and Fatness", in: Obesity Research, Vol. 12, Issue 3, pp. 461-472.

Pratt, J.W. (1964): "Risk Aversion in the Small and in the Large", in: Econometrica, Vol. 32, Issue 1-2, pp. 122-136.

Putnam, J., Allshouse, J., Kantor, L.S. (2002): "US Per Capita Food Supply Trends: More Calories, Refined Carbohydrates, and Fats", in: Food Review, Vol. 25, Issue 3, pp. 2-15.

Raineri, A., Rachlin, H. (1993): "The Effect of Temporal Constraints on the Value of Money and Other Commodities", in: Journal of Behavioral Decision Making, Vol. 6, Issue 2, pp. 77-94.

Rashad, I. (2006): "Structural Estimation of Caloric Intake, Exercise, Smoking, and Obesity", in: Quarterly Review of Economics and Finance, Vol. 46, Issue 2, pp. 268-283.

Rashad, I., Grossman, M., Chou, S. (2006): "The Super Size of America: An Economic Estimation of Body Mass Index and Obesity in Adults", in: Eastern Economic Journal, Vol. 32, Issue 1, pp. 133-148.

Rehner, G., Daniel, H. (2002): "Biochemie der Ernährung", 2nd edition, Spektrum, Akademischer Verlag, Heidelberg, Berlin.

Rejda, G.E. (2008): "Principles of Risk Management and Insurance", 10th edition, Pearson / Addison Wesley, Boston (MA).

Richards, T.J., Patterson, P.M., Tegene, A. (2007): "Obesity and Nutrient Consumption: A Rational Addiction?", in: Contemporary Economic Policy, Vol. 25, Issue 3, pp. 309-324.

Robberstad, B., Cairns, J. (2007): "Time Preferences for Health in Northern Tanzania: An Empirical Analysis of Alternative Discounting Models", in: Pharmacoeconomics, Vol. 25, Issue 1, pp. 73-88.

Robert Koch-Institut (2006): "Gesundheit in Deutschland", Gesundheitsberichterstattung des Bundes, Robert Koch-Institut (ed.), Berlin.

Robert, S.A., Reither, E.N. (2004): "A Multilevel Analysis of Race, Community Disadvantage, and Body Mass Index Among Adults in the US", in: Social Science and Medicine, Vol. 59, Issue 12, pp. 2421-2434.

Rosen, H.S. (2005): "Public Finance", 7th edition, McGraw-Hill / Irwin, New York (NY).

Royal College of Physicians (2002): "Forty Fatal Years. A Review of the 40 years since the publication of the 1962 Report of the Royal College of Physicians on Smoking and Health", http://www.rcplondon.ac.uk /pubs/contents/3e39baff-760c-45df-be23-2395567287aa.pdf, download October 22nd, 2007, 11:19 h.

Ruhm, C.J. (2000): "Are Recessions Good for your Health?", in: Quarterly Journal of Economics, Vol. 115, Issue 2, pp. 617-650.

Rychlik, R. (1999): "Gesundheitsökonomie: Grundlagen und Praxis", Ferdinand Enke Verlag, Stuttgart.

Ryder, H.E., Heal, G.M. (1973): "Optimal Growth with Intertemporally Dependent Preferences", in: Review of Economic Studies, Vol. 40, Issue 121, pp. 1-31.

Sabia, J.J. (2007): "The Effect of Body Weight on Adolescent Academic Performance", in: Southern Economic Journal, Vol. 73, Issue 4, pp. 871-900.

Salmon, J., Bauman, A., Crawford, D., Timperio, A., Owen, N. (2000): "The Association Between Television Viewing and Overweight Among Australian Adults Participating in Varying Levels of Leisure-Time Physical Activity", in: International Journal of Obesity, Vol. 24, Issue 5, pp. 600-606.

Salmon, J., Timperio, A., Cleland, V., Venn, A. (2005): "Trends in Children's Physical Activity and Weight Status in High and Low Socio-Economic Status Areas of Melbourne, Victoria, 1985-2001", in: Australian and New Zealand Journal of Public Health, Vol. 29, Issue 4, pp. 337-342.

Samuelson, P.A. (1937): "A Note on Measurement of Utility", in: Review of Economic Studies, Vol. 4, Issue 2, pp. 155-161.

Samuelson, P.A. (1954): "The Pure Theory of Public Expenditure", in: Review of Economics and Statistics, Vol. 36, Issue 4, pp. 387-389.

Sander, B., Bergemann, R. (2003): "Economic burden of obesity and its complications in Germany", in: European Journal of Health Economics, Vol. 4, Issue 4, pp. 248-253.

Sarlio-Lähteenkorva, S., Lahelma, E. (1999): "The Association of Body Mass Index with Social and Economic Disadvantage in Women and Men", in: International Journal of Epidemiology, Vol. 28, Issue 3, pp. 445-449.

Schneider, R. (1996): "Relevanz und Kosten der Adipositas in Deutschland", in: Ernährungs-Umschau, Vol. 43, Issue 10, pp. 369-374.

Shils, M.E., Olson, J.A., Shike, M., Ross, A.C. (1998): "Modern Nutrition in Health and Disease", Williams & Wilkins, Baltimore (MD).

Sobal, J., Rauschenbach, B.S., Frongillo Jr., E.A. (1992): "Marital Status, Fatness and Obesity", in: Social Science and Medicine, Vol. 35, Issue 7, pp. 915-923.

Sobngwi, E., Mbanya, J., Unwin, N.C., Porcher, R., Kengne, A., Fezeu, L., Minkoulou, E.M., Tournoux, C., Gautier, J., Aspray, T.J., Alberti, K. (2004): "Exposure over the Life Course to an Urban Environment and its Relation with Obesity, Diabetes, and Hypertension in Rural and Urban Cameroon", in: International Journal of Epidemiology, Vol. 33, Issue 4, pp. 769-776.

Spallholz, J.E., Boylan, L.M., Driskell, J.A. (1999): "Nutrition: Chemistry and Biology", 2nd edition, CRC Press, Boca Raton (FL).

Stafford, M., Cummins, S., Ellaway, A., Sacker, A., Wiggins, R.D., Macintyre, S. (2007): "Pathways to Obesity: Identifying Local, Modifiable Determinants of Physical Activity and Diet", in: Social Science and Medicine, doi:10.1016/j.socscimed.2007.05.042, download October 24th, 2007, 15:20 h.

Stipanuk, M.H. (2000): "Biochemical and Physiological Aspects of Human Nutrition", W.B. Saunders Company, Philadelphia (PA).

Strotz, R.H. (1956): "Myopia and Inconsistency in Dynamic Utility Maximization", in: Review of Economic Studies, Vol. 23, Issue 3, pp. 165-180.

Stunkard, A.J., Berkowitz, R.I., Stallings, V.A., Cater, J.R. (1999): "Weights of Parents and Infants: Is there a Relationship?", in: International Journal of Obesity, Vol. 23, Issue 2, pp. 159-162.

Sturm, R. (2002): "The Effects Of Obesity, Smoking, And Drinking On Medical Problems And Costs", in: Health Affairs, Vol. 21, Issue 2, pp. 245-253.

Sturm, R. (2004): "The Economics of Physical Activity: Societal Trends and Rationales for Interventions", in: American Journal of Preventive Medicine, Vol. 27, Issue 3, Supplement 1, pp. 126-135.

Sundquist, J., Johansson, S. (1998): "The Influence of Socioeconomic Status, Ethnicity and Lifestyle on Body Mass Index in a Longitudinal Study", in: International Journal of Epidemiology, Vol. 27, Issue 1, pp. 57-63.

Sundquist, J., Winkleby, M. (2000): "Country of Birth, Acculturation Status and Abdominal Obesity in a National Sample of Mexican-American Women and Men", in: International Journal of Epidemiology, Vol. 29, Issue 3, pp. 470-477.

Surgeon General (1964): "Smoking and Health: Report of the Advisory Committee of the Surgeon General of the Public Health Service", http://profiles.nlm.nih.gov/NN/B/C/X/B/, download October 22nd, 2007, 11:52 h.

Thaler, R. (1981): "Some Empirical Evidence on Dynamic Inconsistency", in: Economics Letters, Vol. 8, Issue 3, pp. 201-207.

Thompson, R.F. (2001): "Das Gehirn", 3rd edition, Spektrum, Akademischer Verlag, Heidelberg, Berlin.

Townsend, M.S., Peerson, J., Love, B., Achterberg, C., Murphy, S.P. (2001): "Food Insecurity Is Positively Related to Overweight in Women", in: Journal of Nutrition, Vol. 131, Issue 6, pp. 1738-1745.

Truong, K.D., Sturm, R. (2005): "Weight Gain Trends across Sociodemographic Groups in the United States", in: American Journal of Public Health, Vol. 95, Issue 9, pp. 1602-1606.

Tsou, M., Liu, J. (2006): "Obesity, Schooling and Health Knowledge: An Empirical Study of Taiwanese Women", in: Education Economics, Vol. 14, Issue 1, pp. 89-106.

Van Hook, J., Stamper Balistreri, K. (2007): "Immigrant Generation, Socioeconomic Status, and Economic Development of Countries of Origin: A Longitudinal Study of Body Mass Index Among Children", in: Social Science and Medicine, Vol. 65, Issue 5, pp. 976-989.

Varian, H.R. (1992): "Microeconomic Analysis", 3rd edition, W.W. Norton & Company, New York (NY).

von Lengerke, T., Reitmeir, P., John, J. (2006): "Direkte medizinische Kosten der (starken) Adipositas: ein Bottom-up-Vergleich über- vs. normalgewichtiger Erwachsener in der KORA-Studienregion", in: Gesundheitswesen, Vol. 68, Issue 2, pp. 110-115.

Wang, G., Dietz, W.H. (2002): "Economic Burden of Obesity in Youths Aged 6 to 17 Years: 1979-1999", in: Pediatrics, Vol. 109, Issue 5, p. E81-1.

Wang, G., Volkow, N.D., Telang, F., Jayne, M., Ma, J., Rao, M., Zhu, W., Wong, C.T., Pappas, N.R., Geliebter, A., Fowler, J.S. (2004): "Exposure to appetitive food stimuli markedly activates the human brain", in: NeuroImage, Vol. 21, Issue 4, pp. 1790-1797.

Wang, Y. (2001): "Cross-National Comparison of Childhood Obesity: The Epidemic and the Relationship between Obesity and Socioeconomic Status", in: International Journal of Epidemiology, Vol. 30, Issue 5, pp. 1129-1136.

Wang, Y., Beydoun, M.A., Liang, L., Caballero, B., Kumanyika, S.K. (2008): "Will All Americans Become Overweight or Obese? Estimating the Progression and Cost of the US Obesity Epidemic", http://www.nature.com /oby/journal/vaop/ncurrent/pdf/oby2008351a.pdf, download August 11th, 2008, 16:43 h.

Wee, C.C., Phillips, R.S., Legedza, A.T.R., Davis, R.B., Soukup, J.R., Colditz, G.A., Hamel, M.B. (2005): "Health Care Expenditures Associated With

Overweight and Obesity Among US Adults: Importance of Age and Race", in: American Journal of Public Health, Vol. 95, Issue 1, pp. 159-165.

Whitney, E., Rolfes, S.R. (2005): "Understanding Nutrition", 10th edition, Thomson Wadsworth, Belmont (CA).

Wilson, D.S. (2007): "Evolution for Everyone: How Darwin's Theory Can Change the Way We Think About Our Lives", Random House, New York (NY).

Wilsgaard, T., Jacobsen, B.K., Arnesen, E. (2005): "Determining Lifestyle Correlates of Body Mass Index using Multilevel Analyses: The Tromsø Study, 1979-2001", in: American Journal of Epidemiology, Vol. 162, Issue 12, pp. 1179-1188.

Winkleby, M.A., Gardner, C.D., Taylor, C.B. (1996): "The Influence of Gender and Socioeconomic Factors on Hispanic / White Differences in Body Mass Index", in: Preventive Medicine, Vol. 25, Issue 2, pp. 203-211.

World Bank (2003): "Curbing the Epidemic: Governments and the Economics of Tobacco Control", The International Bank for Reconstruction and Development, Washington, D.C.

World Health Organisation (2000): "Obesity: Preventing and Managing the Global Epidemic", WHO Technical Report Series, No. 894.

Yaniv, G. (2002): "Non-adherence to a low-fat diet: an economic perspective", in: Journal of Economic Behavior and Organization, Vol. 48, Issue 1, pp. 93-104.

Zdrowomyslaw, N., Dürig, W. (1997): "Gesundheitsökonomie: Einzel- und Gesamtwirtschaftliche Einführung", Oldenbourg Verlag, München.

Zhang, Q., Wang, Y. (2004): “Socioeconomic Inequality of Obesity in the United States: Do Gender, Age, and Ethnicity Matter?”, in: Social Science and Medicine, Vol. 58, Issue 6, pp. 1171-1180.

Volkswirtschaftliche Analysen

Herausgegeben von Elisabeth Allgoewer, Georg Hasenkamp, Wolfgang Maennig, Christian Scheer und Peter Stahlecker

Band 1 Matthias Ross: Unsicherheit und Arbeitsnachfrage. Eine theoretische und empirische Analyse des warenproduzierenden Gewerbes in Deutschland. 1998.

Band 2 Olaf Schlotmann: Die deutsche Zeitstruktur der Zinssätze im Lichte der Wicksellschen Kredittheorie. 1998.

Band 3 Gunar Schröer: Schätz- und Testverfahren im strukturellen Kointegrationsmodell. 1998.

Band 4 Joachim Dannenbaum: Der Strukturwandel in Deutschland und seine Bedeutung für die Arbeitslosigkeit. 1998.

Band 5 Birgit Layes: Kompatibilität von Arbeitsqualifikationen. Eine volkswirtschaftliche Analyse. 1998.

Band 6 Nils Hauenschild: Alterssicherungssysteme im Rahmen stochastischer Modelle überlappender Generationen. 1999.

Band 7 Axel Kunde: Langfristige Auswirkungen der wirtschaftlichen Integration der Mitgliedsstaaten der Europäischen Union. 2000.

Band 8 Anna-Maria Herfeld: Reformansätze zur Alterssicherung in Deutschland und intergenerationelle Gerechtigkeit. 2001.

Band 9 Oliver W. Wojahn: Airline Networks. 2001.

Band 10 Thomas Krause: Dynamische Straßenbenutzungsgebühren zur Reduzierung von Staus. 2003.

Band 11 Markus Klintworth: Schätzverfahren im linearen Regressionsmodell bei partiellen und unscharfen Parameterrestriktionen. 2004.

Band 12 Harm Bandholz: Konjunkturelle Frühindikatoren für die Bundesrepublik Deutschland und die Freie und Hansestadt Hamburg. Eine empirische Analyse unter Verwendung linearer und nichtlinearer dynamischer Faktormodelle. 2004.

Band 13 Heike Ruhrmann: Nationale Innovationssysteme. Eine komparative Analyse am Beispiel Irlands und Finnlands. 2007.

Band 14 Elise Hefti: Economic Aspects of Obesity. 2009.

www.peterlang.de